COUNSELLING FOR MANAGERS

COUNSELLING for MANAGERS

Nigel MacLennan

Gower

First published 1996 in hardback

Paperback edition published 1998 by
Gower Publishing Limited
Gower House
Croft Road
Aldershot
Hampshire GU11 3HR
England

Gower
Old Post Road
Brookfield
Vermont 05036
USA

Nigel MacLennan has asserted his right under the Copyright, Designs and Patents Act 1988 to be identified as the author of this work.

British Library Cataloguing in Publication Data
MacLennan, Nigel, 1961–
    Counselling for managers
    1. Counselling 2. Psychology, Industrial
    I. Title
    658.3′85

ISBN 0–566–07661–6 (hbk)
       0–566–08092–3 (pbk)

Library of Congress Cataloging-in-Publication Data

MacLennan, Nigel, 1961–
    Counselling for managers/Nigel MacLennan.
        p.   cm.
    Includes bibliographical references and index.
    ISBN 0–566–07661–8 (cloth)
    1. Employees–Counselling of. 2. Executives–Training of.
3. Management–Study and teaching.   I. Title.
HF5549.5.C8M26 1996
158′3′024658–dc20   95–49159
                                                                                  CIP

Typeset in Ehrhardt by Poole Typesetting (Wessex) Limited, Bournemouth and printed in Great Britain by MPG Books Ltd, Bodmin.

CONTENTS

PREFACE

The objectives of *Counselling for Managers* are:

- to make counselling both accessible and appealing as a performance enhancement/management tool
- to bring out the natural counselling abilities you already possess
- to give you confidence in your existing counselling abilities
- to show how easy counselling is
- to demystify counselling
- to expose the self-serving myths and propaganda of the counselling community
- to make you aware of the controversial issues normally smoothed over
- to make you aware of the realities of counselling – warts and all
- to provoke thought about, and analysis of, counselling issues
- to make the realization of your mastery of counselling as enjoyable as possible.

Who is the book for?

Anyone who is serious about helping their staff to perform at the highest possible level. All those who are prepared to invest a little time and effort to learn how to protect their most valuable asset: their people. Your intellectual resources (people), like any other resource, have problems. You already have cost-effective methods of rectifying problems with your other resources – for example, you don't throw out a machine that merely needs some rapid and low-cost, non-specialist maintenance. This book is for those who can see that counselling is the rapid, low-cost, non-specialist way of supporting and maintaining your intellectual resources.

What is it designed to do?

Counselling for Managers will enable the enthusiastic reader to attain all-round counselling competence in the workplace. It will introduce the commercially relevant Skills Training Model (STM) for counselling. It will give you eight guiding principles to which you can refer to make any counselling decisions. But, first, it will demonstrate that counselling is not the sophisticated science that its advocates claim it to be. You will see counselling in the flesh, stripped of all pretension and mythology.

The book is designed to be read as a companion to my previous book *Coaching and Mentoring*, also published by Gower. Collectively the two books form a complete work on performance management. As such, there will be only brief repetition here of material which spans both subject areas. For instance 'stress' is a significant field of study which you might expect to find covered in-depth in a book on counselling, but it has already received such treatment in *Coaching and Mentoring*. There are cross-references to the earlier book where appropriate.

What are its limitations?

This is not a book which aims to create experts in counselling for any one problem area; it will not give you enough information to claim expertise in, say, drug counselling at work or redundancy counselling. But it will equip you with more than enough general counselling expertise in the workplace to handle most people problems more effectively than before.

How to use the book

The text comprises four main sections. Part I gives you an introduction to when and how counselling can be a useful tool for the manager at work. It goes on to explore many of the myths and propaganda you may have heard about counselling – particularly those designed to make you doubt whether you, as a manager, are 'qualified' to counsel.

Parts II and III concentrate on counselling skills. Part II starts by looking at the counselling skills you already have and Part III goes on to show you how you can harness those in a more structured way. These two parts comprise the main body of the book and are designed to help you develop your abilities to use the simple, yet powerful, methods and techniques provided.

Part IV contains suggestions for handling specific problems: problems which require counselling; your problems, as a counsellor, with the counselling process and with the people you are trying to counsel. It also examines ways of handling many of the ethical and organizational issues you will and do face.

Those of you who have read my previous works will know what to expect in terms of the format and method of presentation. For the benefit of new readers, I will reiterate that I use the principles of effective education. To wit, the text is made accessible and more memorable with short paragraphs, numerous summarizing headings, easy flowing language, no jargon, cartoons, (attempts at) humour, interactive exercises and occasional summaries. In fact I have deliberately tried to do everything that academics try to avoid because they 'detract from the gravity of the message' in order to make your learning experience more enjoyable and effective.

At key points throughout the book you will find developmental exercises. Some are given their own heading; others are embedded in the text. Completing the exercises will help you become a more effective counsellor.

If you are entirely confident that you can quickly learn to counsel, you do not need to read Chapter 2. If you have reservations about whether you are capable of being an effective counsellor you definitely *should* read Chapter 2 – it will open your eyes. If you wish to plunge straight into the 'how to' of counselling, start reading from halfway through Chapter 3. If your first priority is a good theoretical understanding start by reading Chapter 6. Most importantly, to get the best out of the book, *do the exercises*.

Enjoy becoming a more competent counsellor than you already are.

Anyone wishing to contact the author may do so at:

Commercial Coaching
1733 Coventry Road
South Yardley
Birmingham B26 1DT

e-mail: nigel@maclenan.demon.co.uk

Nigel MacLennan

ACKNOWLEDGEMENTS AND DEDICATIONS

To you, the reader of this book, the manager seeking to improve your skills to make yourself a better leader, without your noble intentions this book would not exist. To the world's best business leaders who have, over their years of service, developed such advanced counselling skills (without even knowing it) that they will never need to read this book, you inspire confidence in us all. To all the professionals everywhere whose self-taught counselling skills have made, and continue to make, the world a better place: although your skills are unrecognized and unrewarded by most, some of us know the value of your work and thank you.

To the governments all over the world whose wisdom blocks the efforts of the vested interests groups wishing to regulate who provides counselling: as individuals, you counsel your families, your friends, your colleagues; you know how important your knowledge of, and interest in, those people is to your ability to counsel; you know how much good you do by counselling and you know what folly it would be to prevent yourself and others from doing the good you and they do. Long may your wisdom prevail.

To all the thinkers in this field, some of whom have taught me how to, others how not to, thank you. To all thinkers past, present and future whose ideas have been or will be superseded, thank you also: without your ideas to build on, progress can never be possible. To those who will go beyond my ideas, thank you for using them as your springboard.

To all the clients whose successful outcomes inspired and enthused me, thank you. To the clients whom I failed to help, you developed my thinking without even knowing it, and I thank you. To the many staff, clients, friends and acquaintances with whom I have had long hours of discussions about counselling, psychotherapy, coaching and training, thank you for your insights and criticisms.

Once again to all the staff at Gower, particularly Malcolm Stern and Solveig Servian, who take wonderful care of my literary babies, thank you. To

David Newton – a real professional – for yet again doing such a splendid job of turning my cartoons into something worthy of that description, thank you. To Sarah Allen for yet again editing the first draft of this manuscript and for supporting my crude efforts with such patience.

Again to my mother, Patricia MacLennan, for the long years of help and care, for the hundreds of positive attitudes and beliefs you taught, for the empowering example you set then and continue to set now, thanks. Somehow, thanks does not seem enough for the thousands of acts of good so unselfishly provided or sufficient for the encouragement provided, by example, in showing that a young widow, with two children, can be a successful businessperson against all the odds, including pervasive sexism.

NM

Part I

The context

You have probably heard much about counselling from the media, from friends and colleagues and others. You may have a counsellor in your company. You may have used counselling yourself. But few people outside the counselling profession know how easy it is to be an effective counsellor and in how many different situations counselling can be a useful performance management tool. Part I of this book is designed to give you that inside information.

1

INTRODUCTION

At various stages in this book we will look at the failings in counselling. The purpose of doing so is to demonstrate that counselling is not the sophisticated science that its advocates claim. If I can show you the realities of counselling you will lose any sense of foreboding or awe of the subject. If I can debunk some of the commonly held myths that previously stopped or discouraged you from counselling you will embrace counselling with the level of confidence which is essential to obtain results (See the section on placebo management, p. 54, for more on confidence as an influencer of outcome.)

What is counselling?

A brief history

Counselling and therapy for people in distress has the most dismal history. Throughout the ages, people with emotional or personal problems have been treated in the most appalling ways. In the Middle Ages, when the world was run by the *religiosi*, 'evil spirits' were thought to be at the root of all problems. The 'cures' ranged from exorcism to execution, all of which were done in the best (?) interests of the victim so that their soul might be 'freed from evil'.

A little later, 'loose morals' came to be perceived as the cause of all emotional or personal problems, particularly for women. The general attitude was that, if someone's standards fell below what was acceptable and 'they fell from grace', they should be locked up to protect them from themselves (well, from us actually). There are still people in mental institutions today whose only 'problem' was to show an interest in sex at an age when today's youth would be regarded as very late developers.

We only started to take a more civilized stance in this century – more civilized but no more rational. We have witnessed a range of entertaining

Early 'counselling methods'

nonsense masquerading as scientific theory. Freud was a master entertainer, proving his credentials with an amusing little ditty about bad toilet training, penis envy, castration complexes and repressed emotions being the cause of all anguish. The (?) 'obvious cure' was to lie on a couch looking at a ceiling while some 'expert' 'ummed' and 'ahed' in the background for three or four hours a week for several years.

Others followed the series with some interesting fairy stories which included a variety of exciting episodes ranging from 'family communication' being the source of all problems through to the truly memory-jolting episode about electrifying aversion 'therapy'. Then there was the 'right yourself in your own time even if it takes forever' sketch laid on by the client-centred therapy production company – a timeless classic.

Some of the more scientific productions have failed to follow even the fundamental principles of science (always good for an intellectual suicide scene). A particularly powerful trilogy started with the 'attention discrimination theory' which suggested that emotional and other mental health problems were caused by the individual's inability to attend to, or discriminate between, the most relevant variables in the environment. The sequel, 'hemispheric asymmetry theory', was a little production about the two sides of the brain not working well together (relationship conflicts always were a good source of theatrical material). The follow-up to the sequel, 'concept formation theory', was closed and consigned to the psycho-thespian dustbin for the same reasons as its two predecessors: it was an observation passing itself off as an explanation. Each element in the trilogy simply described what any theatrical novice could have reported; none offered an analysis of the plot behind the narrative.

But, more seriously, all these theories breach the fundamental principle of science in that observation is passed off as explanation. It's like saying the earth is spherical because the earth is spherical. Or gravity is the attraction of one body to another because gravity is the attraction of one body to another. Any theory of human emotional problems is only useful if it leads to a means of actually helping the client. It is useless if it just offers observation or a description of what is happening. Most do that. Most don't help at all.

You may have been led to believe that all the problems with counselling are in the past. Dream on. As you will see in the next section, even now counselling is a semi-formed art at very best, and at worst a pseudo-science more at home with those trapped in the naive idealism of student life than in the achievement-oriented world of top-class professionals.

Evolution of thought in counselling

The evolution of counselling thought has paralleled the evolution of thought in Western societies as a whole. We have moved from thinking that people problems were caused by religious factors through a range of explanations to more realistic theories. In living memory we have moved from 'breeding' being the

basis of performance (or lack of it) to learned behaviours conditioned by the environment being the cause of people problems, both of which were explanations mirroring the predominant viewpoint in society at the time. Now that we have moved (societally) on to a model of competence based on skill, it is only natural to expect the emergence of a skill-based model of human problems and performance. We now have just that and will present it later in this book.

A definition of counselling

Counselling is extremely difficult to define, for reasons that will become clear in the next section. But a definition we must have in order to be sure we are talking about the same thing. So let's try:

> Counselling is the creation and maintenance of an environment in which a person can be helped to help themselves to overcome the difficulty that led them to seek assistance, for as long as the person seeking help requires that environment.

The more people there are at work able to provide this self-help environment, the better for all of us. For that reason alone, counselling and psychology must be demystified, defrocked and exposed as being made unnecessarily complicated and deliberately ambiguous by those with vested interests. It must be made usable by one and all. So let's practise what we preach by amplifying and clarifying the above definition:

> In practical terms, counselling is the manifestation of knowledge, attitudes, skills and behaviours which are aimed at helping people to manage/solve their own problems, ideally by encouraging them to harness their own means.

EXERCISE

Now devise your own definition of counselling. Once now and then again after you have finished the book. Compare the two and the difference will be a guide to your development progress.

The differences between counselling and conversation

Conversational imbalance

A good conversation is more or less balanced between the two players. Counselling, on the other hand, is highly imbalanced. The person providing counselling is willing to temporarily suspend their needs and desires to help the other person. The client does most of the talking; the counsellor does most of the listening.

The difference in 'balance' between counselling and conversation

Not thinking about your responses

In normal conversation most of us are ready to respond immediately as soon as the other party finishes speaking. Usually we can do so in less than one second. That's remarkably fast and is easy to do if you have been, on some level, formulating your response as the other was talking. In counselling, your response is of little significance compared to the client's need, both to express their position and to have you understand so that you can be able to help them. Paradoxically, in many instances all the client needs is the opportunity to share their problem with someone else; no further action is required. Obtaining that understanding is your prime motive. You therefore have little need to come back with a fast and flowing response. In fact you should preferably take a little time to reflect on the client's statements in order to actually understand them. Taking your time shows you are trying to understand, whereas, in a social context, the same behaviour would be interpreted differently. How can you ensure you take some time to respond? How can you ensure that you keep your mind empty of distractions so you can listen effectively when the client is speaking? (See the listening skills section on page 129.)

Not passively listening while awaiting your turn to speak

Neither is counselling a passive 'just sit and listen' process; active listening is required. Active listening is hard work. It involves trying to follow the client's meaning in every dimension: context, history, links of cause and effect, emotional content, decisions made, decisions not made and so on. Don't worry if that sounds too complicated at this stage; there are easily learned techniques to master active listening. In fact, as you will see in Chapter 2, you probably already have most counselling skills. So, all that is needed is an awareness of what you already do and the willingness to do it at the appropriate time.

Not seeking to just get on with each other

In normal conversation, at least in the early stages of a friendship, much effort is put into 'getting on with each other' – in other words, avoiding areas of disagreement, ignoring personality flaws, avoiding challenging the other person and so on. But as the bonding process progresses, you expect to be more honest with your friends and to engage in less self-censorship. The counselling relationship progresses in the same way, for a specific purpose. You need to develop a mutually positive relationship quickly so that you harness that relationship to effect positive change. That almost always involves confronting the client or encouraging them to change the way they think. This is not something you do lightly or regularly with your friends. Try it for a month and see how many friends you have at the end!

Not seeking entertaining debate

Much conversation between friends is for the purposes of bonding and mutual pleasure. Depending on culture, class, education level, intelligence and so on, the ways in which this is done will vary. Entertaining debate (or intellectual banter) is common among educated people. As a reader of this kind of book the chances are that you too engage in intellectual fencing for entertainment (winning or losing usually being of no consequence). Counselling is not like that. The outcome of your deliberation with the client may have profound consequences for the rest of his or her life. Counselling is not intellectual fencing. Being a counsellor is a bit like being a one-person support team to someone trying to climb Mount Everest. You engage with them to achieve their objective. Having said that, neither should counselling be dull and sombre. It is possible, nae desirable, to have a good time reaching the summit. Try to find the right balance.

EXERCISE

Look to your relationships with your colleagues. How do you strike the balance between getting results and enjoying the process sufficiently to keep motivated towards the objectives?

Have fun supporting your clients

Counselling in the workplace

The needs and benefits of counselling

Counselling provided by managers and supervisors is probably the fastest, cheapest and most cost-effective way of helping employees to solve performance-impairing problems for themselves.

Helping your staff to solve problems themselves brings several benefits:

- It reduces their dependence on you.
- It increases their self-sufficiency and independence.
- It makes better use of your time.
- It helps you to retain your staff and reduces absenteeism.
- It increases the team support spirit.
- It demonstrates respect for, and loyalty towards, your staff.
- It will engender respect for, and loyalty towards, you.
- It can increase productivity.

- It increases the standing of the company in the public eye (with all the recruitment advantages that brings).

Expediency as a motive for counselling

It is said by some leading proponents of counselling that expediency as a motive for introducing counselling into an organization is harmful. Hogwash! The only sensible motive for introducing counselling to an organization is to positively and quickly affect profitability or efficiency, whether that end comes about directly or indirectly. If you try to use 'appeals to social conscience' or 'calls to community responsibility' to incite people to counsel, please expect to be politely ignored. People for whom these motives are decisively appealing generally do not go into business, and neither should they; they would bring down the best of companies. Enlightened self-interest and expediency are the motives which will sell counselling in the workplace.

Who is likely to be the most effective counsellor in the workplace?

You. Yes you, the manager, supervisor or director. You are best equipped to provide counselling at work because *you* know what it is like to work there. You've been there, you're still there. You know the organizational pressures, constraints, demands and deadlines. You've coped with them in the past, and by enhancing your existing counselling skills you'll be more able to help others cope in the future.

Contrast the above with the outside (or even in-house) counsellor's perspective. When they come into your department they are totally ignorant of the practical and cultural realities of your workplace. As a poor substitute they bring along some generalized theories they learned in college and try to make your staff fit those theories. Need I say more?

In situ, you can do what most counsellors would give their hind teeth for: you can observe cause and effect of workplace problems as they unfold; you can compare current behaviour to past behaviour; you can detect the subtle changes in working relationships as they happen; you can monitor changes in performance; you have the information to analyse the troubled person's environment; you have the authority to make any changes necessary; you have the option to put pressure on the client to resolve their problem rapidly; you have the ability to exert pressure on your client to change ...

Most of all you can bring the work ethic to the problem: you can demand that the client takes responsibility for solving this problem in the same way that

you expect them to solve their work problems. Every day, day by day, counsellors all over the world fight the battle of self-responsibility with their clients, gradually and subtly persuading a client that they have to change something about themselves; but you can demand self-responsibility with ease – it is already part of the workplace culture. You are in a position to force the issue. Their cooperation is required; their job security is linked to their willingness to resolve the problem. Counsellors sitting in their offices have to wade through all sorts of second-hand and indirect information. They have to cut through what the client says to reach only an approximation of the truth. You, by comparison, can observe your staff directly. You have first-hand and direct information. You can witness events and behaviours as they occur. You are in a position to understand more than any non-observer. This is the kind of information people conducting research into emotional and other problems value above all else. To what other information or observations do you have direct access which office-bound counsellors would give their eye-teeth for?

In summary, you are the right person to counsel because:

- you can witness events, behaviours and so on, at first hand
- you know the people whom you are counselling
- you have a strong motive for making sure they solve their problem as quickly and effectively as possible
- you have a strong motive for ensuring they acquire problem-solving skill to prevent a repetition
- you can encourage self-responsibility in line with the work ethic

- you can put pressure on the client to do what is required to solve their problem
- you are in a position to take some practical action to help them
- you are in a position to monitor agreed changes in behaviour
- you are in a day-to-day position to help with changes and follow-up as and when required
- you have inside knowledge of what it is like to work in that environment
- you have direct experience of the subtleties of commercial life
- you have advanced persuasion skills.

Counselling as a leadership skill

One of the skills of leadership is to effectively persuade people to do what is best for them, the team and the organization. As we will see later, counselling is virtually indistinguishable from persuasion. Successful commercial leaders with their superior persuasion skills probably make better counsellors than those merely counselling for a living.

Counselling is a leadership skill

EXERCISE

Who is the most effective leader you personally know? How do they help their staff with problems? Compare that person with the company welfare officer or the designated member of staff for counselling in the personnel department (if you have them). Just how wide is the gap in perceived effectiveness? What accounts for the gap? What skills? What attitudes? What behaviours?

Frequently used types of counselling interview at work

You may not realize it, but you already frequently conduct counselling interviews in the workplace. Consider the following:

- appraisal
- problem identification
- problem informing
- crisis management
- post–crisis support
- support input
- decision–making assistance
- rapport formation
- understanding and seeking understanding
- training follow–up counselling
- training input counselling.

In what other circumstances can you use counselling?
  When is counselling appropriate in the workplace?

- when a member of staff is not performing
- when someone is not solving problems they are capable of solving
- when thinking is unclear and affecting decisions
- when decisions are being avoided or seriously delayed
- when someone is not responding to their usual motivations
- when someone is self-sabotaging
- when someone is anxious, tense or moody
- when a marked change in behaviour is noticed
- when someone seems unaware of, or is disregarding, the consequences of their behaviour
- when someone is detrimentally affecting the work of others
- when managing change
- when a crisis or trauma arises
- when someone is retiring, being redeployed, or made redundant
- when a situation requires highly sensitive management.

You choose any from the infinite list of people problems.

EXERCISE

What problems that you frequently encounter have been missed on this list?

When to counsel and when to use other techniques

Counsel when: you trust the member of staff to solve the problem; you want to develop someone or your relationship with them; you wish to empower a member of staff; it is important that the member of staff resolves a problem or you need the decision to be theirs to create maximum commitment; you are, or wish to be, a secondary player in the decision-making process; you need a problem solved, but you don't mind how it is solved.

Do not counsel when: action needs to be taken; objectives are fixed and not open to negotiation; time pressure prevents; those involved are certain to resist if not directed; cost prevents.

Counselling is a great tool: as a servant it serves well. As a master it will sap your strength, diffuse your purpose and blur your vision. Eventually it becomes a master which will destroy you. Do not counsel on every problem or issue. Do not counsel as much as the idealists would implore you to: one look at their lives will tell you why.

Ration your counselling

Counsel only when it is wise to do so – that is, only when it benefits you and the company. The number of problems in any organization expands to fill the capacity of that organization to deal with them. There is an infinite demand for healthcare, emotional support, decision-making support; if you make those things available people, who would otherwise have solved these problems either on their own or with help from elsewhere, will use them.

This is one of the biggest paradoxes in counselling: counselling supposedly helps people to solve their problems themselves, but the availability of counselling reduces the likelihood of their doing so. People move from being self-sufficient to being counselling-dependent. They begin to blame the absence of counselling which is normally provided (or is available to others and not to them) for their inability to solve their problem. They eventually need to see a shrink for a problem which, only a few years B.S. (Before Shrinks), they would have solved themselves or with the help of friends and family. Has counselling created an artificial need for itself? Has counselling weakened society by removing from the family one of its most sacred roles – that of supporting its members? Over to you on those questions.

Possible outcomes of counselling

There are numerous different reasons for wanting or providing counselling, many of which we have listed already. As demonstrated by the following list, the range of outcomes is much more restricted:

- solution of the problem and life enhancement
- solution of the problem
- gradual solution of the problem
- acceptance of the problem (no solution possible)
- gradual acceptance of the problem (no solution possible)
- management of an insoluble problem
- gradually learning how to manage an insoluble problem

- learning some skill
- relearning something forgotten
- learning how to learn about a particular area
- realization that there is no problem – perception change or education required
- realization that there is no problem – gradual perception change or education required
- refusal to recognize the problem
- refusal to recognize that they have the problem
- acceptance of problem but refusal to change or tackle it
- refusal to engage in counselling
- refusal to engage in counselling and further attempts result in trauma.

The most productive, effective and money-saving outcome from any counselling input is that the client becomes their own future problem-solver.

EXERCISE

Put the above list of outcomes in your own words. Identify the outcomes not listed above. In the past what problems have you solved in a way not listed above?

At a very general level the positive outcomes can be grouped and classified as follows. The client changes either:

- the environment, or
- themselves, or
- their perceptions, or
- the way they process/interpret the world.

These positive outcomes are usually achieved by one or more of three routes:

- They harness their own resources.
- They unblock their own resources.
- They acquire the necessary resources.

Summary

Counselling can provide several benefits for you, your company and your staff and can be used beneficially to manage several common workplace problems. You are the best person to secure the benefits. Counselling, like most other social phenomena, is most effective when it reflects the culture of its place and time. Since we are currently in a competence-based culture, counselling is most effective when following that lead. In the workplace there is no room for methods which don't pull their weight. Counselling for most managers is to do with getting results, not about ideology. Finally, counselling is quite different from normal conversation; it is heavily biased toward the needs of one party, but, paradoxically, satisfies the needs of both.

2

DISPELLING THE MYTHS

Introduction

Before we dispel the myths about counselling, I should say that there are many counsellors who are as horrified by the myths and deceits which follow as you will be. There are many good counsellors who freely admit that their profession is far from honest and ethical, who recognize and seek to dispel the myths perpetuated by some of their less scrupulous colleagues. There are many good counsellors who are fully aware that first-rate counselling skills are not monopolized by the so-called qualified. Many are disgusted by the training they received, with its total omission of the most important element: outcome assessment. However, a percentage of counsellors, psychologists and other psycho-blah-blah-ists peddle and perpetuate these myths, knowingly or otherwise, to feather their own nests – to stop you doing what they know you are more than capable of.

If you know what problems and myths plague counselling you will be in a better position to engage productively in the activity. You will not be handicapped by the demotivating propaganda put about by those who have interests in stopping you counselling in the workplace.

You may possibly read all the criticisms of counselling which follow and become demotivated. Don't be. Read them from the viewpoint of someone who wants to know the facts – someone who wants to know what is and what is not possible. Read as an enthusiastic realist who knows that the best way to excel in any field is to know the facts, problems and limitations, however unpalatable they may be.

Let us try a little experiment before you read this chapter. Imagine you are a counsellor or a representative of a counselling organization. Your motive is to protect your livelihood or the livelihood of your members. What myths would you create? What propaganda would you peddle? How would you deter people

Exposing counselling myths

from doing for themselves what you know they are entirely capable of doing? Go on, do it before you read any further. Then compare your answers to the reality.

Dispelling the myths that discourage businesspeople from counselling

There is now a huge and growing industry of so-called professionals making a living from counselling. Naturally they want to protect their interests. So, they'll tell you that counselling is a job for experts; that counselling is a compli-cated science; that counselling is more subtle than medicine and more intricate than quantum physics; that you'll need at least five years' training just to reach beginner level; that all sorts of horror stories will come true before your eyes if you don't use a 'professional'; that ... well ... you invent some 'scare off' story and I'll bet we can find some counselling organization peddling it.

Let us take a look at those and other myths – examine the reality the myths are designed to hide and the motives driving those who start, spread and perpetuate them.

'Years of training are required'

Certainly, years of training are lavished on trainee counsellors, but are they effective? The evidence suggests the contrary. There are several studies (we'll leave the details to the academics) which demonstrate that clients cannot tell who is a trained counsellor and who is not. What? Yes, that's right, and further, when asked to express a preference, clients unknowingly tend to prefer the 'untrained' counsellors. It seems that training in counselling encourages the 'qualified' person to focus more on counselling techniques than on the person being counselled. Clients detect this, and they don't like it. What do you think is the remedy to this problem?

'A knowledge of many different counselling methods is required'

Well, if that were true you would not expect to find any 'experts' advocating or practising just one counselling discipline. And guess what? You do! Worse still, the advocates of different forms of counselling berate each other for being, at best, misinformed. You find the Freudians repressing their hatred of the Rogerians and both being negatively reinforced by the Behaviourists. So obviously a knowledge of the different forms of counselling is not important: ask any of the above; they'll tell you that only their system is required reading.

'There is an observable difference between qualified and unqualified counsellors'

Yes, that sounds reasonable, doesn't it? You would expect people who have been counselling for years to be able to detect those with no counselling experience. They cannot. Even 'experts' cannot tell who is qualified and unqualified when asked to separate the two after watching counselling sessions performed by both. Why would the experts tell you there is an observable difference when they certainly know of this much-repeated research finding? Sorry, no prizes for a correct answer!

'There is measurable and provable beneficial effect of counselling'

Absolutely. The most readily provable beneficial effect of counselling (well, actually the only provable beneficial effect of counselling) occurs in people who receive help after a stressful or traumatic incident. They are much less likely to experience any form of post-traumatic stress disorder, or, if it does develop, they experience it to a lesser degree. However – and that is a big 'however' – it does not matter whether or not the provider of the post-incident chat is 'qualified'. What *does* matter is (a) whether the person providing the counselling has been through the same experience and coped with it successfully and (b) whether they are prepared to listen to, and encourage, the expression of feelings. With workplace traumas you fit those criteria more often than not. You certainly fit more often than a counsellor brought in from outside the department or organization with no first-hand experience of commercial traumas. So, if you were to recommend only one role for your counselling at work, what would it be?

There *is* a measurable and provable effect of counselling, but it need not be provided by a person who earns their living from counselling. However, on a wider scale we are unable to demonstrate that the number of people who improve during counselling and other psychological therapies is greater than those who 'recover' by themselves without counselling input. Oops! Should I be saying this in a book about counselling? Yes. Why? It is the truth and you ought to know it.

The most likely reason for equality of recovery rates in counselled and non-counselled clients is that the latter group receive their counselling from channels that would not be recognized as counselling, such as friends and relatives. That, in turn, means that counselling provided by unofficial sources is just as effective as that provided formally. So counselling given by you is just as good as that provided by so-called 'professionals'.

'Some counselling methods are better than others'

Well, if you listen to the proponents and advocates of the 450-plus counselling styles you would certainly believe that some are better than others (there were only about 250 as recently as 15 years ago). In reality, if any counselling system(s) was clearly superior, the others simply wouldn't be able to survive in the marketplace. The fact that they can survive, and that the number of systems is growing, suggests an equality of effectiveness (or ineffectiveness).

Further, the way in which various counselling methods come in and out of fashion suggests little in the way of differences between them. The core elements of anything which is effective are not subject to the whims of fashion.

'Certain problems can only be resolved with specific counselling methods or styles'

Proponents of one style or another will tell you that their counselling method is the best at solving whatever problem you present. None will be so modest as to claim to be the least effective help for a particular problem. Contact a few counsellors at random and test that comment for yourself. Prepare yourself to hear the myths exposed in this chapter espoused with a passion that would put a religious fundamentalist to shame. Few counselling schools claim to be specifically oriented towards one kind or category of problems to the exclusion of others. Those few that do can offer no evidence that their approach is significantly better than those not claiming such specialist expertise.

'Problems can be clearly defined and measured by experts'

Not so. Emotional or psychological problems don't exist in an absolute sense. That is best demonstrated by looking at the ways in which psychiatric bodies decide what is and is not a problem. (This will shock you.) They vote. That's right, they hold elections to decide if a candidate (problem) is to be re-elected or deselected. In the 1970s US psychiatrists were embroiled in a two-sided campaign. Some were voting for homosexuality to be re-elected as a mental health problem and others were keen to see it deselected. There can be no better illustration that the mental health profession is unable to assess what is or is not a problem. They (well, we – I qualified as a psychologist) can't even agree to what extent the presence of a classifiable disorder constitutes a problem. For instance, the 'occurrence' (diagnosis) rate of senile dementia in New York is twice that of London, although there is nothing to indicate that US citizens are more predisposed to the disease than UK citizens. A smaller percentage difference could be accounted for as falling within the bounds of standard distribution, but difference of a factor of two indicates that something much more profound is taking place. It probably means somebody somewhere is making some 'big time' errors. If we translate that mismatch into terms we can all identify with, you would find physicists in New York measuring gravity at twice the rate measured in London. Would that be acceptable in physics? So why on earth are we prepared to tolerate it in mental health? Because we don't have accurate measuring instruments. Because we can't even define what we are seeking to measure. If we can't measure something with such profound effects as dementia, what hope is there that we can define and measure more subtle problems or phenomena, or even something which most people falsely assume can be measured – personality? (Will you ever have faith in a personality test ever again?)

'Problems have deep underlying causes which take years to uncover'

Ah, yes. This is the school of thought which states that all problems have a deep, dark, sinister and hidden cause which *will* take a long time to uncover. About as long as it takes to pay off the counsellor's mortgage, thank you! It is the school of thought that advocates reliving all the significant traumatic moments in one's life just in case 'that's the one what did it, Guv'. It is the school of thought which states that the milk you spilled when you were five must now be wiped up because it wasn't fair that daddy had to wipe it up for you 30 years ago. Yes, well, the chances are the milk has left as much of a stain on your life as it did on the tiled kitchen floor. It's about as much use trying to wipe up the event 30 (or even three) years on as it is trying to wipe up the milk. Historical investigation of problems as a counselling method is overused, overrated and abused. (See the section on establishing causes, page 215, for more information.)

'Diagnostic consensus prevails'

If counselling were the scientific profession it claims to be you would expect to see a uniformity of problem diagnosis. You would expect to see 95–100 per cent of practitioners agreeing on the diagnosis of a person's problem as you would, say, in medicine. Unfortunately the inverse is true; you would be lucky to find 5 per cent of counselling practitioners agreeing on the nature of a person's problem. However, once the skills training or competence-based counselling model gains wider acceptance, that will change.

'Relevant client variables can be defined and measured'

Any counselling method ought to be able to state what characteristics, personality or other variables in the client are relevant to the problem, and then be able to define and measure them. Yet, none can. Until now. Later we will introduce the Skills Training Model, in which we will show how client variables can be defined and, with sufficient development, be measured.

'Relevant counsellor variables can be defined and measured'

You would also expect each counselling school to state which counsellor variables are relevant to outcomes. Indeed, most do (now there's a surprise). However (didn't last long, did it?), the next logical step would be to say what effect various counsellor attributes will have on client and outcomes. Most don't. The model we will present later won't either. The reason? We can't yet measure personality with any more accuracy than the tossing of a coin. If anyone claims otherwise, ask to see their validation figures – anything with a predictive validity over 50 per cent should make you very, very suspicious. (Now why do you think there are hundreds of test providers who will tell you that they can do better than that?)

'Only "experts" are permitted to counsel'

Some countries have attempted to pass legislation to restrict the use of psycho-logical and counselling techniques. Only those who are 'fully trained' are permitted to describe themselves as counsellors or psychologists. Sounds reasonable enough, doesn't it? No. Has it increased the rate of positive outcomes in counselling (usually less than 30 per cent)? Not one jot. Has it raised the recovery rate (30 per cent) of those counselled above that of the non-counselled? Not even slightly. Has it stopped supposedly unqualified people practising? No way. They simply describe themselves as something else and carry on as before. It is simply not possible to control who counsels using psychological methods. Neither is it wise to even try; a large number of people have to provide counselling. Every parent automatically does it. Every schoolteacher does it (few are trained in counselling, but many are excellent at it). Every physician does it (the vast majority of medical schools offer no training of *any* sort in counselling at any stage of a medical degree). You name anyone in a people-oriented profes-sion, and they do it. Shockingly, even clinical psychologists receive very little training in counselling and psychotherapeutic techniques; most UK schools provide less than 20 hours' tuition! That's roughly a third of the time it will take you to read this book and do the development exercises.

Unbelievable, isn't it? Not only does virtually everybody who deals with people in their professional lives have to and actually do provide counselling, but those who most need to do so receive virtually no training. What does that say about the necessity of training to be a first-rate counsellor? What does that tell you about how difficult it is to master the requisite skills? What does that suggest about the motives of those who insist that only experts should be doing it? What do you think motivates such claims? The protection of counselling clients or the protection of counsellors' income?

'The causal explanation of problems can be clearly defined and assessed by experts'

Most counselling systems will tell you what 'caused' the client's problem. The (not so) strange thing is that they all offer different causal explanations of the same standard problems. The other not so strange thing is that each school of counselling will categorically tell you that the client's problem is caused by whatever particular explanations they espouse. With 450-plus different expla-nations for any one problem somebody is telling porkies. Once we have covered the difficulties involved in establishing the causes of a problem (see page 215), you'll probably conclude that everybody is 'being flexible with the truth'.

'It is possible to provide non-directive counselling'

Many contemporary counselling techniques claim, in part, to be 'non-directive' – that is, the client is not, and should not be, directed by the counsellor in any way. Ho, Hum! Prepare for some entertainment.

This is probably the most widespread and most commonly held myth in counselling. Yet it is the most patently fallacious. We ought to expose and totally demolish it to clear your way to well-informed and effective counselling.

Most non-directive counselling schools advocate long years of training. This begs the question, if the counsellor never directs the client to do anything nor does anything to the client, what skills does the counsellor need that require such prolonged training?

'Oh, very subtle, extremely complicated skills which only a few selected people are capable of mastering,' I was once told.

'What,' I asked, 'are those special skills?'

'There's no point in trying to explain, they're too complicated for non-specialists to understand,' was the reply.

Since when have the guiding principles of any people discipline been too complicated to understand? Far less the principles of a practice which claims to be totally non-directive? This conversation took place when I was a student; the respondent was a very senior health service practitioner (consultant level). Draw your own conclusions about what is taught to those seeking to provide 'non-directive' counselling.

The self-contradictions of 'non-directiveness'

Another little gem appeared in a book published by a professional organization in this field. The author advocated non-directive counselling but then added, ' ... if the client gives you power, use it for their sake'. A sensible piece of advice, but self-contradictory if you have advocated non-directive counselling as that author did. How can you use power and be non-directive?

Inconsistency in 'non-directiveness'

What one non-directive counsellor reflects may be different from another's reflection of the same client's statements. The counsellor's choice of focus will be determined by his or her mood, life experiences and a hotch-potch of other counsellor-related variables. That reflection will then influence the future direction of the discussion. If one counsellor reflects the feeling element of a communication, the client may concentrate on how they feel, or felt, about the problem. Another counsellor may decide the contextual component is more important and reflect that, influencing the future course of the counselling session in another direction. So much for non-directiveness!

Directive effects of technique variance

Even the way a particular technique is used to reflect will influence the future direction of the session. For instance, let's consider the technique of 'echoing', which is one of those techniques supposedly too complicated for non-specialists to understand. Echoing reflects the client's last few utterances word-for-word. What effect will echoing the last phrase have compared to echoing the last two phrases, or the last three? It will most certainly emphasize different meanings. One single phrase will communicate to the client that you wish to further explore the specific part echoed (yes, what you say to the client is interpreted by them as a statement of what you, the wise counsellor, consider to be worth exploring). If you echo the last two or three phrases, the wider meaning conveyed is taken to be the important issue. How many other aspects of your behaviour unwittingly direct people? Can you see how every single word or gesture influences the client? Non-directive counselling is simply not possible.

More internal inconsistencies in 'non-directive' counselling

One final internal inconsistency should be exposed: ' ... a client whom one imme-diately and instinctively dislikes if treated with enough empathy and respect may gradually come to be more likeable' (the name of this author on non-directive counselling has been withheld to protect their otherwise good reputation). What? First, one of the key premises of non-directive counselling is that counsellors can suspend their judgement of people. If judgement can be suspended, why advise counsellors how to react to someone they don't like? Because we are all human and can't suspend our judgement, that's why. It is simply not possible. Second, if one is being genuine towards the client (as all counsellors should be) isn't treat-ing someone one dislikes with empathy and respect insincere and artificial? Of course it is. Third, non-directive counselling advises that one should not fake sincerity. Oops! How then can the counsellor maintain the relationship long enough for the client to 'gradually come to be more likeable'?

There is no such thing as non-directive counselling. It is a myth, a self-delusion and a deceit of vulnerable people. It is a myth supported by the notion that clients need protection. If clients need protection, it is from the very people who are claiming to be acting in their best interests.

We don't sit children in a room and expect them to teach themselves to read and write on their own. Why then should we expect clients who lack the skills to solve a problem (the reason most of them have come to counselling) just because we sit them in a room and listen to them? We direct children to read and write. Once they have mastered the basics, the best of them go on to self-direct to become more proficient. But most – the vast majority – need further direction to develop their skills. Why should we think that adults with prob-lems are any different as a group?

There is no escaping either the inevitability of directing others or the need to do so in most situations. You would not expect new members of staff to solve the problem of how to do their job with no input from you or others, would you?

Dispelling the myth that counselling is a scientific discipline

What would you expect to see if counselling were the advanced science some claim it to be?

Since scientific reasoning is the most successful intellectual tool ever devel-oped by the human species it can probably teach us something about how to solve life's emotional problems. Throughout the world scientists use the following five stages to seek understanding of whatever it is they are studying: observation, definition, explanation, prediction and, ultimately, control.

This is the basis of scientific reasoning. When trying to understand something, you first observe its occurrence. You then try to define what you are observing. Having generated a satisfactory and reliable definition, you then seek to devise an explanation of what is going on. To be of any value, your explanation must lead to predictions which can be either verified or falsified – in short your explanation should lead to the generation of testable hypotheses. Eventually, through experimentation, you find valid explanations which correctly predict events. You are now in a position to control and harness the phenomenon you originally observed.

One of the most powerful tests of our understanding of any field is to evaluate how far it has progressed through the five steps of science. Those protecting their livelihoods not only peddle the myths described above and a few more besides, they also regularly claim that counselling is a skilled profession based on scientific principle. So, let's apply some scientific principles and see if counselling holds up. Let's break the above question down into logical component questions. What would we expect to see? Try answering that question yourself before reading the next section. What *would* you expect to see if counselling were the scientific discipline its advocates like to claim it is?

'Outcome would be the best measure of competence'

If counselling competence was measured by results achieved, you would expect to see all qualification systems treating the outcome of counselling sessions as the largest and most serious element of assessment. You would expect to see a recognizable grading system for judging counsellor effectiveness, wouldn't you? Of course. Is there one? Of course not. You might also expect to see some method of monitoring the differential effectiveness of counsellors. There is none. Neither of the two principal awarding bodies in the UK has any system that takes into account the outcome of counselling sessions during training. How, then, is 'competence' measured? It is not. Knowledge is assessed. Time served is recorded. The number of hours in 'supervision' is recorded. The number of hours of personal counselling is recorded. But at no stage is outcome taken into account. What does that tell us? Clearly that results don't matter in the training of counsellors. As a competent manager you'll be familiar with the commercial truism 'We should expect that which we inspect.' If we don't inspect results we send a *clear* and *unambiguous* signal that we don't expect results. That may be acceptable to the bodies awarding counselling 'qualifications', but it is not acceptable to us in business. We will look at measuring outcomes later.

'Predictions can be made about the best "cure" for specified types of problems'

If counselling were as organized as, say, medicine, you would expect to see a coherent system that would make predictions, based on research data, which would tell us what the best solution was to any particular kind of problem. Guess what? That's right, there is no system.

'Accurate and measurable diagnosis of problems can be made'

If we can't predict which 'cure' is appropriate for specified problems, surely we can at least devise an accurate and measurable diagnosis of any problem? Sorry, no can do. We can't even say what caused a particular problem with any certainty. Oh yes, all the various counselling methods will give you their cause, but we can't assess, measure or prove any causal links with any degree of accuracy (more on this later).

'Personality types can be matched to counselling types'

Surely, if nothing else, we should be able to match different personality types to appropriate counselling methods? No need for a response, you've already guessed it. So how do potential counselling clients find a counselling method they feel suits them? Trial and error. Most would-be clients 'do the rounds'; they keep trying different counsellors until they find one they like. Doesn't sound too scientific, does it?

'Counselling types can be matched to problem types'

Well, you might say, people are peculiar at the best of times; their preferences for dealing with other people are based on the thinnest of grounds. Surely if we take personal preference out of the equation we will find that certain counselling methods are more appropriate for certain types of problem. Not so. There is no reliable and independent evidence for this at all.

'There is a method for mixing the appropriate types of counselling tools for people and problems'

Some counsellors practise 'eclectically' – that is, they choose whatever method or system seems most appropriate for the client and problem. 'Oh, that sounds promising' is the usual reaction. Indeed it is. So what would we expect to see if this were a scientific system? Well, first, all of the above criteria and, second, a coherent decision-making system – this could perhaps be expressed in a complicated flowchart, showing that if the client suffers from X and has the personality characteristics ABC then counselling method Y should be used. Does such a system exist? Of course not. So how do 'eclectic' counsellors decide what is best for the client? On the basis of 'many years' experience', don't you know. Ho, Hum. Even if such a system did exist, and could be proven to work, how could any one human being claim to have expertise in all the different counselling methods available, and keep their skills so up-to-date that they could use them effectively at the drop of a hat? Not likely. Have you lost your reverence for psychologists and counsellors yet?

'It is not possible to counsel without years of training'

You have already seen that experts can't tell unqualified from qualified counsellors, so clearly counselling can be successfully provided without any training. Well, actually that's an oversimplification: it seems most well-adjusted people develop counselling skills via informal training in the course of their lives, without ever realizing it. By comparison, years of formal training, far from being beneficial, may be counterproductive; they may destroy your naturally acquired skills.

'Counselling is a coherent scientific discipline'

A principal characteristic of genuine scientific disciplines is the existence of one coherent paradigm within which most work is conducted. A principal characteristic of a pre-scientific discipline is the existence of a large number of competing paradigms with no way of differentiating between the useful and the useless. Counselling is in the pre-scientific or pre-paradigmatic phase of development as a science. It could not be more clearly so, including as it does so many different schools and philosophies of counselling.

How did counselling measure up to the five steps of science?

- *Observation*: Yes, we can observe counselling taking place and we can observe people suffering from problems for which they seek counselling.
- *Definition*: There is no agreed definition of what counselling is. There is no definition of problems needing counselling. There is no (fill in the blanks from the above).
- *Explanation*: We are unable to provide a provable explanation for the cause or 'cure' of problems (not surprising when we can't define what we are observing).
- *Prediction*: We are unable to predict who responds to which types of counselling (not surprising since we can't come up with provable explanations).
- *Control*: We are not able to control the process of counselling and therefore are unable to control the outcome.

The counselling profession could dismiss all the above unsatisfied scientific needs as having been satisfied many years ago

Finally, if all my criticisms were hollow you would expect the so-called counselling profession to provide immediate evidence that everything which I claim not to be present, actually is, and was finalized and working years ago – or at the very least, was to be resolved in the very immediate future. Don't hold your breath. Indeed, I suggest you pass that advice on to your grandchildren!

Has counselling any value at all?

However, don't take all my criticisms as a dismissal of the value of counselling, or of the potential value of trying to improve its effectiveness. Quite the contrary. Counselling can be of enormous benefit. So why be so critical, you might ask. Often the best way to improve something that is not living up to its promises is to ruthlessly expose its inherent problems for all to see. Pointing out the myths, weaknesses, vested interests, deceits, logical and scientific flaws, inconsistencies, contradictions and so on, gives both you and me the chance to seek better solutions, methods, principles and guidelines. Perfecting your skills, in counselling or any field, can be achieved by being the arch-critic of that same discipline. By becoming aware of the problems, you prime your mind to find better solutions. As you go through this book, take the same ruthless approach to criticizing the solutions I offer; it will help you go beyond my level of understanding.

Paradoxes and contradictions

As you have probably noticed already, counselling is full of paradoxes and contradictions. Here are a few of the more obvious:

- It is a genuine role, yet it has to be faked.
- It is a skill most of us acquire naturally, yet we have to relearn what we are doing to be comfortable doing it.
- It is something we can do naturally but which we have to fake until we gain the confidence to do it naturally.
- It is something from which we can all benefit, yet it is loaded with stigma (in the UK only).
- It is a formal profession, yet professionals are largely less effective than good amateurs.
- It is divided into several schools of thought, yet even 'experts' cannot tell one from the other in practice.
- It has its use restricted in some places, yet anyone can practise it under a different label.

EXERCISE

To help you increase your understanding of the subtleties of counselling open up and keep a counselling paradox file. You will spot several as you go through this book. You will spot even more when you start counselling properly.

Summary

Many myths are peddled by those with vested interests in discouraging you from counselling. Some – but not all by a long way – of these myths have been exposed and exploded. The high priest of all counselling myths is the one which states that counselling is a scientific and organized discipline. As we have seen, it nowhere near approaches that. The deputy high priest is the myth which states that you should provide non-directive counselling. As we have seen, that is quite simply not possible. Once stripped of all mythology and vested interest arguments, counselling and counselling psychology clearly cannot provide what its advocates promise. What can be done, can be done by virtually anyone. All of this means that you can learn to counsel rapidly and effectively. Indeed, as you will see in Part II, you may already have all the ingredients you need to counsel effectively.

Part II

The skills

Now that you have some understanding of the context of and uses for counselling and can see straight through the myths and propaganda, you are probably keen to begin to develop your skills. Part II of this book is designed to give you a format and structure to develop good counselling skills, as well as a practical and usable understanding of the most effective and up-to-date counselling methods stripped of the unnecessary jargon and other baggage that you would usually be required to tolerate.

3

COUNSELLING AND YOU

Counselling: an ancient and innate skill

The human race evolved as a social species – in other words, we evolved by supporting each other in hundreds of subtle little ways, one of which we have recently chosen to call 'counselling'. The urge to support others and seek support for ourselves is probably programmed into our genes. Even the earliest, least civilized human societies had methods of helping those in trouble; these were often better systems than later societies (particularly medieval ones). Counselling is a skill passed on from grandparent and parent to child genetically and socially (many behaviours and abilities are genetically in-built). By the time most of us reach working adulthood, we've already had a lifetime's experience of counselling; we've practised and fine-tuned our counselling and supporting skills with friends, relatives, lovers, parents and colleagues in a wide range of different contexts.

You might assume that counselling is a worldwide phenomenon. It is, but only in first-world democracies is it labelled as such. And even that label is a recent invention. In most parts of the world, 'counselling', as we call it, has no equivalent. Friends and family provide the same support that we take for granted. What does that tell us? First, you already have the skills; second, you just didn't know it.

EXERCISE

Take some time to consider just how much counselling experience you already have. Take the above list of people and ask yourself about the ways in which you support them, and the frequency with which you provide that support, both currently and in the past. Then think about how much support you have received over the years which was essentially counselling without the label.

Counselling is an ancient skill

Counselling skills you already have

What you have is a high-level, pre-articulate, automatic expertise in counselling, acquired over many years. You have the ability, the social skills, the
communication skills, but you don't have the theoretical understanding.
That's OK; too much knowledge of counselling seems to be counterproductive. One of the reasons formally trained counsellors are slightly less
preferred by clients could be that rigid training interferes with natural skill.
The 'trained' counsellor begins to concentrate more on technique and method,
thereby directing less of their attention to the client. Thereby having less of
their mental capacity directed at listening to, responding and interacting with
the client.

Person-focus versus technique-focus

People know when they are being listened to – they know when they are the
object of someone's undivided attention. If you lack a theoretical understanding of counselling techniques, you are forced to focus on the person; it is all
you can do. That explains why unqualified people are just as effective as their
qualified contemporaries. They have no conscious knowledge of techniques so

their person-focus is much more intense. Who really listens to you? Are they counsellors in the formal sense or are they people who would probably never describe themselves as counsellors who are expert nonetheless? The next time you are involved in a conversation with another to the exclusion of all else, suspend your concentration for a second and ask yourself what it feels like. What do you do to achieve that level of person-focus?

Counselling technique

The person providing counselling can be more effective than any method as long as that person somehow provides the following:

- respect for the other person's views
- simplicity and straightforwardness
- avoidance of any pretensions or poses
- ability to put themselves in the other person's shoes
- a good-sized helping of humanity and sensitivity.

(We will elaborate on the 'somehow' in the next few pages.)
    If techniques are so unimportant, as I have argued, why are virtually all counselling courses (and books like this) stuffed full of weird and wonderful techniques? Because possession of techniques seems to give counsellors the confidence required to make the above simple factors work.

- It seems that the techniques force counsellors to provide the above factors. It is almost as though the techniques act as a vehicle with which to deliver them.
- The techniques may also distract the counsellor's mind thereby preventing him or her from interfering with the processes which naturally occur when the simple factors are provided.
- It could also be that the techniques may act as a placebo (see the placebo management section on page 54 for examples).
- Or that the techniques may provide a placebo effect necessary to those counsellors whose person-focus is not very intense.

EXERCISE

Think of other explanations for counsellors' preoccupation with technique.

How you can acquire first-rate counselling skills

The task ahead of you is to understand, harness and enhance your natural expertise without destroying it. The best way of doing this is to maintain a strong person-focus. Remind yourself regularly: 'Person-focus is more effective than any technique.'

Why you don't need years of training

Because you've already had it. Because, as must be more than obvious by now, you already have a lifetime's experience in counselling to build on and fine-tune. The fine-tuning required is partly theoretical and partly confidence-building. And how is that best acquired? Well, as you probably know, the highest achievers in virtually every field are self-trained. Self-training requires an enormous amount of self-discipline. You have doubtless noticed that most people don't have that level of self-discipline or motivation; they have to go on training courses to acquire skills. The chances are you don't have to. Why? Because you are engaged in self-training right now, and that probably means you are a high achiever.

How you can train yourself

You can train yourself by adopting and practising any of the remarkably small number of counselling principles you haven't already perfected. There are

Counselling is an inherent skill

many exercises designed to help you do just that. You will probably be surprised when you discover just how few operating rules there are to guide effective counselling.

Counselling theory is secondary to what is actually practised in counselling

What is actually happening in counselling is a long way from what is said to be happening. When expert counsellors are asked to determine which counselling schools and philosophies are being used by other counsellors presented on videotape, they can't do it – despite the insistence of practitioners that they are practising one style in preference to another. What does that tell us? It tells us that the differences between counselling styles are almost irrelevant. It tells us, despite the claims of the experts, that they are all fairly similar. Or at least it indicates that, in all counselling methods, something fundamental goes on, which transcends the claimed differences.

What fundamental factor makes counselling effective?

Well, actually there are eight fundamental factors common to virtually every counselling system. There are eight principles which, if followed, will make counselling more likely to succeed. Note that I didn't say 'make counselling successful': it is up to the client to determine the outcome; all you can do is provide the environment that makes positive change most likely. The eight principles are:

1 Be interested, genuine and avoid negative judgements.
2 Establish and maintain a good rapport.
3 Provide an environment that allows the expression of emotions.
4 Provide support and reassurance.
5 Provide an atmosphere of positive expectation and hope.
6 Provide plausible explanations of causes and rationales for solutions.
7 Provide opportunities to experience success.
8 Encourage the adoption of empowering beliefs.

As we have seen, there are many ways of providing the eight common principles. What we, as managers, need is a coherent and commercially relevant way of providing them. By the end of the book (if I have done my job properly) you will have one.

Applying the eight principles for counselling in crisis

Often the best way to demonstrate principles is to show them in action. There being no time like the present, let's immediately (and simplistically) look at an application of the eight principles in a crisis situation involving a member of your staff. What should you do?

1   Be interested, genuine and avoid negative judgements. Make it clear that you care, that you are available to help and that you accept the problem as authentic.

2   Establish and maintain a good rapport. Ask open-ended questions, and listen to the responses. Check that you have understood properly by reflecting your understanding and asking for confirmation.

3   Provide an environment that allows the expression of emotions. Acknowledge the presence of whatever emotions are being expressed for as long as they continue to be expressed.

4   Provide support and reassurance. Support the other person in their attempts to come to terms with or resolve the situation and reassure them that they can cope, or do what is required.

5   Provide an atmosphere of positive expectation and hope. Convey your genuine expectation and belief that they will come through the crisis. Believing intensely will automatically generate the appropriate attitudes, body language and so on that will convey your expectation to the other person.

6   Provide plausible explanations of causes and rationales for solutions. If you are asked to explain the events/crisis, provide a plausible explanation; it doesn't have to be the provable truth (whatever that is), any reasonably intelligent explanation will do. To a lesser extent you should (only if asked) provide a rationale for solving the crisis. Ideally the rationale for the solution should be based on the explanation of the cause.

7   Provide opportunities to experience success. There are innumerable ways of doing this, ranging from the success of the interaction itself to providing small solution-oriented steps which you know the person will be able to complete successfully.

8   Encourage the adoption of empowering beliefs. Believing one can cope is obviously more likely to lead to success than its opposite. The best way to encourage the adoption of whatever empowering belief is most appropriate is to ask in which other ways the events could be interpreted, or in which other ways interpretations would be more empowering.

Following the above eight principles roughly in that order is probably as good a crisis counselling strategy as you're ever likely to see. The order is obviously important to some extent; to ask the questions outlined in point eight at the start of a counselling session would clearly be inappropriate. Nevertheless, as you will see, the ordering of the principles and the timing of their application can be altered to suit various different circumstances.

EXERCISE

Help yourself to remember the eight principles by rewriting them in your own words, or by devising your own visual representation of them.

Common mistakes that can be simply avoided

By following the above eight principles and avoiding the following common counselling mistakes you will already be well on the road to being an effective counsellor in the workplace (I told you it was easy and simple!). We will look at problems to avoid in more detail later but, for now, avoid:

- talking about oneself and how one solved this or that problem
- attempting to cheer up the other person
- immediately providing or seeking a solution for the problem
- trying to do something (anything) for the person
- taking counselling too seriously
- failing to take the client's problem seriously enough (note the difference in the last two points)
- suggesting that the problem is in the client's imagination
- an environment not conducive to listening
- sarcasm, blaming and moralizing
- anticipating responses or hearing what you want to or expect to hear.

A counselling problem to avoid

EXERCISE

Consider what attitudes, mannerisms, behaviours and so on would put you off about someone trying to help you. What has put you off in the past?

Summary

You, as a typical reader of this book, already possess most of the skills necessary to become an effective counsellor. There are only eight simple principles to follow. Knowledge of this single fact gives you enough to perform effectively in all your future counselling.

4

FOLLOWING THE EIGHT COMMON PRINCIPLES

Common principle 1:
Be interested, genuine and respectful

This section introduces basic listening skills. The more advanced listening skills (the finer points of which you probably practise already without realizing it), we will cover in the appropriate section of the commercially relevant eight-stage model (Chapter 5).

Respect versus unconditional positive regard

Many counselling approaches advocate an 'unconditional positive regard' for clients. Yet, although it is one thing to make someone feel that you view them as being important, it is quite another to view someone positively regardless of what they have done or are doing. Would you have an unconditional positive regard for a teacher who beat your children? Or for a social worker taking your children into care for some unfounded allegation of 'ritual satanic abuse'? Of course not. And neither should you. Most people would think you were a loaf short of a picnic if you did! More importantly, *so will your clients*. Clients may need help, but they haven't lost their sense of social norms. If you pretend to not be affected by something the client knows very well should have affected you, they will immediately suspect your motives and doubt your trustworthiness. Unconditional positive regard is so sycophantic as to be transparently deceitful. By all means show respect, but beware the counsellor bearing unconditional positive regard. Cue for an exercise: when have you been distrustful of someone who showed approval for you or your actions, when you know they should have disapproved?

Genuineness versus non-judgementalism

Here we have a similar point to make about the one on unconditional positive regard: be genuine to your clients. Conventional counselling 'wisdom' tells us to be non-judgemental. This is not a very realistic stance, for obvious reasons: no one can be expected not to pass judgement on others; we need to pass judgement to survive. Despite its physical weakness, the human species evolved because of its ability to make judgements about threats from and in its environment. Judging is a very deep-set and basic human behaviour. It is simply not possible to be non-judgemental. If you don't believe me, try it. Try going to the roughest neighbourhood in your area and walk the streets. See if you can last just one hour without passing some kind of judgement. 'Oh, that's different,' the vested interests will cry, 'you're asking someone to put themselves in a dangerous situation and not pass any judgements.' Yes, I am, and no, it is not different. If you lived in one of those areas would you be prepared to listen to the call to non-judgementalism? Of course not. Why do we have to pass judgements on the street? To avoid being hurt and to avoid the need to have to hurt anyone else (accidentally or in self-defence). Why do we have to pass judgements in counselling? To avoid being hurt or avoid hurting anyone else either accidentally or in self-defence. There is no difference between the two situations: judgement is necessary for survival.

Other less threatening issues also force us to be judgemental in counselling. For instance, let's assume you communicate in a manner which denotes a high level of education. Your grammar is precise, your vocabulary is complex and colourful, your sentences are long and consist of many interwoven phrases and your vocal characteristics would be judged by most as representing the élite in your country. Would you use the full complexity of your language to counsel a 16-year-old filing clerk? No way. You would tailor virtually everything about your presentation to facilitate communication with the person you are trying to help. And how do you do that? Well, as you've probably guessed, *you make judgements*. You have to judge education level, linguistic sophistication and so on to make the adjustments that will enable you to communicate effectively.

In short, non-judgementalism is a naive ideal which emerged from the overenthusiasm for counselling in the 1950s and 1960s. We now know better. We now know that clients respond much better to genuine people offering counselling than to those who seem artificial because they pretend not to do what we know everybody does – that is, pass judgements.

EXERCISE

The next time you are in conversation with someone who is either way below or way above your educational level, notice what changes you make to facilitate communication. Notice how you change your language to talk to children. Notice how the younger the child, the more dramatic are the changes you make. How did you know what changes to make? What cues indicated to you that you should make changes? Catch yourself in the act of passing the judgement the non-directive brigade will tell you they don't make!

Speak to clients in their language

Genuineness is the ability to consistently communicate a true picture of your feelings or views on any issue. Cynics would suggest that genuineness is the ability to be perceived as being genuine. Or that the hardest part of being genuine or sincere is faking it.

Be yourself – but apply different skills to different situations

We are told that we should be completely genuine in counselling. Of course you should, but that doesn't mean that the skills you apply to counselling shouldn't be different from those you apply to other situations. As a manager who has to use a wide range of skills for the job at hand, you will know how important it is to alter the beliefs, attitudes and behaviours required to do differing tasks. You wouldn't use the same level of diplomacy with your work colleagues that you would use with troubled customers; you would tailor your behaviour to fit the situation. In reality we have to use different skills in different situations. That does not mean that you are non-genuine in some roles – quite the contrary. If you know what skills must be used to get results and adopt them to achieve that end you are being entirely genuine in your attempts to help the client.

Avoidance of criticism

How do you react to criticism? Does it fill you full of trust for the critic? Does it inspire and motivate you to form an effective problem-solving relationship with him or her? Hardly! It is more likely to make you reactionary or obstinate, or, at very least, less cooperative than you might otherwise have been. *Stop!* Doesn't that contradict what we've just said about not showing 'unconditional positive regard'? *No!* Allow yourself to be affected by whatever the client throws at you, but don't turn that reaction into criticism or hostile negative judgement. What is the difference in terms of action between disapproving and criticizing?

Reflection

Reflecting and summarizing

What is the best way to convince someone you are genuinely interested in, and understand, what they mean? It is to paraphrase, reflect or summarize their message and ask for confirmation of your understanding. There are many different ways of reflecting and summarizing. There are also many different aspects of the client's message which can be reflected. Novice counsellors assume you should merely reflect what is said. But reflection counselling is open to anything you notice, as it is in a social situation. You can reflect what you notice, or what you would expect to notice but which is absent. We'll cover what and how to reflect later.

Good listening habits

Most of us consider ourselves to be good listeners. Why, then, are most of us so surprised when someone actually listens to us? Could it be that not many of us actually are good listeners? If you have reached any position of seniority in your company, the chances are that your listening skills are already part of your 'good habits repertoire'. If you are on the way up, you'll probably have discovered how effective listening is as an influence tool: people listen to people who listen to them. Let's expand and formalize those guidelines. Basic good listening habits are constituted as follows:

- Create the right environment for listening.
- Be interested in, and show interest in, the person speaking and the content of their speech.
- Take time to fully understand what is said before responding.
- Check your understanding regularly and summarize from time to time.
- Maintain concentration both when complex ideas are being expressed or the speaker becomes boring.
- Prevent your prejudices and other emotional reactions from interfering with your listening.

What else could you add to this list?

Listening is not diagnosing

Novice counsellors (those learning to do formally what they already understand informally) tend to think that their role is to diagnose the client's problem. It is not. It is, and can only be, the client's responsibility to diagnose their own problem during the listening stage. Your role as a manager providing coun-selling is to understand the problem *as the client sees it*. Diagnosing the problem in terms of the Skills Training Model (see page 70) is acceptable, but only *after* you have established a strong rapport, communicated your understanding of the client's problem and encouraged the client to explore other ways of looking at the problem.

Labelling and interpreting

Don't do either! Don't deliberately label your clients – even in your own mind. Why? Labelling has the strange effect of deluding us into thinking we understand something when in fact all we have done is given the thing we don't understand a name. Judge if you have to, but avoid labelling. Impulsive labelling blocks further attempts at understanding. Given that you are seeking understanding of the client's problem as they see it, you won't be tempted to label them, will you?

The same applies to interpreting. Don't deliberately interpret. Don't try reading between the lines, because the chances are you'll be wrong. Most models of human behaviour work for some people in a specific place at a particular time under highly specified circumstances. If you do want to interpret the meaning of something the client has said (and that is an all too human temptation), *ask the client to do it*. Their interpretations can lead to something positive. Yours, frankly, are little more than intellectual masturbation at this stage.

EXERCISE

Name five things which we humans have labelled but don't really understand. Gravity is one.

In this stage of counselling, interpretation and evaluation are not appropriate. You haven't gathered all the facts from the client. You know that, but more importantly they know that too. In their eyes, therefore, you are not yet capable of any form of evaluation or interpretation. Later, when the client knows you have the facts and knows you understand their problem, they will accept your evaluations, but not now. Even later, the client may choose to acknowledge your interpretations but disagree with them.

Common principle 2:
Generate and maintain a good rapport

Although this may seem obvious, unless the counsellor and client operate together as a team to understand and then in some way solve the client's problem, the chances of success are limited. Nonetheless, this has to be said because there are several counselling styles in existence which do *not* operate on a cooperative basis. There is no place for any such style in the modern workplace. Indeed that may be a strong pointer as to the counselling methods we should be using. They should reflect the level of cooperation and team participation that is present in the contemporary work environment. The client should feel they can call upon their team-mate to help solve their problems for the better performance of the team.

Developing a strong rapport

'A relationship with a caring listening other is often all that is required for clients to solve their problems. The relationship, in some cases, is a necessary

Counselling is a team exercise

and sufficient healing device.' Unfortunately that observation has been taken too far. Because a good relationship was sufficient for some, it was deemed necessary for all. A large number of counselling schools sprang up preaching the message 'all that is needed is a supportive relationship with a caring other'. We've now moved on to a more sophisticated level of thinking where we recognize that a good rapport is absolutely essential but only rarely sufficient; the other seven common principles should also be applied (in whole or in part). We will show precisely how to develop a strong rapport later. (Refer to the section on rapport development starting on page 117.)

Expertness, trustworthiness, attractiveness

In research study after research study, the three counsellor factors that are repeatedly demonstrably effective are expertness, trustworthiness and attractiveness. Your clients or staff will attribute expertness when you are articulate, comprehensible and knowledgeable about the subjects being discussed. So, in a counselling situation being expert is derived from listening to and understanding their problem. They will attribute trustworthiness when you reveal both your positive and negative motives, and especially when you disclose information that most people would consider it would be safer for you not to reveal. They will attribute attractiveness when you are human (not machine-like), humorous, approachable, and make your appearance attractive. Note that we did not say you have to possess movie-star looks, but that you should use what you do have attractively. Who do you consider to be expert, trustworthy and attractive? What is it about their behaviour that makes you think so? We will look at the details of how to develop these later. (See page 188 *et seq.*.)

Personal revelations

No, not that kind! Keep your really intimate details to yourself. What kind of things can you reveal in counselling to improve the relationship? Perhaps we can answer the question with another question. What kind of information would you reveal to a friend who was just outside your innermost circle of friends?

EXERCISE

Think of someone who has had a really profound effect on your life. If the rapport had not been so good, do you think that you would have let that person influence you? What was special about the rapport?

Common principle 3:
Provide opportunities for the expression of emotions

The emotional bypass in other forms of helping

In medicine and dentistry there is a strong emotional component to whatever disorder leads the client to seek help. The emotions stem from the anxiety which any serious symptoms create and, depending on the person, the reaction can be minor or extreme. While physicians and dentists don't have to address the emotional component directly, they have to be sensitive to it. Why? Because the client is in emotional distress while the disorder is present and because, as soon as the disorder is treated, the anxiety and related emotions disappear. In effect, the healthcare professional completes an emotional bypass. The last time you had a new symptom and sought medical intervention how did you feel before and after treatment?

Emotion in counselling

By contrast, in counselling the emotion is the disorder. Yet, it can be bypassed in the same way. Yes, it can be altered by changing the perception which gave rise to it, or the beliefs on which it is based. Yes, the emotion can be dissipated by allowing the client to express it to the point of exhaustion. But one way or another the emotion, once it has arisen, has to be acknowledged, treated as valid and not bypassed. (Later we will discuss techniques of emotional management.) Unfortunately that truism is taken too far by some counselling schools which suggest that re-expressing emotions from years or even decades ago is necessary for a full recovery. Some go as far as insisting their clients 're-live' the 'birth trauma'. Utter nonsense! If it wasn't true you'd think that such concepts had sprung straight from a Woody Allen film!

EXERCISE

Think about the last time you had an emotional imbalance (we all get them). Did it take more or less time to be resolved than the feelings you had when you consulted the doctor?

So, how do you give the client as much opportunity to express emotions as they wish? By not shrinking away from the expression of emotions. How? By resisting the temptation to do anything for clients who are expressing strong emotions. By avoiding all the normal 'there, there, it'll be all right' and other 'please stop crying, it's upsetting me' type statements. You don't have to do anything about the client's feelings other than listen to and acknowledge them.

Feelings, especially extreme ones, tend to muddy the waters of reason. But once they are expressed and/or exhausted, clarity returns. Let the emotional sediment settle in its own time. Simply be there as an understanding person sharing a journey with a troubled friend.

How do you provide opportunities for the expression of emotions? What methods are available for eliciting feelings?

- Simply ask the client to report their feelings.
- Invite the client to express their feelings explicitly during discussions. Most people express their feelings indirectly via tone of voice. But tone is insufficiently precise.
- As most problems produce a range of feelings, ask the client to list the range of feelings being experienced about whatever area you are exploring.
- Feelings occur in patterns in the same way thoughts do. This is hardly surprising since feelings are based on thought patterns. Ask the client to sequence their feelings on the issue you are exploring. What happens first? Then how do they feel? And then?
- Feelings vary in their frequency. Ask the client to note the frequency of particular feelings.
- After a conversation, ask them to report what they were feeling during the various stages of the discussion.

EXERCISE

Think of other ways in which you encourage the expression of feelings.

Common principle 4:
Provide support and reassurance

Most people with well-developed practical counselling skills have a theoretical perception that counselling is about providing support and reassurance. While support and reassurance are extremely important, even central, to successful counselling, there are times when it should be given and times when it should not.

Requirements in one stage can be taboo in another

For instance, offering support is essential when you understand the problem, but offering it before you know the full details will be interpreted as insincerity or worse. Don't offer support until you know that the client knows that you understand the problem *and* its full scope. How do you feel when someone tells you 'it'll be all right' in response to a problem you know is unresolvable? Or in response to a problem about which you know they know nothing?

Shared experience relief

Often clients come for assistance because not only have they never encountered a problem like their current one, they do not know of anyone else who has. Typically that line of thinking evolves into 'I'm the only one with this problem.' When you detect such thinking, one of the most effective things you can do is to gradually explain that others also suffer this problem. It seems that just knowing this gives enormous relief and reassurance. Others too suffer this problem. Others too feel they are alone. Others too find some comfort in

Support and reassurance

realizing that they are not on their own. Naturally, in an ideal world, you would like to see the client coming to that realization themselves. What can you ask clients that will help them towards that realization?

How and when do you provide support and reassurance?

Support is best given by demonstrating that you are listening, that you really are trying to understand and that you are there to help them solve their problem in their own way. It can also be demonstrated in other ways. You can ask how they have already tried to solve/manage the problem; on a practical level you can ask the client what you can do immediately to help them, such as by making a few phone calls on their behalf or acting as a mediator. There will be other possibilities. You may not be able to do anything, but offering in itself demonstrates support.

Reassurance can be provided once the client knows you understand them and their problem (not before) by letting them know you have faith in their ability to solve the problem, that you are sure they solved a problem similar to this one last year/month/week, that others have faced this problem before, felt exactly as they do and eventually found a constructive way through.

Be very careful with your reassurances. Go too far and it will sound as if you are denying the validity of the client's reactions. Don't go far enough and the client may feel you don't believe that they can handle the problem.

Common principle 5:
Provide positive expectation and hope

There is a very strong connection between this principle and the next – providing plausible explanations and feasible solutions. The successful generation of a positive expectation and hope for the future depends largely on offering plausible explanations and feasible solutions. But they can be and regularly are given separately.

You can create a sense of expectation and hope by your non-verbal behaviour. How? Genuinely believe there is a positive future for the client and your body language, tone of voice, facial expression and so on will automatically convey the message. You can also hold such an expectation – possess such a faith – without any evidence or rationale. Religions all over the world depend on unquestioning faith to heal and minister to troubled souls, largely to good effect.

The power of thoughts and hope

Thoughts vary in their effects on the mind, body and spirit. At their best they can lift the spirit, cure the body and develop the mind. At their worst they can torture the spirit, disable the mind and kill the body. For most of us, life is lived somewhere between the two extremes. Which extreme do you prefer? Shouldn't you then learn how to harness your thoughts to live in the condition you prefer? Some choose not to. Some develop psychosomatic disorders from not doing so.

The word 'psychosomatic' conjures up images of people with stress-related physical illnesses. It is far more wide-ranging than that. From our point of view, people can come to counselling with emotional and other workplace problems which have a psychosomatic origin. Some clients will actually be directly responsible for their own emotional and physical illnesses. But to say that is extremely threatening, and we need to present that information more subtly. After all, how would you react to the following questions? Who was your last close relative to die? Could their death have been psychosomatically caused? How would you react if you were told that all of your ailments, past and present and future, were psychosomatically caused?

How do we subtly influence our members of staff to choose to realize what effects their thoughts and expectations have on their lives and to learn to control them? One way is to ask staff if they would like to know how some of the world's greatest minds have viewed the management of the mind. 'There is nothing either good or bad, but thinking makes it so', said Shakespeare, quite a long time ago. 'The mind is its own place, and in itself can make a heav'n of hell, a hell of heav'n', added Milton – not that new a thought either. Another from the distant past is 'Great men [people, please!] are they who see that spiritual is stronger than any material force, that thoughts rule the world' – Emerson. And perhaps the parting shot should be from the person who did more to enlighten human thought than anyone else in the history of our species: 'The highest possible stage in moral culture is when we recognise that we ought to control our thoughts' – Darwin.

With thoughts and thinking, as with every other aspect of human life: control it or it will control you.

One way of helping clients to accept that some of their behaviours may be causing, or exacerbating, their problems is to give them the information indirectly in a non-threatening context and then help them to see how the behaviours/thought/feelings concerned also apply in their current situation. A discussion about the client's general health is expected in counselling. Use that discussion to communicate and explain the influence of the mind on all aspects of health using the psychosomatic influence matrix below.

The psychosomatic influence matrix

This matrix consists of two interacting dimensions: psychological factors and physiological factors. The psychological behaviours in which one engages can be harmful, inhibiting, neutral, or health-enhancing. The same applies to the physiological factors.

Ask your clients to examine their behaviour to determine what they do which is harmful or inhibiting to them. Which factors in their environment are harmful or inhibiting? And, more importantly, what do they propose to do about them? See the irrational beliefs and dangerous thoughts list in Appendix II.

What should they do about those harmful influences?

Change the beliefs underlying them, then adopt new constructive replacement behaviours. It is extremely important to adopt replacements for any change in

	PSYCHOLOGICAL INFLUENCE			
ENVIRONMENTAL INFLUENCE	PSYCHOLOGICAL CAUSES	PSYCHOLOGICAL INHIBITION OF CURATIVE POWERS	PSYCHOLOGICALLY NEUTRAL FACTORS	PSYCHOLOGICAL ENHANCEMENT OF CURATIVE POWERS
ENVIRONMENTAL PHYSICAL CAUSES	PROBABILITY OF ILLNESS (MENTAL & PHYSICAL) VERY HIGH	PROBABILITY OF ILLNESS (M&P) HIGH	PROBABILITY OF ILLNESS MEDIUM	NEUTRAL
HEALTH INHIBITING FACTORS ENVIRONMENT PHYSICAL	PROBABILITY OF ILLNESS (M&P) HIGH	MEDIUM	NEUTRAL	PROBABILITY OF GOOD HEALTH (M&P) MEDIUM
ENVIRONMENTALLY PHYSICALLY NEUTRAL FACTORS	PROBABILITY OF ILLNESS MEDIUM	NEUTRAL	PROBABILITY OF GOOD HEALTH (M&P) MEDIUM	HIGH
HEALTH ENHANCING PHYSICAL/EXTERNAL FACTORS	NEUTRAL	PROBABILITY OF GOOD HEALTH (M&P) MEDIUM	HIGH	PROBABILITY OF GOOD HEALTH (M&P) VERY HIGH

human behaviour or belief; without them the old behaviour has a ready-made place to fill or refill. Behaviours and habits (mental or physical) are never stopped. They are only ever replaced. One of the main objectives of counselling is to replace destructive mental and actual behaviours with constructive alternatives; to replace harmful habits with helpful ones; to replace disempowering beliefs with empowering versions.

Beliefs and their effects on results/outcomes

Positive expectation and hope are highly effective placebos yet, ironically, they are a genuine cure for low spirits and troubled souls. If people believe they will get better, their chances of getting better are dramatically increased. If people believe they will feel good, they will feel good. If people believe you can help them, you can help them. Much of counselling is belief-management, expectation-management and hope-management.

Vicious circles and virtuous circles

Beliefs are so powerful because they become self-fulfilling prophecies. In one direction the prophecy completes a virtuous circle and, in the other, a vicious circle. Once a problem starts it can become self-perpetuating. Once hope and positive expectation take hold they become self-perpetuating. What beliefs of yours have turned out to be self-fulfilling?

Harnessing self-fulfilling prophecies in counselling

Transmit belief in positive change to clients if you want them to improve. If you believe they will improve, they will detect that through the mechanisms we have covered elsewhere and will then be more likely to believe a solution is possible too. How do you transmit such a belief? There are several ways. But first let's look at the power of the placebo effect.

The placebo effect and powerful placebos

The placebo effect is probably the most studied phenomenon in both psychology and medicine. It is enormously powerful. For those who haven't come across it before, it is the beneficial healing effect which takes place when people believe they have received something which they assume will benefit their condition. Its most commonly perceived effect is shown when a person taking harmless and inert 'sugar pills' in the belief that they are a 'real medicine' experiences a clinical improvement, or even cure.

If people choose to believe something, it can profoundly affect both their behaviour and their metabolism. For instance, people who were deceived into assisting in an experiment to investigate the effects of hunger and thirst on perception demonstrated marked differences in behavioural and physiological measures depending on what they believed. When the allotted time for the experiment was up, the participants were divided into two groups. The first group were given strong motivational reasons for continuing ('It is expected as part of your course.') The second group were offered no reasons and therefore had to generate their own motives for continuing with the pain of hunger and thirst. When the experiment was completed the second group not only ate and drank less than the first but also had lower levels on metabolic measures of hunger in their blood.

What happened? Those given no reason for continuing generated their own internal motives for doing so – 'I'm not hungry anyway. It is a great way to lose weight' and so on. Those thoughts then affected changes in their bodies. Self-generated thoughts and beliefs in this instance had a greater effect on the participants than other-generated thoughts.

We could fill the rest of this book and a few more besides with evidence for the power of the mind over the body. From innumerable studies we know the mind can control, or at least strongly influence, the immune system, the endocrine system, the nervous system (even at single-cell level!), the muscular system, the blood circulation system – in fact, every system.

Some really bizarre things that ought not to happen, sometimes, do. For instance, some people can use their minds to control the temperature of specified parts of their bodies, leaving surrounded parts unaffected. We don't understand quite how these effects are brought about, but we know they are.

EXERCISE

Assuming you don't have any heart problems, try to control the speed of your heart just by thinking. Take a watch and by monitoring your pulse rate with your first two fingers on the pulse point in your wrist, concentrate on either speeding up or slowing down your heart rate.

Placebo management

The evidence for the placebo effect and its influence of the mind on the body is very strong. So how do we manage this phenomenon? First we ought to find out what makes a placebo optimally effective. There are three interrelated variables:

1   The source of the placebo is authoritative, expert and credible.
2   The placebo is 'belief-matched' with the client.
3   The placebo administration process elicits commitment.

The factors which make a placebo source authoritative, expert and credible are discussed in the section on persuasion in counselling starting on page 188. For now we'll look at the other two requirements in detail.

Belief-matched placebos

The acceptability of a placebo and the level of its effectiveness depend on the match between the recipient's beliefs and the rationale behind the placebo. For example, you would not find a non-religious person accepting or being helped by a religious leader's blessing, but you would expect to see a religious devotee being heavily influenced by a religious ceremony aimed at a cure or amelioration. You would also witness an increase in the effectiveness of the 'placebo' with increases in the seniority of the religious figure performing the ceremony. Status assists the placebo effect.

A believer in science may be influenced by science-based placebos and a believer in astrology will be influenced by a favourable reading by a famous astrologer. As a counsellor, you should try to identify the staff member's belief system so that you can choose the placebo most likely to be effective. But, as we have said elsewhere, there are only a few placebos which you will be able to provide with any credibility. That therefore means there has to be a match between the provider and the recipient's beliefs about that provider.

The client, too, can provide an effective placebo and is, after all, best placed to provide one matched to their beliefs. If clients can generate their own reasons/placebos, they will wholeheartedly accept them as a remedy to their problem. Your role as placebo manager is to reinforce the client's rationale – to add your credibility and weight to it.

The nastier the cure, the ...

Eliciting commitment to a placebo

If people perceive the cure as being nasty, but they are prepared to have it, that must mean that they believe it will work. There is a direct link between the nastiness of the 'cure' and the strength of its placebo effect. The nastier it is perceived to be, the more they have to believe it will work in order to do it. So the best placebos are those which taste worst. Or, in our terms, the best placebos are those which require most effort.

People also need to rationalize their action: 'I have just done this so I must believe that I have done so for a purpose.' Harness this phenomenon by creating a situation in which your clients do something which is supposedly beneficial for them without telling them why it is beneficial. The internal reasons which they have to generate for engaging in the activity, because they are devised and owned by them, have much more power than any you can suggest.

People required to make statements of renunciation toward their problem and statements of affirmation toward the solution are affected by the same need to rationalize: 'I said these things voluntarily, so I must believe them.' So invite your clients to curse the problem and praise the potential, but as yet unspecified, solutions.

People are highly influenced when they can identify and vilify an enemy, either internal or external. Once the cause of the problem has been identified and vilified, recovery is much more likely. Humans are at their best and worst in war. Declare war on the problem and harness the power of the shared enemy.

People are also more easily influenced when they feel they are part of a special group from which others are excluded. Those who have experienced and survived a disaster, for instance, are special to each other. They share a common strength acquired from the experience – a bond others cannot understand or share. You can harness this phenomenon via support groups or if you have suffered the problem yourself. See also cognitive dissonance (p. 99).

Certainty of effect

The strongest characteristic of the placebo effect is certainty. The more certain you are that it will work, the more certain it will be to work. The same applied to the client. What you are going to give them or do to them *is* going to solve their problem. If you are in any doubt about the power of certainty or the placebo effect, I suggest you take a trip to Haiti and learn about voodoo culture. It is *not* a big screen fantasy.

EXERCISE

When have you been helped by something which turned out to be a placebo? Who was/is the best physician from whom you received help? Did they help you to believe a 'cure' would be effective? If so, how did they behave? What made you sure they were right?

Common principle 6:
Provide plausible explanations and feasible solutions

Why is it necessary to provide or facilitate the development of a rationale and feasible solution?

Amongst the many reasons your staff have sought help are two that are very common. Either they don't understand the problem and its causes or they cannot see a solution (or they see a solution and can't accept it). Helping them to explain and understand the problem makes it more manageable. Giving or devising a solution provides hope – and it also helps to harness the placebo effect. When you go for help of any kind, why do you like to hear explanations and solutions?

Whatever the current received wisdom on non-directiveness, the client will look to you for explanations and possible solutions. If (at this stage) you withhold those when it is clear to the client that you have something to offer your credibility and trustworthiness will be detrimentally affected. If you decide to advise them to come to their own conclusions, you had best be prepared to provide a good case for doing so. If you fail to convince them, your motives for counselling will be called into question. In my experience, clients want your opinion as a starting point in their search for a believable rationale. It is most unlikely that they will accept your rationale without objection and detailed consideration. Remember, they seek an understanding and resolution of their problem that is acceptable to them.

One commonly used way of finding an acceptable explanation is to seek out a range of possible contenders and evaluate them until only a few likely candidates remain. Your staff members may expect you to provide some of the contenders. Even so, it is still preferable to encourage your client to come up with their own rationale, but not if withholding your rationale is going to damage your relationship. You can, of course, prompt and offer suggestions.

Which solutions and explanations are plausible?

Given all the problems which plague counselling (see earlier), what kinds of solutions and explanations are going to be acceptable to the clients? Any which fit with the culture of the workplace. Any which are skill- and competence-based, objectives-based and outcomes-based. That rules out 99 per cent of all known counselling methods; most are process-based. You may be interested to know that the psychological profession largely abandoned conducting outcome-based research into counselling because measuring and proving a beneficial outcome turned out to be virtually impossible. Instead they focused on processes, which led to an increase in the numbers of counselling methods oriented towards process at the expense of outcome. But now that we have competence-based models in the workplace, now that we can measure whether or not someone possesses a skill, we can start measuring outcomes again. Skill-based solutions to people-problems are by far the most credible in the contemporary workplace.

As we saw in the previous section, the plausibility of a solution is heavily influenced by its source. What does that tell us about which solutions we should be offering? You, as a manager, are a credible source of skills-based explanations and solutions. Your role is to ensure the proper application of your team's skills to achieve specified objectives. You would not be a credible source of hormonal or metabolic explanations. You would not be a credible source of family-conflict-based explanations, or early childhood experience-type explanations. No, you are a successful practitioner of skills in an environment where the application of skills is the route to achievement; you therefore are most credible using, and offering, skills-based explanations.

To advise or not to advise, that may (or may not) be the question

Advice is the offering of a solution or the means of determining a solution. The more feasible it is, the more acceptable it is. Offering feasible solutions is a central requirement of effective counselling, but the slightest false move may unleash a potential battle:

> To advise or not to advise,
> that is the question.
> Whether it is better for results
> to suffer the tortuous road to self-counsel,
> or take arms against the uncertainties of life
> and by advising seek to end them.

Apologies to Shakespeare. But I hope it illustrates the point: you have reasons for wanting to give advice and reasons for not doing so. How do we decide when to advise and when not to, for surely there are times when it is appropriate? We have all sought advice at some time. Ay. There is the nub. When invited, advice is acceptable. When not, it is not.

When you have sought advice and then trusted and used it, how did you separate the good from the bad? Is the best advice not that which you wanted to hear? If so, why did you seek advice in the first place? Or is the best advice that which gives you what you did want without demanding that you give up something else you wish to keep? Oh dear. It becomes more complicated by the minute. Indeed, the rest of this book could be dedicated to the psychology of choosing which advice to listen to. We can't do that. But what I can offer is two little lines which Confucius might have said, but MacLennan actually did:

> Never trust advice from person immunized from the consequences of that advice.
> Make self immune from persons seeking consequences for themselves with their advice.

Causal explanations/rationales should be linked to the encouragement of empowering beliefs

For any solution to be longlasting, it should offer the client a better philosophy for living than the one that brought them to counselling in the first place. Virtually all counselling styles – including the skills-based model we will introduce later for use in the workplace – provide their clients with this. However,

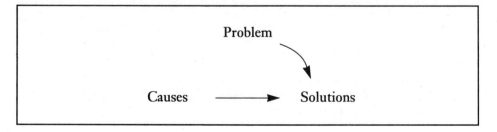

an improved philosophy for living is useless on its own. It needs to be tied to, and based on, the causes of the client's problem. Solutions that are not based on the components of the problem have no credibility.

What explanations are plausible? Those which are obviously derived from both the perceived cause and the perceived problem.

To believe or not to believe your own publicity

You will now see why I used 'perceived cause and the perceived problem' in the last sentence. If you do present a rationale, explanation or cause of the client's problem, don't get trapped into believing that what you have offered is true. We cannot establish a definitive causal pattern for any emotional or psychological problem – but that is not important. What is important is not that your causal explanation or the one supplied by the client is correct, but that the client is satisfied with it, believes in it and is willing to use it to solve or manage the problem. One of the best ways to get your client to believe either your causal hypothesis or theirs is for you to believe it yourself. However, while it helps to believe that your explanations of the client's problem are true, you should be aware that no causal explanation is provable; few are even 'logically determinable'. Your clients will most usually need to find a plausible explanation: together you may even be deceived into believing it.

Here is yet another contradiction in counselling: absolute certainty is pivotal to the delivery of the placebo effect. *But certainty is absolute self-delusion when attributing cause.* We will explore this further in Part IV, Issues and Problems, page 215.

No matter how much you delude yourself your causal explanation will certainly be wrong

Does that mean you should not delude yourself? Does it mean you shouldn't even venture a causal hypothesis? *No!* It means that you should do so; offering an explanation of cause is a significant part of the placebo effect. But every so often you should remind yourself that your explanation is almost certainly wrong. Why? Because you need to remain flexible. You must be able to alter your view of the client's problem should the client decide to do so. Remember, what is important is that the client believes whatever explanation is most constructive in terms of helping them to solve their problem. What you believe, while being influential, is of secondary importance.

EXERCISE

Devise a list of plausible causal explanations for the list of the most commonly encountered problems (see 240). Don't worry that this is not your field; your pragmatic business thinking will lead you to produce many plausible causes.

Common principle 7:
Provide opportunities to experience success

Relationship chats

Show your staff member that they are able to have a successful relationship with at least one person – you. Of course, they have successful relationships with others, but they probably don't *feel* as though they do. They need to know that at least one aspect of their lives is going well. So, in your periodic relationship maintenance chats, point out the things that are going well in the relationship. Tell them the positive feelings you have towards them and their actions. For some problems such a demonstration of success will not be necessary and may even raise suspicions. But it almost always helps.

Success in making at least one other person understand

Counselling is not something people enter into lightly (at least in the UK). Distressed people think long and hard before seeking the kind of help you are offering. Counselling is partly sought because the client can find no one else who understands the problem. There is a feeling of success to be had from being able to make just one other person understand when, up to then, nobody else has. Your acknowledgement of their success should be genuine; don't underestimate how difficult it is to even start to explain a complex problem you don't really understand when you are in deep emotional pain. When have you been speechless with emotional pain? When have you been so troubled that you couldn't think clearly? If you can't answer both of those questions think very carefully before counselling others; not because you lack the experience, but because you are not being honest with yourself.

Success in understanding the various components of the problem

Prior to counselling, the client's level of emotion usually prevents them from seeing clearly, which in turn increases the level of emotional turmoil. The multi-faceted nature of the problem is just one big haze to the client. With your help, they will gradually begin to organize the problem in their minds and start to see the various components. That can be perceived as a significant success by the client. You can point it out if they have missed it. Naturally, it is best pointed out with the use of questions:

- 'What do you understand about the problem now?'
- 'What progress have we made?'
- 'What strengths does that tell you you have?'
- 'In which ways do you feel better now?'
- 'In which ways will that realization help you solve the rest of the problem?'
- 'How can we build on that?'

The principle of pointing out success with questions is simple. Either ask the client to tell you about the success, or ask them to acknowledge it by considering how it can be useful.

Common principle 8:
Encourage the adoption of empowering beliefs

Virtually every counselling system has some mechanism for encouraging the client to adopt empowering beliefs. We will explore how to encourage the adoption of such beliefs later. For now, let us look at some of the surrounding issues.

Who is in control? The further up the following list of counsellor behaviours, the more the client is in control:

We'll explain what each of the behaviours in the left-hand column means later

Listening	Client Controlling
Reflecting	▲
Clarifying	
Summarizing	
Drawing out	
Questioning	
Suggesting	
Advising	▼
Prescribing	Counsellor Controlling

but, for now, the main issue is: the more control the client has over the process, the more likely it is to be effective. That does not mean that offering prescriptions is always a counsellor-controlled event or that listening is always client-controlled. For instance, the counsellor can adopt a 'listening only' mode thereby forcing the client to talk (so-called non-directive counsellors do this). Alternatively, the client can demand a prescription/solution and the counsellor can take control by refusing to give one.

How do you ensure that you give the client as much control as possible?

If the client demands that you prescribe a solution explain that you are not in their position and only they can come to a sensible decision. If they insist, give your honest opinion with the caveat that you are not them. If seeking your advice empowers the client, give your advice.

The same principle applies when you are providing a highly powerful placebo. 'What?' you might say, 'Giving a placebo takes away power from the client!' Not so. If the client believes that your solution will work, they have adopted a belief that helps and empowers them. Yet another paradox!

Encourage the adoption of empowering beliefs

Encourage the client to take notes as a route to empowerment

You may fall into the trap of taking notes during a counselling session. Be careful. You are supposed to be providing a confidential service. How can you guarantee confidentiality if you commit the proceedings to paper which will be stored in your office? If you do take notes – and some at least are necessary to cover your back – you should not put *anything* on the notes that might disclose the client's identity. Obviously you will need a coding system so you can identify one set of notes from another, but it is often advisable to keep the code-key off the premises. And, in any event, why should only you be taking notes? After all, it is the client who needs to keep track of the process and monitor their thoughts. Most counsellors are horrified at this prospect. Why? Because it means they lose control, and are seen to do so (yet they will claim the client ought to be in control). Ask yourself, would you expect to solve a complex problem at work without using some means (computer or paper) of recording your thoughts as you explored various solutions? Of course not. And that's exactly why you should encourage your client to keep track. It may be that solving problems in a systematic way is a skill they lack. In which case getting them to take notes in itself is a step towards developing that skill.

Help the client take responsibility for choosing

Your role is to help the client solve their own problem in their own way. You can, of course, help them by providing a structure to solve the problem, but the solution must be theirs – they must own it, believe in it and arrive at it by themselves. The client may, however, require some assistance before reaching the point where they are prepared to take responsibility for making the appropriate choices. What else can you do to encourage clients to take responsibility for choosing?

At the start of the counselling, clients will demonstrate one of a range of responsibility-taking behaviours:

- Some will take no responsibility for their problem or its resolution.
- Others will take some responsibility, but don't want to come to a solution/resolution.
- Many will perceive that they are taking responsibility but are not actually doing so.
- Some will take partial responsibility, but not in the areas that will make a difference.
- Others will take partial responsibility, but not enough to make a difference.
- Some will take total responsibility and just want a listening ear to help them through.

Each of those client types has different needs. Those at the end of the list need support and understanding. Those near the top of the list need understanding and gradual persuasion towards taking responsibility for their problem. An overriding principle in counselling is that clients will only solve/resolve their problems if they take responsibility for doing so. They have to adopt empowering beliefs and behaviours. What else can you do to encourage clients to adopt empowering beliefs?

How many counsellors does it take to change a light bulb? None, if you can get the light bulb to take up DIY!

Summary of the common principles

Equipped with the eight common principles, you could easily devise your own counselling method. As long as the system you adopt includes them in some plausible format, your system will be as effective as any of the many others. Less ambitiously, you now have all you need to counsel effectively. As long as you follow the eight common principles your counselling will be at least as effective as anyone else's.

Whichever counselling methods you go on to use (including the STM), if you ever lose your way during counselling fall back on the eight common principles. Doing so will re-establish your person-focus, the temporary loss of which was the reason you went astray.

5

THE EIGHT-STAGE MODEL

If you forget everything else in this book, remember this point. Actually listening to your staff is so rare, and so effective as a helping tool, as to be virtually priceless. If you do nothing more than just listen, you will help many of your staff to solve their own problems. Listening is so important that you can only proceed through the stages we are about to present after the member of staff knows you have listened and understood. A few years ago, I heard a wonderful little ditty that encapsulates this notion wonderfully: 'Your staff don't care how much you know until they know how much you care.' By 'care' I mean the willingness to listen and to try to understand.

Some harsh realities

Care as you may, you will be faced with some painful dilemmas, no matter how much you listen and understand. In the workplace, problems have to be confronted and solved as quickly and as effectively as possible. That may mean that you can't afford to wait ten sessions for a staff member to tell you what the problem is. Harsh and heartless as it may sound, you are running a business or the department of a business, not a welfare organization for troubled employees. We ought to remind those who take the contrary view that if there were no businesses making profits and paying taxes there would be *no* social welfare provision whatsoever. So, with a difficult/reluctant/resistant client, you will have to decide whether it is best to:

- continue hoping they will eventually take control and resume their normal work performance
- compromise your belief in giving the client maximum control and tell them what to do to get back to performing

- refer them to some other service (state or privately funded) outside of the company
- suggest that they take sick leave until they resolve the problem
- suggest that they take sick leave for a fixed period after which you will expect either normal performance or resignation
- acknowledge that they are unlikely to resume normal performance and take appropriate action
- acknowledge that the time and costs of resuming normal performance are greater than the cost of replacement and retraining
- take whatever decisions are necessary to enable you to fulfil your obligations to your company.

That's the real world of counselling at work, at its most cost-conscious. Most of the counselling you provide at work will have a more successful outcome. The above are the worst-case scenarios – the decisions that no one fulfilling the role of counsellor and manager ever wants to have to face. The good news is you won't face these dilemmas very often, if at all. But you do need to be prepared for them. And you do need to carry out the tough decisions. If you do not, you will not have a job; your company will eventually be brought down by the welfare burden placed upon it.

The eight-stage model in overview

Let's take an overview of the model and then explore in-depth how to provide counselling in a commercially relevant way. First, we will list the stages, then we will specify the objectives in each stage and the factors which indicate when transition to the next stage is appropriate. Second, we will look at how to actually provide what is required in each stage – which mental skills you will have to use and how to use them. Remember that you already possess many or most of these skills, but may never before have articulated them or ordered them in the format you are about to see.

Stage	Activity
0	Pre-counselling awareness
1	Rapport formation
2	Understanding
3	Reframing
4	Solution searching
5	Solution planning and commitment development
6	Implementation
7	Evaluation and adjustment
8	Ending and consolidation.

Now we will detail the objectives of each stage and the indicators that tell us when we should move on to the next stage.

EXERCISE

Guess what each of the above mean and compare your answers to the following.

---

0   Pre-counselling awareness

The client gradually becomes aware that they have a problem which they are unable to solve on their own. When that point has been reached they will be receptive to counselling, or indeed seek it out. If you have a staff member who is having difficulty, your objective could be either to support them as much as possible or help them to realize that they have a problem for which you can offer help. Be ultra-careful if you take the latter path; people resent others pointing out their problems, uninvited.

1   Rapport formation

The objective here is to form a relationship in which the client feels comfortable with you and your role as counsellor. No progress is possible if you fail to establish a counselling rapport. You will know you have one when the client starts to tell you about the problem with a level of honesty which goes beyond that which you would usually expect from your normal relationship.

2   Understanding

Your objective here is to understand the problem *from the client's perspective*, and for the client to know that you do. You can find out when you have achieved this objective by asking the client. You will be unable to progress unless you *do* understand the problem, and any attempt to move forward will be resisted by the client.

3   Reframing

Your objective in reframing is to encourage the client to see the problem from a perspective that makes its management possible. By definition, if the client already had such a perspective they would not have come to a counselling session. When you have helped them to a more manageable perspective they will be ready to move to the next stage. No progression or problem resolution is possible until the client changes their perspective of the problem.

4   Solution searching

Identifying a solution at the most general level is the objective of this stage. A solution type is sufficient. You will arrive at this point having explored various solution types. Progress to the next stage depends on the client being committed to a particular type of solution. They will resist your attempts to progress until that point.

5   Solution planning and commitment development

Once you have identified a type of solution your objective in this stage is to plan a specific solution and develop the level of commitment necessary to see it through to a successful conclusion. Progress is only possible when the client has expressed their commitment to the solution.

6   Implementation

The obvious objective here is to carry out the plan generated in the previous stage. Specifically your role here is to help the client with their motivation, focus and persistence. Before your progress to the next stage you should have already made a good attempt to implement the plan. The client may push you to the next stage if they are not happy with the results.

7   Evaluation and adjustment

Whether you are pushed into this stage or not, the time will come when the implementation as planned has been completed or has reached an impasse. This is the time when, together, you begin to evaluate and adjust the plan, if necessary. The objectives in this stage can vary enormously, from abandoning a plan the client has lost faith in, to fine-tuning a minor aspect of the plan, to addressing the reasons why the client seems to find fault with every plan. You will only progress to the next stage when the problem solution has been successfully implemented.

8   Ending and consolidation

Now that this particular problem has been overcome, it is wise to help the client consolidate the skills they have learned or the solutions they have adopted. A sensible option is to put the client in a position where they can solve the same or similar problems if (or, more likely, when) they re-emerge.

As you have probably realized by now, there are likely to be occasions in which something emerges in one stage which indicates that an early stage has not been properly handled. In these circumstances, re-addressing the previous stage is the obvious solution. There will also be circumstances in which stages have a closed feedback effect on each other. For instance, the client may initially prefer a particular solution type, but when they come to plan a solution, they discover the courses of action dictated by that solution type are unacceptable to them. You then have to return to the previous stage to seek new solution types. Alternatively, their reasons for not wishing to confront a particular course of action may indicate that they need to pay further attention to their perception of the problem; they may still be viewing parts of the problem from the angle that brought them to counselling in the first place. In short, you will find a strong need to jump back and forth amongst the stages. You will also find that some stages for some problems have to be combined because the feedback between them is so strong that they are clearly functioning as one single stage.

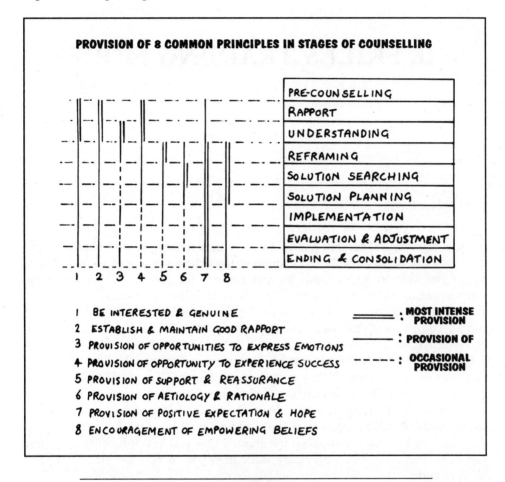

PROVISION OF 8 COMMON PRINCIPLES IN STAGES OF COUNSELLING

PRE-COUNSELLING
RAPPORT
UNDERSTANDING
REFRAMING
SOLUTION SEARCHING
SOLUTION PLANNING
IMPLEMENTATION
EVALUATION & ADJUSTMENT
ENDING & CONSOLIDATION

1 2 3 4 5 6 7 8

1 BE INTERESTED & GENUINE
2 ESTABLISH & MAINTAIN GOOD RAPPORT
3 PROVISION OF OPPORTUNITIES TO EXPRESS EMOTIONS
4 PROVISION OF OPPORTUNITY TO EXPERIENCE SUCCESS
5 PROVISION OF SUPPORT & REASSURANCE
6 PROVISION OF AETIOLOGY & RATIONALE
7 PROVISION OF POSITIVE EXPECTATION & HOPE
8 ENCOURAGEMENT OF EMPOWERING BELIEFS

————— : **MOST INTENSE PROVISION**
———— : **PROVISION OF**
– – – – : **OCCASIONAL PROVISION**

EXERCISE

How would you pull together the eight common principles to provide a coherent model of counselling? Would you keep the eight stages I advocate, or would you subdivide some of them or merge others?

Having outlined the sequence of stages of the commercially relevant model, we ought to examine some of its most important principles and tools. The most important tool is the Skills Training Model (STM). In the next chapter we will give a general overview of the STM. Then we will move on to a stage-by-stage guide on how to use the model.

6

THE SKILLS TRAINING MODEL

Introduction

What is this Skills Training Model we have been talking about? A few simple questions can often provide more answers than the answers themselves. What makes you able to understand the material on this page? Your reading and comprehension skills. You spent a long time in school perfecting these skills. What benefits do those skills bring you? Substantial benefits. In fact, so many and so consistently that you probably take them for granted. The skill has become invisible to you.

How much time did you invest in learning your current job? The answer to that may not be so easy. Yes, you may have completed a training programme in a specific time, but is it only the skills learned in that period that are used in the job? Most unlikely. What about the other skills, such as social skills, communication skills, diplomacy skills and so on? All were learned at some stage in your life. All are so taken for granted that you have probably forgotten you have them. Yet these necessary skills help you to succeed or, at the very least, to cope.

Now imagine what the consequences would be if you lacked social skills – or if you lacked diplomacy skills. Problems can be caused by a lack of the requisite skill – what would be the consequences if you had, say, poor persuasion skills as a salesperson or poor spatial reasoning skills as a design engineer? You would have a big problem. Another possible problem area lies in the ability to decide when to use certain skills. Imagine the consequences of using the wrong skill at the right time, or the right skill at the wrong time, because you have poor higher-level skills of realistically perceiving the environment and its requirements. Life would not be comfortable. Your lack of skill would cause you all sorts of problems. Worse still, you would not understand why. You would have a big problem – the kind of problem that may lead you to counselling.

On the chessboard of life, if you don't possess the skills of the game, every square is fraught with danger, every move is another potential disaster. The very heart of your king, your self-esteem, is exposed to the mercy of the mildest pawn. People who have emotional problems with life need only acquire the necessary skills to solve them. Skills deficits or inadequacies can lead to problems, and the solution is to be found in skills training.

The consequences of skills deficits

The Skills Training Model makes the following assumption: clients have some (not all) problems because they lack certain skills. If, together, we can equip them with the skills required, they will be able to solve their problem now, and solve similar problems in future. What will that mean? It means that some people will only ever need counselling once, while others will need counselling several times with different skills areas being addressed in each batch of counselling.

Skills are acquired by:

1   parental (guardian) input
2   other family member and peer group input
3   educational input – formal

4   educational input – informal
5   experiential input – actual
6   experiential input – imagined
7   experiential input – vicarious
8   self-education.

From what other sources have you learned skills?

How are skills acquired?

Shown below are some of the early models, which are still being used today. They serve to explain the basics.

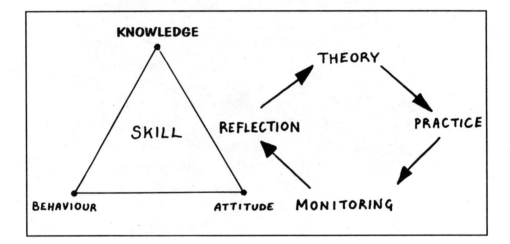

All skills consist of three elements: knowledge, attitude and behaviour. Well, that was the conventional view. It is now clear that beliefs play a very large part in the execution of skills. So we have amended the old model.

Similarly, it was thought that skills acquisition followed four stages, and at a very general level that is true. But it is too general to be a useful guide to helping your staff members acquire a skill to solve a problem. We need a more sophisticated understanding.

So, to repeat the question, how *are* skills acquired? In simple terms, skills are acquired in the same way as virtually anything else: by choosing a purpose and following a method:

1   A purpose is chosen (consciously or otherwise).
2   The elements of the skill are learned (beliefs, knowledge, attitudes, behaviours).
3   Contextual understanding of the skill begins.

4   A mental hierarchy of the contexts is developed.
5   Performance of the skill moves from being elemental and analytical to contextual and patterned.
6   With practice, a comprehensive repertoire of patterns is established. Skill is then a matter of automatic responses to the recognition of patterns.

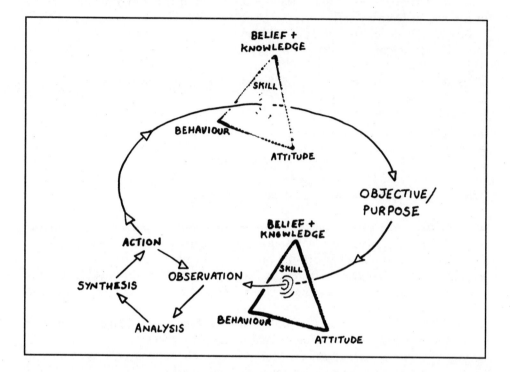

If you were to decide to acquire a skill, how would you do it? Your method might look like this:

1   Choose a purpose.
2   Consider and learn the elements of the skill.
3   Create a model.
4   Mentally prepare/rehearse the performance/commit to action.
5   Carry out the skill.
6   Focus on the relevant elements while performing the skill.
7   Observe self in action.
8   Define the outcomes and process.
9   Decide whether the method/behaviour/skill needs to be improved or altered.
10 Decide if the model or theory is to be altered or improved.
11 Continue practising until a contextual understanding of the skill is established.
12 Continue practising until a mental hierarchy of the context is formed.

13 Reach a point where the practice of the skill is an automatic response to the recognition of a pattern.
14 Practise regularly to keep the responses automatic.

As you can see, we have moved a long way from the first early models of the skill acquisition process. How does this model compare with your own model or method of learning skills?

In terms of skills, the kinds of problems you and your clients confront fall into several categories:

- problems – the normal range of human trials and tribulations
- problem management skills deficits
- specific skills deficits (total)
- specific skills deficits (partial)
- inappropriate skills for context
- inappropriate context trigger cues for skill.

These can be expressed in more detail, as follows:

- *Problems – the normal range of human trials and tribulations.* Many of the problems you will deal with have nothing to do with skills problems, defects and so on. They are the normal problems we all have.
- *Problem management skills deficits.* Some clients lack the skills necessary to cope with life's trials and tribulations. They lack high–level problem management skills.
- *Specific skills deficits (total).* Other clients will have a total lack of particular skills; they are totally unable to deal with a situation.
- *Specific skills deficits (partial).* More usually, clients will possess some skill but not enough to handle whatever they are facing.
- *Inappropriate skills for context.* Some clients will have skills which work well in another context and try to apply them to what they perceive to be a similar situation, but unsuccessfully.
- *Inappropriate context trigger cues for skill.* Occasionally you will encounter a client who applies a skill inappropriately because the cues which they use to trigger the practice of the skill are quite simply the wrong cues.

Your role as skill educator

Part of your role as a cost–conscious counsellor is to find the best way for staff to solve their own problems. That means they should be equipped with the skills to do so, and you may have to provide some kind of training in those skills. We know from a growing body of research that successful people – those who cope well with life's challenges – are those who have acquired the intellectual skills to do so. The means of acquisition varies from individual to individual. Some acquire the skills from parents, others through education, others by deliberately developing the skills, some possess the skills only by accident or by virtue of some aspect of their personality. The point is that those skills are linked to healthy well-adjusted people, and your clients will be more likely to fit that description if they acquire them.

So what kinds of skills do we need to cope with and thrive in life?

Well-adjusted people tend to exhibit several overlapping skills, most of which are easy to acquire with a little practice. They can be expressed in very general terms:

- They engage in activities which maintain physical and mental health.
- They take appropriate amounts of rest and recreation.
- They foster a sense of usefulness, satisfaction and purpose.
- They establish and maintain a sense of involvement.
- They develop and maintain a confidant relationship.
- They attain a level of objectivity about themselves (but not too much, as we will see later).
- They take responsibility for their life and all its problems.
- They maintain a sense of humour about themselves and don't take themselves too seriously.
- They live in the present while enjoying the journey into the future.

This list can act as a good introduction to the notion of skills as a means of solving and preventing problems for clients. Use it as a checklist of their skills at the most general level: 'In which ways do you engage in each of these activities?' Most of your staff members will only engage in a few on the list. For the vast majority of people you will see the following range of reactions to the list:

- 'I've been meaning to get round to doing those things, but just can't find the time.' (Common)
- 'I used to do all these things regularly, but now ... ' (Not so common)
- 'That's all very well, but I'll still have my problems even if I do these things.' (Not so common)
- 'Oh yes, I've let my life get out of control – no wonder I've got problems.' (Rare)
- 'Ah, so those are the skills I need to acquire to live a full and successful life.' (Almost never)

The reaction to the skill list indicates what you need to do to help the client. The less the client recognizes the need to engage in these activities, the harder will be your job of persuading them to take self-responsibility and acquire the skills necessary to make their lives better.

Experience shows that you are more likely to help clients see their problem in terms of skills if they have some generalized skills to start with. Unskilled people who are not used to making progress through the acquisition of skills are going to be harder to help than those whose lives have progressed via skill development. But remember, the actual counsellor and following the eight common principles are more important than *any* technique. This technique, like all the others, may only be effective because it provides a vehicle with which to deliver you with your mastery of the common principles. But unlike all the other methods, the STM will always leave the client better able to cope with life after counselling than before; they will at least have acquired some skills.

To examine the skills in more detail, first we should separate them into two main categories and define them: interpersonal skills and intrapersonal skills. Interpersonal skills are those which help us get on effectively with others. Intrapersonal skills are those which help us manage ourselves effectively.

For the purposes of conveying understanding, we will separate the skills into component parts. However, be aware that most of the skills operate in conjunction with others. There is a huge overlap in most of the skills listed. For instance, inner dialogue control is involved in virtually every skill; relaxation skills are a component of both emotional management and health management skills. This raises the point that this list is by no means exhaustive; it is meant as a simple sample – a manageable introduction to those skills most relevant in workplace counselling. Neither do we have enough space in this book to explore all the skills listed in-depth. In fact, each skill would need a book of its own to explain it properly. There are many such books already available.

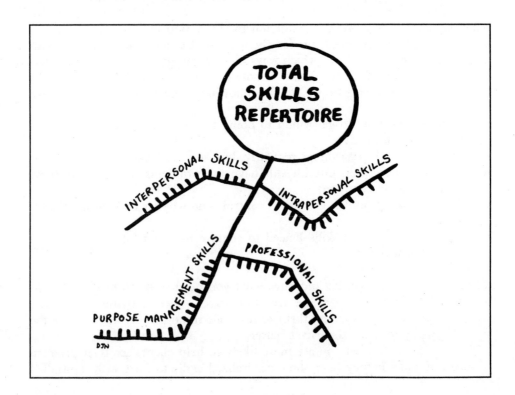

Interpersonal skills

- Communication skills
- Emotional expression skills
- Social skills
- Meeting people skills
- Relationship development skills
- Relationship maintenance skills
- Assertiveness skills
- Negotiation skills
- Team-leading skills
- Team participation skills.

Intrapersonal skills

- Thought-based skills:

    - rational thinking
    - inner dialogue control
    - belief consequence analysis
    - rules/values adopted evaluation/awareness
    - awareness of effect of 'filters'.

- Reality awareness skills:

    - perception skills
    - cause attribution skills.

- Emotional management skills:

    - happiness management
    - emotional protection
    - relaxation management.

- Problem management skills:

    - problem anticipation
    - problem prevention
    - problem solving.

- Achievement management skills:

    - time management
    - goal/purpose management
    - persistence management
    - self-reward management
    - skill acquisition skills
    - knowledge acquisition skills.

- Health management skills:
    - physical health maintenance skills
    - mental health maintenance skills

EXERCISE

That is my organization of the skills. How would you do it?

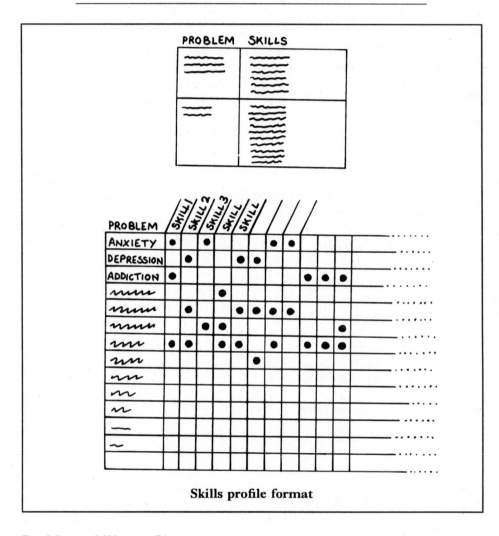

Skills profile format

Problem skills profiles

As you might imagine, some problems are caused by skills deficits. More usually the problem is caused by some indeterminable combination of factors (more on this later) but is maintained because the sufferer lacks sufficient skill to do something about it. Each problem can be described in terms of its 'problem skills profile'. Here are two typical problem skills profiles:

Anxiety   Stress management skills deficits
                        Stress prevention skills deficits
                        Time management/priority management skills deficits
                        Thought control skills deficits
                        Rational belief formation skills deficits.

Depression   Happiness management skills deficits
                        Self-stroking skills deficits
                        Energy-level management skills deficits
                        Realistic goal-setting skills deficits
                        Social skills deficits.

Asking the client to draw up a problem skills profile often prompts them to realize that they lack certain skills and that their solution lies in acquiring or improving those same skills.

EXERCISE

In which area of your life do you currently have problems? Draw up a 'problem skills profile' for that problem. What does the profile suggest you should do to remedy or minimize your problem?

A general explanation of the STM

Each skill has a belief, knowledge, attitude, behaviour and contextual component. The mental equivalent of behaviour is a thinking pattern. One of the important tasks for you as an STM counsellor is to make clients aware that mental behaviour determines what happens to them in life. Many (probably most) people simply don't make the connection between what they do in their heads and the outcomes they achieve. Even fewer realize that they have mental skills which can be developed. Of course, most people are aware that their work skills have an effect on their lives, but few make the leap from work skills to self-management skills. Your job as an STM counsellor is, at least partially, to educate them.

Clients often have problems for the opposite reasons I've just suggested. That is, they overinternalize their problem; they blame themselves for situations about which they could have done nothing. 'It must be something I'm doing.' They expect too much of their intrapersonal skills. They expect themselves to control the uncontrollable. Which skills do you think those clients overestimate?

As there are innumerable publications on some skills – assertiveness skills, leadership skills, communication skills and so on – here we will explore those which you are unlikely to find information about elsewhere. We will cover:

- Thought management skills:

  - problem management
  - beliefs
  - inner dialogue
  - language usage.

- Emotional management skills
- Purpose management skills.

Thought management skills

Which mental behaviours constitute thought management skills? How do highly successful people manage their minds? By the use of thinking skills such as:

- perceiving events/behaviours realistically (not allowing personal filters to obscure the facts)
- interpreting and explaining events/behaviours realistically
- predicting events/behaviours realistically
- taking responsibility for choices – ownership of own decisions
- making realistic decisions
- managing problems effectively
- using constructive and empowering inner dialogues
- holding and using empowering beliefs/values/rules
- setting realistic goals
- accepting the need to change/acquire new skills as required to achieve goals.

To cover thought management skills we would need a whole book. What is relevant is that you understand the general principles so you are able to work out which ones are lacking. To get you to that point we will investigate four of the above: problem management, beliefs, inner dialogue and language usage.

Problem management

As someone whose job it is to solve problems, there is little I can tell you that you don't know already. So let's use your knowledge of problem management to illustrate the principles of establishing the specific skills behind any significant skill set. 'Managing problems effectively' or 'problem-solving skills' can be broken down into three components:

1 anticipatory thinking skills
2 prevention thinking skills
3 problem resolution skills.

EXERCISE

To give you an insight into the power of skills over your life, take note of what you do the next time you have anticipated, prevented or solved a problem at work. Which mental processes did you go through to achieve your outcome? Try to draw out a sequence of events, for example:

Anticipatory thinking skills

1   Observe the environment on an ongoing basis.
2   Compare what is observed against the objectives for the department.
3   Project what is observed into the future.
4   Compare that against the objectives for the department.

Complete this sequence and work out the component skills in problem prevention thinking skills and problem resolution skills. Once you understand the processes you can pass them on to your staff.

Beliefs

Previously, we expressed the sequence of events of human behaviour as a straight line. Of course, very few systems in nature have a linear effect; most systems have an influence on other systems. Most commonly, each system is in some way self-affecting – it provides some kind of feedback to itself. Human behaviour is exactly like that. We should therefore close the ends of the sequence of events. Doing so forms a pentagon as shown below. Now let's give our amended construct a fancy name to help clients remember the concept: the Pentagon Principle. It states that through a five-stage sequence, the manifestations of your thoughts always come back to you, be they positive or negative. You must therefore control your thoughts to control your life.

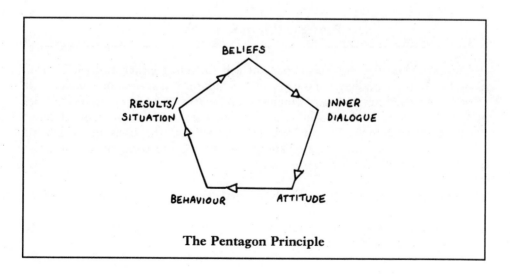

The Pentagon Principle

Draw the Pentagon Principle diagram for your clients; help them to see the effects their thinking has on their life. Ask the client to think through some recent experiences in terms of the Principle.

Some schools of counselling suggest that you can seek to alter the outcomes people achieve in life by changing the way people feel, by changing their behaviour and so on. All these methods fail unless they also incorporate a change in the client's belief/thought patterns. Let me illustrate. Between each adjoining point of the pentagon there is interaction. There is also feedback interaction going on between every two points. As if that isn't complicated enough, there is also interaction going on between pairs of points with other pairs of points. In fact every conceivable interaction is occurring at some stage in the cycle. That much interaction is beyond control (how many possible interactions are there?). Anyone who thinks they can control this process once it has started is deluding themselves. The only realistic way to control the process is to control it from its starting point – beliefs.

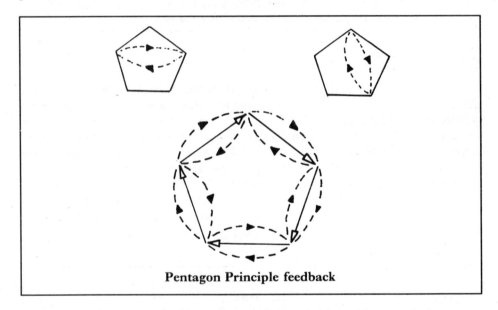

Pentagon Principle feedback

Once established, most beliefs become self-satisfying either on their own or as part of larger paradigms. To explain: a paradigm is a system or model. Each of us has a model in our heads which represents the world, or a significant part of the functioning of the world. Our paradigms are a collection of interrelated beliefs through which the world is interpreted and the basis on which all decisions are made. The level of knowledge about, and consciousness of, the beliefs which make up paradigms varies:

- Some are known and consciously applied (those relating to the practice of new skills).
- Most are, or were, known but are unconsciously applied (those relating to the practice of skills).

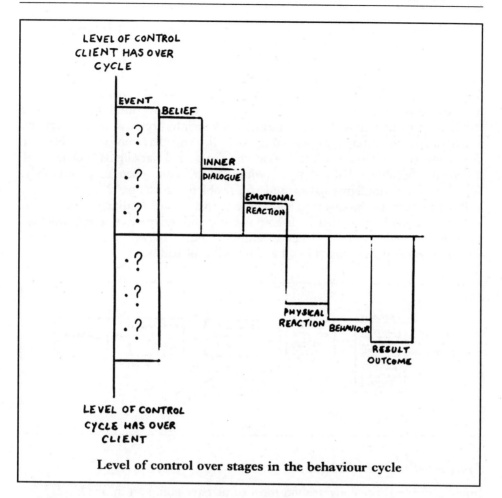

Level of control over stages in the behaviour cycle

- Many are unknown and unconsciously applied (those common to cultures and subcultures).
- Some are unknowable and unconsciously applied (those common to all humanity).

EXERCISE

To illustrate just how difficult it is to determine beliefs toward the end of the above list, try to list those at the start of the list. List the beliefs that guide you in managing your staff. Now try to list those underlying why you work at all. Try to list those underpinning the human desire to produce children.

Any paradigm is made up of a collection of beliefs and epistemes (those beliefs of which we are not conscious) from the above categories. Most of us have several paradigms for the different areas of life and most of the paradigms are related to form a master paradigm – the one which shapes the formation of new paradigms or allows alterations to its subordinates.

Paradigms continue to be used as long as they work. However, virtually nothing can convince the holder of a strong paradigm that it does not work. Anything that happens can be interpreted as fitting the paradigm. If you believe that the way to stop the Martians poisoning your mind with magnetic waves is to wear a sieve on your head, you will interpret any claims that the Martians have no interest in poisoning you with 'they have no interest because they know it won't work while I wear the sieve'. All paradigms, not just the ridiculous, become self-fulfilling – yours, mine, your client's, everybody's. Which of your paradigms has caused you problems in the past?

If a paradigm is empowering and constructive, it will facilitate achievement – that's the good news. If it is disempowering and destructive it will sabotage achievement – that's the bad news. Some of your staff will be the victims of self-destructive paradigms. They have lives full of bad news.

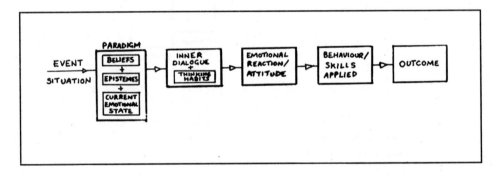

From belief to inner dialogue

Inner dialogue is the conversation most of us have going on in our heads most of the time. It consists of two components: the habit part and those dialogues triggered by events filtered through our belief systems. Although the two components appear separate, they are in fact linked. The habitual inner dialogue became so through multiple repetition. But for the purposes of consideration, we should keep them separate. Both parts are open to control. Any habit and any belief can be changed. Inner dialogue can therefore be controlled. But, neither part can be altered if the owner is unwilling to do so. Try it. Change what you say to yourself about some politician you dislike.

The inner dialogue dictates which emotions are aroused and, subsequently, which decisions will be made about what behaviours and what skills will be engaged. Even those who have highly developed emotional management skills, thereby bypassing the emotion link in the chain, are directly influenced by their inner dialogue. *Everyone* is influenced by their inner dialogue.

Let's take an example. You are in a difficult meeting, negotiating hard with the other parties. Suddenly, they look at each other and get up as if to walk out the room. You think, 'Oh gosh, I've blown it. What am I to do? I know,

Inner dialogue

I'll offer a better deal.' The clients accept and sit down to consolidate the details. Later your boss calls to ask why you are striking loss-making deals and suggests your talents are better suited to charity work.

Let's rewind. You think, 'They obviously need time to consider their position. I'll ask them if they would like a room for a private discussion.' They accept and return a short while later with a mutually beneficial proposal. Later your boss calls to congratulate you on such a well-struck deal and asks you to handle the prime account.

In the first scenario you believed that people walking out of a room was a statement of no deal. In the second you believed it meant people needed to clear their heads or have a private discussion. The belief determined a chain of events. One belief was empowering, the other disempowering.

What a small difference a few thoughts can make! Business careers are built one thought at a time over a lifetime. But a couple of poor thoughts can put you out of business for a lifetime. Belief is the basis of skill and success. What do you have to believe to be an effective counsellor?

Beliefs are involved both in the practice of skills and the decision about when to use them. They are central to everything human beings do. Every skill has some underlying beliefs. The more strongly the belief is held and applied, the more effective will be the skill in the long run. When you are helping clients develop or improve or transfer skills to solve their problems, you should encourage them to focus on what is best to believe for maximum effectiveness of the skill in hand.

Language usage – volatile vocabulary

Words are virtually omnipotent. Words led a highly educated, civilized country to commit the worst atrocities in the history of the human race. Words led people who had sworn an oath to help save the lives of others to systematically butcher children. The fact that those words were German and were spoken by a tyrannical madman over half a century ago is irrelevant. Words in any language, at any time, have enormous power over those hearing them. Madmen, like Hitler, know how to make you think what they want you to. Yet, the most influential words you will ever be subjected to are those you will utter yourself. You believe your own words more than any others.

So how can words affect me? If you say something is horrifying, how does that make you feel? If you say something has been devastating, how does it make you feel? If you say something is terrifying, how does it make you feel? Just as the word says, horrible, devastated, terrified. 'Extremizing' (this verbal reasoning flaw) is astonishingly common. Many people detrimentally affect their lives by 'awfulizing', 'horrorizing' and 'terribilizing'. Others place heavy burdens on themselves by engaging in 'perfectionizing', 'demandingnation', 'musterbating', 'oughticizing' and 'shoulding' (based on 'I must', 'I ought', 'I should' …).

How often have you heard people using these words inappropriately? Very often, I'll bet. They experience a minor inconvenience such as a scratch on their car, but they describe it as 'devastating'. How do you think that makes them feel? It is obvious. A customer is disgruntled at some small problem, but the customer service executive describes themself as being terrified of losing the customer. How do you think that makes them feel?

Listen to the words your clients use. Ask them if they meant 'devastated' or 'slightly upset'. Ask them if they were 'terrified' or 'a touch apprehensive'. Ask them if they 'should' or 'must' do something or would feel better about themselves if they did. Ask your client to scan their vocabulary for self-destructive patterns of the type just described. And practise what you preach – which disempowering words do you use?

Some examples of disempowering words with more empowering replacements

must	would like to
should	would prefer to
have to	motivated to
awful	not as good as it could have been
terrible	different from expectations
horrible	could have been more pleasant
terrified	a little anxious
embarrassed	highly aware of
failed	a minor stumble
depressed	preparing for, or recovering from, action
overwhelmed	developing new capacity.

Can you see how describing what is seen in a different way alters the emotional reactions which follow?

Emotional management skills

The preventive way to interpret powerful emotions

Every powerful emotion exists for a reason. The reason is that your belief system has triggered a reaction in order to stimulate an intellectual or physical behaviour for your own good. The only logical evolutionary explanation for the existence of emotions is that they helped us to survive in the past. Speculation beyond that is futile. What we do know is that high achievers use emotions to thrive in the present. So how do we use them constructively? By asking your clients to change their reading of their emotions – to place the following positive interpretations on their darkest feelings:

- Fear
  They are anticipating something for which they need to prepare.
- Inadequacy
  Their mind is encouraging them to improve and they believe they can.
- Overload
  They're stressed out, it's time to prioritize their tasks and concentrate their mind on what they can control.
- Discomfort
  Something or some perception of theirs needs to be fine-tuned.
- Frustration
  They have a strong sense that they can do better.
- Anger
  They haven't got their own way; someone has broken one of their core rules for life; time to communicate.
- Disappointment
  It's time to set a new or revised target.
- Hurt
  They should revise their expectations of someone or communicate their disappointment to them.

- Guilt

    They have broken one of their own core rules for living; they should commit themselves to strengthening it.

- Loneliness

    People are important to them; it's time to make contact with others.

EXERCISE

Name five other strongly negative emotions and put empowering interpretations on them.

Choosing how to feel

Learning to choose how to feel

Many people go through their entire lives never realizing that the way they feel is up to them. They experience feeling as something that the outside world imposes on them in a way that is beyond their control. As you obviously know by now, that perception is just not true. Yes, the outside world has an influence on the way you feel, but it does not have control unless you give it that control, as many people do. No, your emotional life is like every other aspect of your life; either you take control of it or it takes control of you.

Make your clients aware of that choice. Ask them when they have been happiest. When have they been most miserable? What do they do to cheer themselves up when feeling low? Then immediately follow up by asking them what other things they do to change the way they feel. Before you know it, they will have agreed that, yes, they do take at least partial control over their emotional state and that, yes, obviously if partial control can be taken with virtually no effort, then total control is probably possible for those determined enough to achieve it.

How can your staff choose how to feel?   They can:

- decide that they want to change the way they feel
- decide how they want to feel
- decide what they will have to think, imagine or do to feel that way
- do it, and keep doing it as often as is required for as long as they want to feel that way
- repeat this cycle as required.

'It's so simple it can't possibly work' is a reaction you will regularly witness. 'If it was that easy, everybody would be doing it' is another. We won't go into the reasons people choose not to be happy, or at least in a pleasant emotional state. Suffice to say, it is that simple, and successful people *do* use this or a similar method. Find someone who has recently become a happy, well-adjusted person and ask them how they do it. There is little point in asking someone who has been this way for some time, because their skill has been so well practised it is now subconscious and automatic. Next time you are in an emotional state, try the above five-point plan.

Emotional protection skills – Freud's defences

Much of what Freud wrote was, well, less than useful. But we won't throw the Oedipus complex baby out with the anal-retentive bathwater. he did devise an excellent list of the ways we protect ourselves from emotional pain. These protection devices are highly effective emotional management skills but, as with most such devices, if you take them too far they become self-imposed prisons. Some of your team will need help because their defence mechanisms are not strong or sophisticated enough to protect them. Others will need help because they have overused a defensive tactic to the extent that it has caused more problems than it was adopted to solve – perhaps even to the extent that it presents a serious obstacle to effective counselling. What are those defences? Here is a list with a short description:

• Repression	Not allowing themselves to think about a problem area
• Denial of reality	Simply denying to themselves the facts
• Isolation of feeling	Admitting the facts to themselves, but totally blocking out any associated feeling
• Reaction formation	Reacting against the desire to act in one way by forming strong desires for the opposite
• Compromise	Backing off and settling for less to avoid the pain of standing their ground
• Act of limitation	Deliberately limiting abilities as a defence against failure or rejection
• Turning against self	Aggressively blaming themselves for whatever may be less painful than passive guilt
• Rationalization	Creating explanations for behaviour which sound better than the real reasons
• Thought dissociation	Dissociating themselves from what they did/said/thought (genuinely no memory)
• Regression	Reverting to a means of coping which worked at some stage in the past
• Projection	Attributing characteristics/motives to others which they possess themselves
• Introjection	Overidentifying with some heroic figure to avoid facing themselves.

EXERCISE

Which defence mechanism do you use? What was the most emotionally painful experience of your life? How did you defend yourself against the pain?

Managing emotions

The above defence mechanisms are mainly ways of blocking emotions. There are more constructive ways to manage emotions, and there are several ways to change any emotion being experienced. Here are the most effective:

- Interrupt the emotional state.
- Change the mental image which gives rise to the emotion.
- Change the action which results from that emotion.
- Change the belief that gave rise to the image which gave rise to the emotion.
- Change the inner dialogue based on the beliefs and image behind the emotion.
- Change the overall paradigm of which the belief is a part.

All of which are things the client can do for themselves if they have acquired the necessary emotional management skills. If they have not you could suggest that the client uses one of the techniques just discussed which will usually help with the immediate emotional pain. But unless the client develops more comprehensive emotional management skills, the relief will last only until the next emotional crisis emerges. You should therefore assess to what extent your staff possess these skills. If you identify the problems and strengths in their thinking skills (thinking precedes feeling, with only a few exceptions), it will help to develop the client's awareness of emotional management issues. That's the why, here's the how:

Assessing emotional management skills

- Ask the client to report their feelings.
- Ask the client to express their feelings explicitly during discussions (many express feelings indirectly via tone of voice).
- Ask the client to list their range of feelings on whatever area you are exploring.
- Ask the client to sequence their feelings on the issue you are exploring.
- Ask the client to note the frequency of particular feelings.
- After a conversation, ask them to report what they are feeling.

When you both have a clear picture of the client's emotional management skills, you can identify the deficits and devise a programme to remedy them. Your programme could consist of belief change, inner dialogue practice, role rehearsal, situation management rehearsal and so on. (This will be covered in

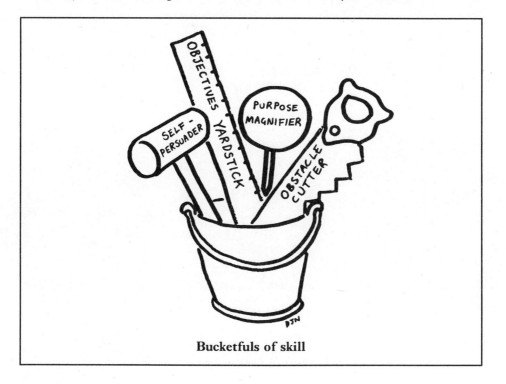

Bucketfuls of skill

more detail later.)

Purpose management skills

The world's most effective people are those with a clear purpose in which they totally believe. Every aspect of their behaviour is arranged around maximizing their likelihood of achieving their purpose. The precise direction in which they concentrate their efforts will change depending on circumstances, but the purpose remains constant. They seek to reinforce their purpose, they seek confirmation that they are achieving their purpose, they seek better ways of achieving their purpose, they turn obstacles into helpers towards their purpose. In fact, there are a whole host of skills associated with purpose management. Ultra-high achievers have developed these skills in bucketfuls, and the chances are that your clients need to make a start on the same skills.

EXERCISE

Take the list of mental activities of high achievers just mentioned and express those as skills. Now expand the list until you have a good picture of what purpose management involves.

7

DEALING WITH SKILLS PROBLEMS

Uncovering skills problems

A sequence of events leads to the client's problem. Although we can never be precisely sure of what factors caused the sequence of events, we can be fairly sure of the stages the sequence follows – if a skills deficit was the cause. You uncover the skills deficits by going backwards through the sequence of events as they are reported to have occurred. Refer to the diagram below. Even where skills deficits are not causal, they may be playing a maintenance role – that is, a lack of skills is preventing a successful resolution of the problem.

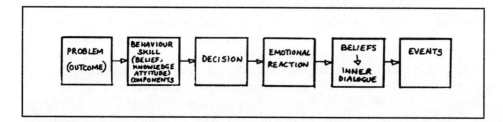

Start with the problem as the client describes it. That may be an event, a result, a reaction by another person, a reaction in the client and so on. Ask them to identify which behaviours led to that outcome. Those who have yet to realize they are totally responsible for their own behaviours may take some persuasion (see reframing on page 148 and persuasion on page 188) for an explanation.

When you have an explanation of what behaviours preceded the outcome, ask the client what skills those behaviours were based on. Again, you may have either an education or a persuasion task on your hands. You should use examples to demonstrate your point. For instance, as in the example given earlier, reading is the skill that enables you to assimilate information from the written page and subsequently engage in thinking behaviour. You will find examples of the kinds of skills underlying various behaviours later.

What kinds of emotional and physical reactions or states have motivated the adoption of the skills which were used? With what level of intensity were the emotional and physical changes experienced? Few people will deny, or fail to realize, that their emotional reaction is involved in their behaviour.

However, many will react against your suggestion that their inner dialogue – the words they utter inside their heads – is what causes their emotional reaction. But it does. To wit, if you tell yourself that you have come into an enormous amount of money, how does it make you feel? If you tell yourself your boss is looking for ways to promote you, how does it make you feel? If you tell yourself you are destined for the greatness you desire, how does it make you feel? Wonderful! But if you were to tell yourself the opposite, how would you feel? Less than wonderful? Of course. The words we utter to ourselves control our emotional reactions (except where an emotional reaction has become so habitual that it bypasses reason and thought). Managing inner dialogue is a valuable skill. Ask your clients what inner dialogue they had immediately prior to their emotional reactions. Encourage them to explore the effects that alternative inner dialogues would have had. Managing your inner dialogue is a specific skill with its own techniques, such as thought stopping, positive affirmation and thought substitution.

Now ask your clients what beliefs led to those inner dialogue statements. What we believe about a subject determines what we tell ourselves about it. If you believe the weather has no bearing on your mood, you will make no inner statements connecting your mood to the weather. If you believe the weather affects your mood, you are likely to make inner statements affirming that belief – 'It's a *horrible*, wet, overcast day', 'It's a *wonderful*, bright, warm day.' If you habitually associate your mood with the weather you may not have noticed the emotional loading and linkage in the statements. If that was the case, you will now realize how difficult it is for clients to make the leap from acknowledging that their inner dialogue does have an effect on them to conceiving that their beliefs determine inner dialogue. Managing beliefs to empower oneself is a skill in its own right. It involves monitoring the effect various beliefs have on your behaviour and then altering them on a regular basis to create optimum results.

How do you do it? How do you identify what skill is being used or rather not being used by your staff member? By asking yourself, and simultaneously the client, such questions as:

- 'The lack of which skills would make it difficult to socialize with others?'
- 'Which skills do you think you would benefit from in trying to get over this loss?'
- 'Which skills do you think make it possible for others to achieve their sales targets?'

Identifying the missing skill in principle is easy enough. Try it yourself. Which skills do you need to be a good boxer? If you wanted to learn how to box, which basic skills would you have to learn? Let's try another. If you wanted to write songs, which skills would you have to acquire?

Identifying thinking patterns and thinking skills problems

That is the process in overview. In detail we need a few more tools to uncover the beliefs behind any skills deficit. How do you identify thinking patterns and thinking skills problems?

- Seek self-report information.
- Ask the client to think aloud (direct inner dialogue access).
- Ask the client to list their thoughts on whatever area you are exploring.
- Ask the client to clarify their thoughts.
- Ask the client to sequence their thoughts on the issue you are exploring.
- Ask the client to note the frequency of particular thoughts.
- After a conversation, ask the client to report what they were thinking.
- Together, make inferences about their thinking skills from their behaviour.
- Ask the client to respond to your inferences.
- Together, form and test hypotheses on thinking skills problems.
- Ask the client to react to the theories you both postulate on their thinking.
- Test them by making predictions about which other areas in the client's life they experience difficulties in.
- Continue testing until you have agreed that the deficit has been identified.

EXERCISE

Identify what else you have used in the past to discern how others are thinking.

What to look for in thinking skills

The client's thinking skills are revealed by a wide range of indicators. Compare the client's actual skills against the following thinking ideals:

- I take responsibility for all beliefs, thoughts, attitudes, behaviours.
- It is my responsibility to anticipate problems.
- It is my responsibility to prevent problems.
- It is my responsibility to manage problems.
- I make decisions based on realistic assumptions.
- I predict the outcomes of decisions and variables in the environment realistically.
- I establish realistic goals.
- I identify and overcome internal barriers to achievement.

- I am sufficiently flexible with my beliefs and values to accommodate change.
- I hold and regularly review a set of values which suit the environment.
- I manage my inner dialogue.
- I choose what to think about how to achieve whatever goals have been set.
- I own the choices which could be made and which already have been made.
- I am honest about my beliefs, thoughts and attitudes.
- I am aware of self-contradictions, hypocrisies, double standards and so on.
- I accept human fallibility and deal constructively with failings and failures.

The comparison will highlight some thinking skills problems. The next set of links in the thinking skills chain are not so easily identified. More often than not, the decision on what skill to use, the emotional reaction and the inner dialogue uttered are all bundled up into one tangled knot. But untie that knot we must. The critical link in the knot is the beliefs the client holds; everything which follows stems from belief.

How do we identify the beliefs behind the skills problems? By following a few signposts or clues:

- *Inner dialogue.* Ask your client to report the inner dialogue surrounding the problem, and in the period leading up to its emergence, so that you can infer their underlying beliefs.
- *Emotional reaction.* Emotional reactions are good indicators of underlying beliefs. Explore the beliefs surrounding the emotional reactions involved with the skills problem.
- *Weaknesses and other problem areas.* Explore beliefs behind areas in which the client feels they are weak to obtain insight into the beliefs behind the weakness which has brought them to counselling.
- *Strengths.* Strong performances or skills indicate the presence of empowering beliefs. Harness or generalize such beliefs to help with the skills problem area.
- *Opportunities seen and unseen.* The visibility of opportunities is a strong reflection of an individual's mind-set specifically, and beliefs generally. What opportunities they can see in various contexts, departments, in relation to their objectives and so on. Take this list and ask your client to infer what beliefs made the opportunities visible.
- *Perceived threats from and motives of others.* An individual's perception about other people is more influenced by the beliefs informing those perceptions than the 'facts' of the situation. Ask your client what they perceive as the motives of others then infer the beliefs behind such perceptions.
- *Expectations of self and others.* As above. What we expect of ourselves and others are based on our beliefs. Infer those beliefs from a compiled list of expectations of self and others.
- *Estimations of own and others' capabilities against the reality.* Compare your client's estimations of their abilities against those as reported by others, to infer the nature, range and accuracy of their beliefs about themselves and others.

- *Plans for behaviour – the future against the reality.* Often we intend to behave in one way and end up behaving in another. By exploring changes of behaviour we can draw powerful conclusions about beliefs and paradigms. Similarly, we often claim to be operating using one theory, but our behaviour makes it difficult to avoid the conclusion that another theory is actually being used. The gap between the espoused theory and the theory in use is highly revealing of beliefs.

EXERCISE

Think of other signposts that might reveal beliefs underlying skills problems.

Now we have some information from the cues and pointers to the specific belief problems, we need a method to interpret that information.

Identifying the disempowering beliefs surrounding a skills problem

1 Identify suitably revealing behaviour from the above indicators.
2 Agree with the client that the behaviour occurred as claimed.
3 Explore the client's motives for the behaviour.
4 Explore the inner dialogue associated with the motives.
5 Ask the client to infer the beliefs behind the inner dialogue and motives.
6 Since there are usually several possible beliefs behind any one behaviour, list as many as possible and then ask the client to choose the one they think is most likely.
7 Continue this process as required until you have a list of disempowering beliefs.

At this point you can act to help the client change their beliefs for more empowering alternatives if it seems that only one or two beliefs need to be addressed. But, as we saw earlier, beliefs usually cluster together to form a paradigm – a complete model of one part of life. Into what kinds of categories do you think beliefs group?

How do you turn knowledge of beliefs into an awareness of a coherent paradigm? By carrying on from steps 1 to 7 above:

8 Pull them together to form a hypothesis of the paradigm.
9 Test the paradigm by predicting how the client would behave in various situations/contexts.
10 Seek confirmation or denial that they have behaved like that in the past.
11 Continue with steps 1 to 10 until you are both sure you have the right paradigm.

Once you have established a paradigm how do you change it? Well, first, *you* don't change it, the client does. You can never change another's beliefs; only they can do that. And, second, it is easier to change a few beliefs than to change a complete paradigm. Comfortingly perhaps, the best way to help someone change a paradigm is to help them turn its belief component from disempowering to empowering beliefs one at a time.

At a general level, you can change beliefs as follows:

- Identify the disempowering beliefs.
- Demonstrate their disempowering nature with the Pentagon Principle.
- Seek empowering replacements.
- Adopt the most empowering replacements.

Specifically you change beliefs, or rather your client does, as follows:

1   Analyse and infer in the way we have just discussed.
2   Explore the options for change.
3   Decide on the most empowering beliefs for the skills required.
4   Decide how holding those beliefs will be rewarded.
5   Strengthen beliefs by use of reference experiences (see following section).
6   Mentally rehearse and practise in application the skill which depends on the new belief until it is automatic.
7   Guard against the re-emergence of the old belief by regular practice of the skill.

There are a number of techniques you can use to assist the above process and to help people change their beliefs or paradigms. Here we will consider a few; more are considered later in the book, in the reframing section.

Reference experiences

Reference experiences are those experiences upon which we build our beliefs. Most people think that experiences shape them – that the link between an experience and its effect on them is direct. Not true. It is not what happens to a person that shapes them, but how they interpret their experiences. One person might allow a disability to cripple their prospects, another might use it as a spur towards their chosen objective.

Your clients can change what they believe by changing what they draw from their reference experiences. Being unpopular at school can be interpreted as 'I'm not liked, so why bother trying?' by some and as 'I need to learn about human relationships and what influences them' by others. The first person ends up in roles that require little human contact and the second becomes a supersalesperson. Were you at school with anybody who seemed totally inept at the activity at which they later became high achievers?

Ask your client to identify reference experiences which they can interpret and use to support the adoption of the new belief. If you ask them 'Which

Reference experiences

events in your past confirm that this (belief) is true?', their minds scan their (entire?) memory base and find reasons to support the belief. As we said before, the mind will always answer questions it puts to itself. And it can always find reasons to believe anything it wants to believe.

If your staff member can find no reference experiences to support a belief what does that tell you? Clearly that they do not want to hold the belief. That, in turn, means that they believe something else which conflicts with the belief that would make the practice of the relevant skill effective. The obvious remedy is to follow the above procedures to identify that conflicting belief and demonstrate how it is disempowering in this context.

Cognitive dissonance

Once people have made a decision they usually go through a period of justifying that decision to themselves. This is a phenomenon which is harnessed by brainwashers and cultists. To put it simply, an individual is asked to agree with a reasonable statement and then it is demonstrated that this agreement must mean they believe something else. For instance:

Cognitive dissonance

'Capitalism is not all good and communism is not all bad – is that reasonable?'

'I suppose so.'

'So there must be some good things about communism, yes?'

'Obviously.'

'And there must be some bad things about capitalism, yes?'

'Yes, some.'

As the individual realizes they have agreed with something which has implications for other areas of their thinking, they experience a sense of discordance, or dissonance, which must be resolved. The dissonance is resolved by subtle changes in belief. Before long you have a highly committed Western, democratic capitalist agreeing that communism is OK or even preferable to capitalism.

You think that is unlikely? Guess what techniques were used by the Vietcong? This, and only this, technique was used to persuade American officers to voluntarily and completely change their views. No force or coercion is needed or was used (in this regard). Cognitive dissonance does it all.

Social facilitation

Achievement levels are generally improved when an audience is present to witness the performance of whatever is being attempted. Social contact facilitates performance. You can harness this effect by getting your staff involved with overcoming each other's problems. First consult all your staff with the idea of group motivation for overcoming problems. Seek their consent as a group, and consent from each individual seeking help as that request comes. If everybody is helping everybody else to adopt empowering beliefs, you will soon have a super-performing team.

Please don't leave this section thinking that all empowering beliefs are rational – that is not the case. Most well-adjusted people hold three irrational beliefs, either deliberately or accidentally. They hold these three beliefs because they empower, because they make life more manageable and because they facilitate happiness. Such people have:

1 an unrealistic optimism about the future
2 exaggerated perceptions of personal control
3 an unrealistically positive view of themselves.

Establish to what extent your clients hold these beliefs. What do you think a lack of those beliefs will lead to?

The general principles in identifying which skill areas are the problems

There are so many skills in human life that to cover them all would take a few more books of this size. Obviously we cannot do that. But what we can do is much more useful – we can give you the general principles with which to identify whatever skill(s) is/are lacking. The skill problem is identified by working backwards through the original sequence of events leading to the problem, as in the following diagram. Note that the skill being utilized (or not) is made up of several elements in the chain.

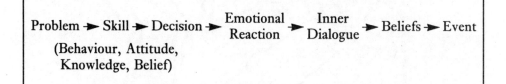

Problem ➤ Skill ➤ Decision ➤ Emotional Reaction ➤ Inner Dialogue ➤ Beliefs ➤ Event
(Behaviour, Attitude, Knowledge, Belief)

More specifically, the STM method for people problem solving follows a sequence of stages, during each of which you and the client seek agreement on:

1 defining the problem
2 defining the problem in terms of skills (which may also involve beliefs and paradigms)
3 identifying which skills the client is having problems with

4   identifying and rectifying the belief problem behind the skills deficit if
    necessary
5   devising a means of developing the requisite skills
6   implementing the chosen method
7   evaluating and improving as required
8   consolidating the client's skills base as a preventive measure.

Yes, the sequence is just as you have seen it before, except that the above is
written from an STM perspective. The eight-stage model seeks to achieve
exactly the same objectives but it is designed to help you maintain a client-
focus with or without the STM. How would you like to organize the STM?
    Not all skills problems are belief-based. Some skills deficit problems are cue-
based, others are reward-based.

Identifying cue-based problems

What makes you get up and go to work in the morning? The alarm clock going
off? The sun shining through your window? Whatever it is, that something is
a cue to start the behaviours which lead you to your workplace. Every behaviour starts with some cue or stimulus. That cue may be internal or external –
in other words, it is either generated in your mind or in the environment. Your
client's problem behaviour/thinking/feeling is also triggered by some cue. The

Behaviour/skill cues

application of all skills starts with some cue or combination of cues. Problems with cues include:

- responding to inappropriate cues
- responding inappropriately to cues (wrong skill)
- confusion over which cues signal which skills
- unawareness of which cues to respond to
- unawareness of the existence of cues.

By identifying the relevant cues and cue problems you can begin to alter the problem. How do you identify the cues? By asking questions aimed at discovering what event, signal, or thought started the process that led to the chain of subsequent behaviours. Where there is an absence of response, ask yourself questions about what triggers the use of that skill in you, yourself.

Once you have identified the cue problem, you can start helping the client to train themselves to recognize and attend to the relevant cues. What are the appropriate cues? That question is best answered by other questions. How do you know when it is time for you to go to bed? How do you know when to answer the telephone? How do you know when it is appropriate to use your negotiation skills? You now know how to identify cues.

Objectives as skill cues

Applying skills is usually linked to attempts to achieve objectives. Some event signals that it is time to attempt the objective. Not using a skill therefore often signals:

1 *Lack of an objective.* If there is no objective there will be no need to establish a response cue.
2 *Lack of a clear objective.* If the objective is not clear, it is difficult to decide which cues to attend to.

EXERCISE

Think of other factors which might cause someone to fail to apply a skill in the relevant and appropriate context.

Reward management – maintenance factors-based problems

When clients develop problems, their natural drive is to solve them as soon as possible. However, there may be motives for keeping the problem. I'm not suggesting the motives are conscious – they rarely are – but the rewards the person receives for having the problem make it easy to continue with it. They are effectively encouraged to maintain the problem.

To eliminate the factors maintaining your client's problem it is first necessary to identify them. If you can find a way to remove the maintenance factors

Maintenance factors

or distance the person from them, solving the problem becomes much easier. Which of your undesirable behaviours do you maintain on account of the rewards they bring?

Help your clients to make their desired solution belief/behaviour/skill as rewarding as possible. Help them to create a situation in which the new skill or belief is maintained through reward.

Paradigm change only happens when the rewards are strong enough

People change their principal beliefs or paradigms only when the evidence for change is overwhelming – that is, when the perceived rewards for changing overwhelm the perceived benefits of maintaining the status quo. People, organizations, scientific progress all change in the same way. You must:

- encourage the client to recognize that the rewards for change and the penalties for not changing are equally large
- invite them to create a situation in their minds where the balance of reward is tipped in favour of change.

Helping and hindering factors

The following technique helps in the assessment and rectification of skills deficits problems. By examining the factors which help and hinder the application of skills your clients can learn a great deal about their skills and their use of them. Invite your clients to explore the:

- actions or behaviours employed which help the application of appropriate skills
- actions or behaviours not employed which help the application of appropriate skills
- actions or behaviours employed which hinder the application of appropriate skills
- actions or behaviours not employed which hinder the application of appropriate skills.

The same technique can be used to encourage clients to think about the ways in which they acquire skills. This will help improve their skill acquisition. Ask them to consider:

- actions or behaviours employed which help the acquisition of appropriate skills
- actions or behaviours not employed which help the acquisition of appropriate skills
- actions or behaviours employed which hinder the acquisition of appropriate skills
- actions or behaviours not employed which hinder the acquisition of appropriate skills.

EXERCISE

Think of other ways in which you can use this helping and hindering factors tool.

Ways to rectify a skills problem

Training techniques

As a competent manager, you will probably be fully aware of the training techniques available. If you have operated in a large company where training has been centralized, you might want to refer to *Coaching and Mentoring*, pp. 92–107, or any other book which covers training techniques. Here are a few:

- lectures
- demonstrating and evaluating skills
- experimenting with different methods
- assessing after outcomes
- projecting and predicting outcomes
- expressing inner dialogue to reveal and improve the attitude and belief components of skills
- biblio-education.

EXERCISE

List the other skills development tools which you currently use.

All training techniques are aimed at helping the trainee create a suitable mental model on which the practice of their skills will be based. So, for one of the thinking skills we looked at earlier (see page 80), you might want to help the client learn how to 'interpret and explain events in the environment (more) accurately'. How could you do that? You could:

- help the client become aware of the effect of their interpretations by asking them to interpret hypothetical (projected) events
- help the client establish their habitual perception patterns and errors by asking them to express their inner dialogue in response to some commonly experienced situations which cause them problems
- demonstrate the difference between truth and perception by asking the client to seek opinions on their version of the truth as seen by other people and have the client speculate about why each person involved has a slightly different perception
- help the client to check perceptions against their common errors and then ask them to predict what consequences would derive from their common errors upon acting on a particular perception.

Solution searching in terms of the STM

The above is a specific example of a solution. What are the general principles for generating STM solutions?

1 Identify and establish skills absences.
2 Identify skills weaknesses.
3 Identify skills to harness.
4 Identify inappropriate skills usage.
5 Identify the absence of skills usage.

You do not need to know whether a skills deficit caused the problem. All that matters is that the deficit exists and that remedying it will go at least part-way towards solving the problem. The solution type will depend on the precise nature of the skills deficit. Deficits fall into five broad categories:

Skill deficit	Solution type
Identify skill absence	Skill training
Identify skill weaknesses	Skill improvement training
Identify skill strengths	Skill transfer/generalization to problem area
Identify inappropriate skill usage	Skill use cue/application awareness training/objective clarifying

| Identify absence of skill usage | Skill use cue/application awareness training/objective setting. |

Seeking skills to harness, transfer or generalize

With the client, seek skills strengths and positive skill assets which can be harnessed. This gives clients a chance to experience success – a fundamental counselling requirement. Even the most emotionally handicapped have skills on which to build their recovery. With your help, your clients can use their existing skills to develop new or improved skills in the problem areas of their lives. They can take skills from other areas of their lives and, with a few adjustments, apply them to the current problem. For instance, an accountant having difficulty making a serious decision could be asked to transfer their balance sheet compilation skills to problem solving. He or she could evaluate each possible decision on the basis of its assets and liabilities.

Often, highly skilled people appear quite ineffectual because they don't know when to apply one set of skills in preference to another. They don't know what cues to look for. They have to learn when to start using their skills – in other words, they need to identify the trigger cues.

An assessment of the STM

Educating clients in the STM is extremely useful in the workplace whether or not you are providing any counselling. It will encourage self-responsibility, self-development, self-problem solving – etc. It fits your existing responsibilities to ensure your staff are sufficiently skilled to do their jobs.

The chief difficulty with 'non-directive counselling methods' is that they don't direct the client to find the problems in both their intra- and interpersonal skills. The big advantage with the STM is that it does try to help the client identify their skill competencies and improve them.

We are working in the real commercial world. There is no place for 'non-directive' methods in the workplace. Just imagine. You are a property developer with a problem: you don't have a design for the building which will occupy a piece of land you have bought. Your architect listens to your problem, but never offers you a solution for fear of depriving you of your 'self-responsibility'. Instead, he or she relies on you using your 'actualizing tendency' to somehow pick up the skills most architects take seven years to learn. Non-directiveness (even if it were achievable) is utter nonsense in the workplace. The STM is used 'non-directively' while the nature of the problem is being determined and then becomes highly directive at the appropriate time. To return to the previous analogy: the architect listens to your problems non-directively and then presents you with some potential solutions for you to choose. The disciplines of architecture and counselling may be worlds apart, but the people management principles are universal.

The STM makes bold, unequivocal and testable predictions

The Skills Training Model brings counselling closer to a scientific discipline. It follows scientific principles; it makes predictions which are eminently testable. If a model can't be tested it is, at best, an interesting hypothesis and, at worst, an idle fantasy. Most – no, virtually all – counselling and therapeutic methods fail to make testable predictions and are therefore useless as mechanisms with which to advance our understanding of how to help people with problems and in need of counselling.

The STM makes bold, unequivocal predictions

Freudian theory cannot be tested; it is a tautology. That is, it is a circular hypothesis – it defines itself in terms of itself. If methods stemming from a theory are to be advanced, that theory must be testable. For the first time we are able to test a viable counselling theory.

Behavioural theory was testable, but it was not viable because it viewed clients as passive subjects of the laws of learning. People will not accept that they are like Pavlov's dogs – they are not. Free will allows us to choose what will influence us and what will not. Some people allow a disaster to destroy them emotionally, others use it to build their character. Behavioural theory predicts that all will respond the same way to any learning experience and, as you always knew, we don't. The Skills Training Model recognizes free will. People have to actively and voluntarily engage in the process; they are not passive recipients.

The STM predicts that the lack of skills in a certain area of life will cause specific problems in managing those same aspects of life. People who are equipped with relevant skills will suffer fewer problems and cope with those problems experienced much more competently than those lacking the same skills in the same circumstances.

People with specified problems have a typical skills deficit profile. The specific skills within a problem profile vary from individual to individual. The typical skills profile for each problem is the central point on a range of skills combinations. The variation within the standard profile for any problem will depend upon the individual, experience, education, culture and so on. By analysing an individual's skills profile we can predict the likelihood of their suffering specified problems. By measuring the skills of a group of individuals and comparing those skills against typical depression profiles, anxiety profiles and so on, we can in theory estimate the probability of their suffering each of those problems in certain contexts and compare the predictions to reality over time. We can predict which individuals will succeed in certain situations because they have specific skills. We can predict that, if they acquire specified skills, the manifestations of a problem will either be reduced or the problem will disappear altogether. We can't fully test these predictions yet, but at least we can make the prediction for anyone to test when the scientific tools are available. When the tools are fully developed we can test most of the STM hypotheses on a large scale. We can test whether – as those of us who use the STM instinctively feel – the most effective prevention of, or remedy for, any emotional or life crisis (which requires more than a listening and understanding ear) is to identify skills deficits and rectify them.

Unlike other counselling methods the STM processes are transparent and their effect can be measured from start to finish to help rule out the influence of other factors on the outcomes:

1   The client's skills level can be measured before the start of counselling (as a society, we can measure some skills and are still developing tools to assess other skills).
2   The client's skills level in the areas where training was provided can be re-measured.
3   The problem can be measured (quantitatively and qualitatively) along several dimensions, both before and after skills analysis and training have been provided, to assess effectiveness.

Some skills levels can already be measured using various tools, more of which are being developed. Such measurement fits perfectly with existing business practices. Most vocational qualification awarding systems include an element of skill assessment. In short, the STM is the most transparent, testable and accessible model of counselling ever devised.

The link between skills and life problems could not be clearer. It is so clear that it beggars belief that we have waited so long to reach what must seem to all outsiders an obvious solution to life problems: equip people with the skills to remedy their problems whatever the original cause. It seems so self-evident that a lack of social skills will lead to social isolation, lack of reward from the environment and potential depression or apathy, and that social skills training is the remedy. Lack of anger management skills will lead to frequent verbal confrontations with colleagues, then to gradual isolation and resentment as one possible outcome or physical aggression as another. The remedy? Anger management training.

Those who do not believe their problems can be solved/managed with skills they currently do not possess will not engage in STM counselling. Experience shows that such people will be incredibly resistant. Yet, if they accept the STM, it brings them to the awareness that all their previous problems may have arisen because – and were certainly prolonged because – they lacked the skill to manage or resolve them and that all future problems not solved or managed effectively will be so because they are doing or not doing something. That is a difficult realization to cope with. It is so much less painful to refuse to accept the STM premise and attribute misery and lack of performance to factors beyond their control. It is almost as though some clients see an undesirable future of tough decisions, a future of self-responsibility, where there is no one else to blame, and so reject the model.

It is tempting to devise a method to screen out such people from counselling. You'll want to. I still want to. Don't. Let them self-select or self-deselect. As counsellors we must always remember that people will defend to the death their right to screw up their lives in any way they see fit. If a member of staff does not accept the model, you have a choice. Either offer no more counselling, or offer counselling based on the eight-stage model without the STM.

Matching the STM to appropriate problems

The STM is not useful for all problems. It is most useful for difficulties based on skills deficits or best remedied by the provision of skills training. It is *not* appropriate for problems which require only a listening ear, such as bereavement and loss, unless the sufferer is experiencing extended grief because they lack the skills to overcome such a loss in the normal manner. They may, for instance, lack the skills of mourning (sounds strange I know, but most of us engage in a series of behaviours which collectively constitute bereavement skills, such as expressing the sense of loss, engaging in rituals which acknowledge the transition, funerals, and so on); they may lack the skill to engage the support of others; they may lack the skills needed to change their beliefs and expectations.

Far from perfection

The STM may be the most promising and commercially relevant approach to counselling we have, but let's not get carried away. Many of the criticisms of counselling made earlier also apply to the STM in its current state of development. We still cannot define with any certainty the causal sequence of any problem. All we can say is that somehow this person failed to acquire certain skills, or acquired the wrong skills, or learned to apply the right skills in the wrong context and vice versa.

Neither should we get carried away by thinking that we have pinpointed the lack of which skills will cause precisely which problems with what kinds of people. We have not. We are still at the stage where logical links rather than proven effectiveness dictate which skills are trained for what combinations of people, problems, contexts and so on. It will be a long time before we can hold up a table showing exactly what problems will arise from the various combinations of skills deficits. As we said before, tell your grandchildren not to hold their breath! The STM is not perfect. It is still being developed. But at least we've moved out of the nonsensical phase of the development of counselling as a science. At least we can move out of the pre-paradigm phase and can start testing a viable and improvable model. At last we've moved from the testing experience of trying to make sense of 1001 nonsense theories to being able to test one theory in a 1001 no-nonsense ways.

Good ideas always receive the same treatment, and always in the same predictable stages. Initially they are treated with derision and ridicule. Then, when it becomes clear that some people are taking the idea seriously, the idea is violently opposed (verbally, and even physically in some cases). Finally, the idea is accepted as a self-evident truth against which, surely, no reasonable mind would take a stance. The STM is no exception. It is being resisted by many vested interests. That is to be expected. Currently, nearly every counsellor I speak to dismissed the STM as 'a ridiculously simplistic way of solving human problems: it totally fails to address the deep underlying cause of the problem'. (Does that sound familiar?) The resistance to good ideas always comes from those whose comfortable lives will be disrupted by the improvements. And it comes most forcefully from those whose livelihoods depend on continuing the old, less productive ways of doing things. There are no examples in history I know of which contradict that rule.

Summary

At the most simplistic level, the skills a person possesses or lacks, uses or fails to use, will determine how well they cope with and influence the environment in which they find themselves. The problems experienced by your staff in the workplace will largely be determined by their skills. The causes of problems are of little significance beyond determining which skill will solve or manage them. Ultimately, all that matters is that your staff member returns to full functioning as soon as possible, and stays that way as long as possible.

Now you have an overview of both the STM and the eight-stage counselling delivery structure, we should pull them together. Before we do, I should restate that your person-focus is more important than any technique. Without strong person-focus you won't be given the chance to help the staff member by means of any technique.

Part III

The process

Part III brings together everything that we have discussed so far. It shows you how to apply the eight counselling principles using the commercially relevant eight-stage model. This section also explains how to use the STM in conjunction with the eight principles and the eight-stage model.

8

GETTING STARTED

Stage 0: Pre-counselling awareness

Objective

To help the client reach an awareness of the problem.

Stages of awareness of the problem

People gradually become aware of the elements that are causing problems in their lives, but only when they reach the final stage in the following sequence are they in a position to start accepting that there *is* a problem or to start doing something about it.

They begin by being ignorant of their ignorance of the problem. Then through exposure to the problem and as a consequence of others' comments or behaviour, they become aware that something is wrong without actually knowing what it is – they acquire knowledge of their ignorance. Through further thought and exposure they come to recognize a problem and its manifestations but are ignorant of its components, ramifications and causes. The final stage in pre-counselling awareness of the problem is knowledge of the problem, its manifestations, components, ramifications and maybe even its cause.

This is the state in which most people arrive for counselling. They know they have a problem, they know what the problem is, but they are unable to do anything constructive about it (perhaps having tried other solutions that worked for them in the past but which have failed on this problem). How does that description compare to your experience of suffering problems? How does the sequence of events just outlined compare to your growing awareness when you have a problem?

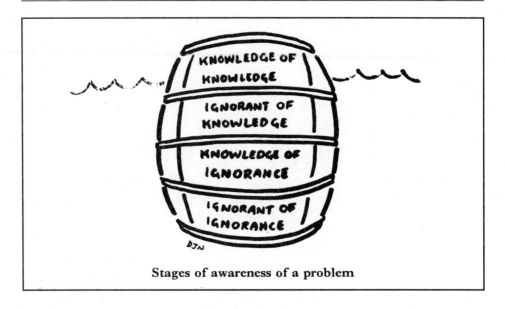

Stages of awareness of a problem

For whom is this relevant? A member of your team may have a problem about which they know nothing. Worse still, their problem may be having a deleterious effect on the performance of others. What should you do? How do you tell someone they are causing a problem without alienating or demoralizing them? Not by telling them, but asking them. By asking them what effects a particular type of behaviour (the one in question) would be likely to have on them, on others, on the department and on the company. By asking them what they think would be certain indicators that this problem was occurring. By asking them what they would do to cope with it if they were in charge and had to deal with it. Ask them to consider the issue and return to you with some constructive suggestions. For most, that will be sufficient for them to tackle and resolve the problem on their own. A few will return to request counselling or some form of assistance. In most cases, you won't have to complete the above line of questions for the staff member to realize both that you are think-ing about them *and* that you care enough about them to do it discreetly.

Preventive counselling

As a manager you will often see members of your staff behaving in ways which are clearly going to incur negative consequences. What do you do? Do you intervene and point it out to them? Or do you let them make the mistake and then ask them to analyse what went wrong? The ideal answer is the second. Why? Well, people seem most receptive to constructive input when they believe it will help them improve, the key being the extent to which they believe there is a need to, and a means of, improving. If they haven't yet made the mistake, the likelihood of believing they need to improve is lower, and they are therefore less receptive.

But you have departmental and organizational responsibilities to think about; you can't always wait for, or afford to wait for, someone to make an expensive mistake before intervening. Clearly a judgement has to be made. Is it better for the company in the long run to accept this mistake as the price of developing staff or is the cost too high to justify? Let staff make the small mistakes, but intervene to prevent the 'biggies'. Let them behave in ways that harm themselves if the level of harm is not too serious and the value of the lesson is greater than the cost.

Acceptance and transition to the next stage

Acceptance that a problem exists, and that the person concerned desires some help to solve it, is necessary for progression to the next stage. Clients who wish to terminate at this stage are those who have resolved the problem for themselves, those who do not wish to have counselling for whatever reason and those who you are unwilling to counsel for whatever reason.

Stage 1: Rapport formation

Objectives

This stage should be more appropriately named, since it really concerns *basic* rapport formation – what you need to do to start up the counselling relationship. Rapport development is taken even further when you start the next stage. For now, we will provide the necessary elements to create a counselling relationship.

Four initial ingredients for an excellent rapport – basic rapport, genuineness, empathy, respect

Forming an excellent rapport requires four fundamental helping attitudes. To form a basic rapport you must do whatever is necessary to make the other person feel worthwhile, unique and valued. What is necessary?

Relevant appearance

Do you look as though your purpose is to counsel a staff member? Physical appearance is important. Do you look too formal to pay attention to emotions? Or too relaxed to care about the emotions of others? A happy compromise is required.

Eye contact

Eye contact during rapport formation should be prolonged, but not so long that it is taken as either aggression or sexual attraction. Ideally, you should scan the face of the other party in an interested manner.

Make good eye contact

Smiling and other non-verbal behaviour

Smile in a genuine way and avoid any body language which forms a barrier between you and the other party (crossed legs, folded arms, turning your body away from the other, hiding behind a desk, continuing to work while the other makes themselves comfortable and so on).

Handshake

Making physical contact is very important in rapport development (at least in Western cultures). Your handshake should convey to the other person that you really want to reach out and touch them. It should not be the automatic handshake reserved for parties and other similar occasions. Make the handshake firm, yet warm.

Verbal greeting

Your greeting should convey a level of pleasure appropriate to your knowledge of the person and the context in which you are meeting to provide counselling (if that is known in advance). Address the other person by name when it is appropriate; people like being called by their names, but hate it being overused.

Initial exchanges

Your initial exchanges should consist of the usual superficial social issues, phrased in open questions. Use your usual cultural exchanges before a discussion. To do anything else would disconcert the client.

Your attitude

Be genuinely interested in the other person. Your attitude will be communicated appropriately if you feel genuine interest in, and respect for, them.

Verbal greeting

Your behaviour

Ask open questions. We will deal with questions in great detail later. For now, it suffices to say that open questions are those which require an answer beyond 'yes' or 'no'. They say to your staff member, 'Hey, I'm interested in you and what you think.' When they reply, really listen. Show them you've heard and understood by bouncing back what has been said as part of your next question. I call these pick-up and carry-on questions. As the rapport develops, show the client you are human – disclose information about yourself. Invite the client to express how they feel on the issue you've just covered. Be honest, be prepared to talk about your flaws, foibles and fears. Be prepared to make fun of yourself (more on humour soon).

Clear communication

Make brief, clear, relevant and coherent communications. Keep what you say short and simple, and try to end anything you say with a question. That achieves two objectives: it keeps the other party interested in the conversation and it keeps the conversation flowing.

Matching and pacing

Have you ever noticed two people getting on really well together? Have you noticed how their body language is virtually identical? And how the speed, structure, intonation, breathing rate, volume and so on of their speech is indistinguishable? The two participants are matching and pacing each other. They match every aspect of the other's communication. Usually both start off by matching the other. Eventually one person leads or sets the pace; they are slightly in control. With good, balanced relationships there is a regular changeover of responsibility for setting the pace. If you initially match and pace your clients you will shorten the time taken to develop a good rapport. Whether you are master of this art or not, just trying to match and pace yields enormous benefits: it forces your attention on to the individual, and it is difficult not to learn about and appreciate someone whose behaviour you yourself are exhibiting. (See *Coaching and Mentoring*, p. 56,) for more details.

Build trust

The most effective tool you have for building trust is honesty. Be honest about your fears, weaknesses, motives and so on. Revealing information about yourself which the client can recognize is not in your best interests to disclose is the fastest route to gaining their trust. If you have some such pieces of information, use them.

EXERCISE

Decide which of the above you are best at. Which require some work?

How can we convey 'genuineness'?

Perhaps we first ought to ask, 'what is genuineness?'. It is the trait people attribute to you when they feel your motives are pure and fully exposed. Who do you perceive to be totally genuine? What do they say and do to lead you to that conclusion? What body language do they display? What facial expressions? Do they appear equally genuine at all times, or does their level of genuineness vary? What makes them appear less genuine at some times than at others?

Genuineness has nothing to do with liking. The most genuine person I know is someone with whom I fundamentally disagree on virtually everything. We don't get on at all, but I respect that person immensely. Genuineness often conflicts with diplomacy. The advice given to trainee diplomats is often the exact opposite of the guidelines you should follow if you wish to be perceived as genuine:

- Be yourself – respond naturally.
- Be spontaneous – that is, as spontaneous as you are naturally.
- Talk about yourself in the way you normally would at the appropriate time in the conversation.

- Express and share your feelings as and when is appropriate (as you normally do).
- Avoid pretending to be something or someone you are not.
- Avoid being either defensive or aggressive – be comfortable with who and what you are.
- Expose your motives – even if they are not what you know the client wants to hear.

EXERCISE

Choose the most genuine person you know and write down the attributes that make you think they are genuine.

How do we convey empathy?

Not in the way it is usually presented. Not in that sickly, nauseating way typified particularly by the TV and radio (unintentional) caricatures of counsellors (someone, somebody, anybody should tell them!). You don't have to act sweet and sentimental to convey empathy. Effective leaders are able to convey their understanding of their team's predicament to them without sounding as though they're talking to tearful toddlers. As I keep saying, just be yourself. Convey empathy by reflecting your understanding of the client's feelings back to the client. You will be most effective if you also reflect the reasons why you understand the client is feeling that way. Try to see the world the way the client sees it. Appreciate why they feel the way they do.

EXERCISE

Who empathizes with you? Who makes you feel that they really understand you? Or, if like most people, no one really understands you, who comes closest to that ideal? Analyse what it is that they do, what they say and how they behave. What can you learn from them?

Respect – how to feel and show it

Respect is an attitude which is based on what you believe about the other person. If you believe they can solve their problem if they are given the right environment, time and assistance you will automatically show respect. Subsumed in that belief are the following assumptions: that this person is worth listening to (if they are one of your team with a problem they most certainly are); that this person has their own unique view of the world that is as real to them as yours is to you; that everyone has the right to believe, think and feel any way they please (they may have to face the consequences of their beliefs, thoughts, feelings and behaviours, but they have the power to do as they please). Hold those beliefs and you'll automatically show respect.

Following is a list of behaviours you would probably automatically adopt to show respect, whether counselling or not:

- Pay positive attention to the other person.
- Follow social courtesies and norms.
- Introduce yourself by name.
- Remember and use the other person's name.
- Be prepared to spend time with the other person.
- Invest effort in trying to understand; ask questions.
- Listen actively.
- Avoid inappropriately negative judgements and destructive criticism.
- Avoid interrupting the other person.
- Avoid manipulation (particularly when you have a clear motive for manipulating a certain solution).
- Avoid being manipulated or used.
- Refuse to be used as a crutch and encourage self-responsibility.

Note the similarity of the above list of behaviours with conventional social skills. What does that tell you about counselling as a skill that requires special development? Who do you believe has greatest respect for you (other than your young children if you have any)? What conveys that respect?

Refuse to be used as a crutch

The logistics for a good rapport – fixed length sessions and work cycle sessions

Imagine what would happen to your newly formed counselling relationship if at the point the client was revealing their core problem you said, 'Sorry, we'll have to end it there; I've got another meeting.' Not exactly a relationship-enhancing manoeuvre. So how should you end a session? The tried and tested method is to set a fixed time period. Both parties will anticipate the end, accept the end-point when it comes and move on.

Counselling sessions can benefit from the same work-cycle planning that improves any other work activity – that is, four phases that merge into each other: preparing, energizing, activity, rest and recovery. The four phases will overlap several of the counselling stages we will be discussing but, for the purposes of simplicity and brevity, we will not explore the work cycle in terms of these stages here. However, I suggest *you* do so at some future stage.

EXERCISE

Draw a diagram which represents where, in the work cycle, the eight common principles in counselling occur. You may want to base it on the eight common factors in the eight-stage model shown on page 69.

Preparing

The preparing phase involves nurturing each other for the task ahead (and is usually led by the counsellor because the client is too absorbed in their own problems to see any need to support the counsellor). In this stage, the mini-team bonds are strengthened (in later sessions) or established (in the case of the first counselling session). Where you are counselling a member of your existing team, some time is dedicated to outlining the nature of the interaction. When counselling someone who is not part of your team, more time will be needed to form a strong relationship before attempting to progress.

Energizing

This phase involves planning, agreeing objectives, discussing and agreeing methods, summarizing where you got to last time, anticipating a positive outcome and so on. These activities are most important if you are to gain coop-eration from, and empowerment of, your client.

Activity

Activity, of course, means the actual business of counselling, which, as you could reasonably expect, will take up most of the time.

Rest and recovery

This should be conducted shortly before the formal end of the session. It involves recognizing the end-point, tying up loose ends, mutual praise for the effort just made, celebration and recognition of the results just obtained or learning from the events that led to no results being obtained. This phase is particularly important for team bonding and for laying the groundwork for the next session.

A 'bad self-esteem day'

Relationship chats

Every so often in counselling, it is wise to check the status of your relationship with your client. You might even want to invite the client to engage in what you will both call 'relationship chats'. Some people find this suggestion odd. They feel awkward discussing relationships. But we know that the most successful relationships engage in exactly these kinds of discussion. Even the staff in successful businesses engage in relationship chatting with each other (usually at all levels). There may be other names for the chats, such as 'working parties' or committee meetings, but they do take place. It's rather like periodically examining a business process to see if it's working well or if it could be improved. Relationship chats are an opportunity for both parties to examine the counselling process to see if it's working.

The frequency of chats will vary from relationship to relationship. Very secure, self-confident people need fewer relationship chats than insecure people with low self-esteem. Most people coming for counselling have experienced one or more 'bad self-esteem' days. How do you establish the right level of relationship chatting? By trial and error. If, when you ask, 'How is our counselling relationship coming along?', the client responds, 'Fine. Why do you ask, again?' or something along those lines, you know you are 'too regular'. Monitor your other relationships to see just how frequently you have relationship chats. Notice what factors affect the frequency of the chats, such as undertaking new projects together, doing particularly difficult tasks, or having conflicts of interest or intention.

Personal revelation

Personal revelations

Revealing aspects of yourself undoubtedly builds trust and rapport. However, too much exposure of yourself and the client might wonder who is providing counselling for whom! A useful guideline is to disclose only as much as you would to someone just outside your innermost circle of friends.

Humour

Probably the most powerful therapy ever devised. If you don't believe me ask Norman Cousins, the American guy who recovered from an almost always irreversible condition (ankolysing spondelitis) by watching non-stop comedy films. If you find that hard to believe ask yourself the following question. No matter how severe your problems, how do you feel after you've watched a brilliant comedian? Ask any parent what's one of the best ways to help their upset or hurt children feel better, and you'll be sure to hear 'make them laugh' or 'do something funny' amongst the replies. Why, then, has counselling such a sombre image? Well, just in case you didn't know, 'counselling is a very serious profession and laughter in such circumstances demeans its credibility'. Hogwash! Refusing to use a tool that is known worldwide to be highly effective demeans its credibility. Make your clients laugh. Laugh at yourself; see if you can encourage them to laugh at themselves. Use humour in your counselling to break the ice. Use it to create rapport. Use it to enliven the proceedings. Use it simply because it's fun.

How? By tuning in to and using your own style of humour. If you don't know what your style of humour is, you now have an opportunity for some personal development. We all have a sense of humour of some kind. What makes you laugh? Who makes you laugh? Do funny cartoons amuse you? Or do authors who (mistakenly) think they are creating funny cartoons make you laugh? Does self-deprecating humour make you laugh? Find out what makes you laugh and use it. You don't have to have a good memory for jokes to be humorous – just be spontaneous. Look for what is funny about yourself, your situation and your behaviour. Invite others to do the same for themselves and you. Perhaps you could start by keeping a log (mental or actual) of what makes you laugh or a log of lead-ins you can use to create humour with your clients. If laughter is the world's best therapy, you can become a more effective counsellor/manager if you become a part-time student of comedy.

Clarifying role expectations

What will clients expect in counselling? Although you might expect clients to have more faith in their own solutions, some will come to counselling expecting you to provide answers, particularly if your normal role as manager is as their problem solver. How can you remove that expectation without disillusioning them or being perceived as not a 'proper counsellor' because you won't solve their problem? Simply spend a little time at the start of the counselling sessions talking about what counselling can and cannot do, about who will and will not be solving problems and about what input you can offer and what you cannot. In short, invest time in clarifying and modifying the client's expectations about counselling.

Role expectation clarification

Acceptance and transition to the next stage

Before you can move on to the next stage, the client must have formed a rapport with you. They must have accepted that counselling in general and that you, specifically, will be beneficial for them. Only those clients who feel that both you and counselling will help them, will go to the next stage.

Clients who wish to terminate at this stage will be:

- those for whom your lack of rapport (as their manager) was the problem. Now that you have both established a rapport there is no need to carry on
- those who perceive (rightly or wrongly) that they cannot form a true rapport with you – their personal agendas may differ from yours, or they may detect a clash of belief systems
- those who only need to know that there are others willing to support them to be able to solve their problems
- those who feel your role as their manager will conflict (to their detriment) with your role as counsellor.

9

UNDERSTANDING THE PROBLEM

Stage 2: Understanding

Since this stage is the most important, it will contain more detail than the others.

Objectives

The first objective is to obtain as total an understanding of the problem as is humanly possible – not for your benefit, but for the client's. The second objective is to communicate your understanding of the problem to the client, both while it is being sought and once it is achieved.

General principles

The general principles to guide your input at this stage will be covered under the following headings:

- Listening skills:
    - listening
    - reflecting
    - using questions
    - clarifying and summarizing.

- Eliminating barriers to understanding:
    - barriers in you
    - barriers in the client
    - barriers in the environment.

Maintaining and developing your rapport and genuinely seeking to understand your clients are more important than all the techniques you are about to acquire. The techniques will help you achieve the objectives, or maybe only give you confidence that you can achieve the objectives. But the objectives are, and must always be, secondary to your person-focus.

Many clients come to counselling with their thoughts clouded by the perceived complexity or insolubility of their problem. While obtaining an understanding of the client's problem is important for you as a counsellor, it is much more important that the client has a chance to come to understand the problem. Part of your role is to ensure that you provide your client with an environment which facilitates reaching that understanding.

Stages of understanding

Both you and your client will go through several stages in your search for understanding. Naturally the stages will vary from problem to problem. Here is the general sequence:

Client	You
A problem	General area of problem
Ownership of problem	Client's level of ownership
Separating and ordering the elements	Determining the elements
Clarifying and checking hypotheses	Confirming the elements and the client's theory
Problem is defined	Overall understanding.

Observe the client and make it easier for them to reach an understanding of the problem. This will give you many insights when it comes to the redefining/reframing stage.

Listening skills

The only way you can hope to understand the client is by listening to them. This goes beyond listening to their words – 'listening' involves very much more than using your ears to pick up soundwaves generated by vocal cords. It means paying complete attention to the non-verbal language and emotions of the client as well. Listening achieves many beneficial effects. It further builds rapport, it enhances the client's ability to express themselves, it creates trust and (useful to any manager) it enhances your influence.

Listening to what? Listening for what purpose? You listen not for one aspect in particular, but to achieve understanding in total. Paradoxically though, understanding comes from seeking the interrelationship of the component parts of any life picture. So, which components should you seek to understand in your search for that holy grail of counselling – understanding? Listen to what the client feels to be the most important: feelings, reasons behind feelings, and beliefs behind feelings.

Listening is the key to making it easy for the client to talk

Then, listen to the other elements, such as:

- environmental, person- and life-stage contexts
- facts and absence of facts
- content
- emotion and absence of emotion
- cause and effect links
- non-verbal communication and its absence
- manner of communication (tone, choice of words, grammar structure, ordering of key points), variation from their normal speech patterns, variations from their normal non-verbal behaviour
- congruent or incongruent communication (does their non-verbal behaviour conflict or match speech?), values/beliefs...
- values and beliefs.

Rewarding listening

How do you help the client to talk? How do you make it easy and safe for them to do so? How do you help them express their problem? How do you help them draw out the finer points of the problem in such a way that they can calmly and rationally 'get a handle on it'? By rewarding them for talking. Your listening should take on a rewarding quality. You don't have to act or force yourself to listen rewardingly. If you are genuinely interested and trying to understand, you will automatically listen in a rewarding way. To illustrate: you've probably done a considerable amount of public speaking in your time (most managers have to). Have you noticed that when you look at the audience, your eyes tend to be drawn to one or two people? No matter how determined you are to follow the rule to 'scan the audience with your eyes', you still want to focus on those one or two people. Have you ever wondered why? It is because they are offering you the most rewarding listening. In various ways they are communicating to you a total picture, which says, 'I am really listening to you. I am interested in what you have to say. I'm determined to understand.'

What ingredients make up 'rewarding listening'?

- Making good eye contact – that is, active looking, not staring or passive (fixed eye) looking.
- Interested body language – facing the client, using body language that reflects both your involvement and the mood of conversation.
- Holding beliefs that lead to the client's respect and acceptance.
- Continuing subjects and issues raised by the client.
- Reflecting the subjects, content, context and emotions proffered by the client.
- Avoiding negatives, 'don'ts' and criticisms.
- Praising when appropriate – acknowledging when the client has overcome some barriers.

EXERCISE

Who do you know who truly listens to you? What do they do to convey that impression? Analyse what it is about their voice, body language, eye contact and so on that conveys the impression that they are completely listening.

Non-verbal behaviour – how to convey a willingness to listen

First, we should say that if you are genuinely willing to listen, your non-verbal behaviour will express that desire automatically. If you have to fake listening until you do it naturally, here are the key signals. But use them with moderation; an impression that you are faking is worse than being disinterested.

- Body posture:
    - arms and legs not folded or crossed
    - facing client
    - relaxed but attentive posture (not slouching or peering)
    - head very slightly tilted.

- Eye contact:

  - attentive but not staring.

- Facial expression:

  - neutral or in tune with the client's message
  - not overexaggerated.

- Signals:

  - head nods at end of sentences/blocks of speech
  - acknowledgements ('Yes', 'I see', 'Go on', 'Mm') at end of sentences/blocks of speech
  - echoing/last phrase repetition
  - reflection of client's message.

Reflecting

Previously we've said that we should reflect the client's communications to demonstrate that we are listening. Doing so actually forces you to listen, helps you to further build a good rapport, and gives you involvement without taking disempowering control of the counselling process. But what should you reflect? The most commonly used and effective ways of providing rewarding listening yield the following ways of reflecting:

- Paraphrase the client:

  - reflect the meaning of their communications
  - reflect feelings
  - reflect context.

- Echo the client:

  - verbatim reflection of what has just been said.

- Summarize:

  - various types (see pages 141–42).

What does reflecting mean in practice? Well, suppose that I came to you and said, 'I'm having problems writing this chapter. I just can't see how to convey the finer point of reflection without overburdening you with unnecessary detail.' In response, you say, 'Your writing's not bad, but don't give up your day job!' No, seriously, you would, if you were reflecting well, say, 'In trying to stick to the key points, you're finding it difficult to express the subtleties of reflection?' Note the question mark at the end of the statement. It is meant to signify that your reflections should take on a questioning tone. You can either ask your confirmation question verbally with an 'add on', such as ' ... Is that right?', or non-verbally by means of tone and intonation. Either way, that response reflects the content. Emotion was also present in my original statement to you. To reflect that aspect, you might phrase as follows: 'The conflicting needs of the chapter are leaving you frustrated?' or 'Your attempts are leaving you frustrated?'

There was also a context to my statement. You may have missed the contextual part of the message because we share an understanding of the context – or at least we think we do. What context do we share? Well, you are seeking information on reflection techniques in counselling and I am trying to present the same information in a way that you will find both interesting and informative. If we had not both had our minds in the same place, you would have seen the context and reflected it. The same situation exists in the workplace; you may share contextual understanding, but check that you do by reflecting your understanding of the context. Restating what you take to be the assumed context can often highlight the misunderstandings upon which a problem is based.

Context of client's problems

Important as it is to try to understand the complexity of emotions that the client is experiencing, there is a wider arena in which emotions exist. Problems always occur on a stage which is cluttered with all sorts of other characters, props and background scenes. The context of most problems is highly intricate. Your client needs to know that you understand the context. More often than not, the client will want to use you as a means to help them to understand the context. Listen to the context in which their problem occurs. When the client knows you understand both how they feel and the context which led to the problem, they will be able to promote you in their minds from listener to helper.

The elements making up each contextual factor are too extensive to list; it takes a large fraction of your life to learn this information. (That is another reason why counsellors in the workplace should be experienced businesspeople first and counsellors second – people without the necessary business experience can't even hope to understand the contextual subtleties involved.) Here are some general contexts/factors:

- health contexts/factors
- work and work colleague contexts/factors
- political contexts
- career contexts
- financial factors/contexts
- social factors/contexts
- family factors/contexts
- spouse/partner contexts/factors
- extended family contexts
- racial and cultural factors
- social class factors

- educational level factors
- age context/factors
- experience factors/contexts
- sex/gender factors
- sexuality factors/contexts
- religious contexts/factors.

EXERCISE

Take the above list and name three issues which will influence each context. For instance, three factors in sexuality could be intensity of drive, focus of sexual desire, frequency with which drive has to be satisfied for healthy adjustment.

Expression of incorporated feelings

Clients regularly convey a covert emotional message with the content of what they say overtly. It may be contained in the tone of voice, in the facial expression, or in body language. As a counsellor, you should try to identify what those feelings are and check with the client that you understand them. When a client has stated something covertly, be it fact or emotion, it is wisest to highlight or reflect what you think you have detected with a question: 'Do you

Seek to clarify any communication you don't understand

mean ... ?', 'Are you saying ... ?'. And if you don't understand, ask: 'What are you saying by your tone?' 'What do you mean by that facial expression?'

If feelings are the most important factor to the client, we should know something about them. Let us take a walk through our emotional landscape.

Dimensions of emotions

Emotions are complicated. We still don't understand them. Yes, there are some people out there who will regale you with rather convincing hypotheses about the mechanisms of emotions. Hypotheses they will remain for a long, long time. All we understand about emotions is that thoughts normally precede them, except where emotional reactions have become a conditioned response. But we can observe that feelings vary along several dimensions. You will find more complex and structured descriptions of emotional dimensions in other books, but the following is sufficient for our role as counsellor. Remember, we don't want to fill our heads so full of theory and method that we lose sight of the client.

Emotions vary along some of the following dimensions:

● Ability to experience feelings	People vary in their ability (inability?) to experience emotions.
● Clarity of feelings	The clarity of emotions varies within and between individuals.
● Level of acceptance of feelings	The degree to which people acknowledge and accept their feelings varies.
● Control perceived over feelings	Some perceive feeling to be totally within and others totally outside of their control.
● Awareness of causes of feelings	Some always know why they feel a particular way, and others never know.
● Awareness of consequences of feelings	The degree to which people are aware of the effect specific feelings will have on them varies.
● Intensity of experience of feelings	The level of intensity with which feelings are experienced varies dramatically both within and between individuals.
● Level of persistence of feelings	The period for which feelings last varies both within and between individuals.
● Occurrence rate of predominant feelings	The frequency with which people experience significant feelings varies.

• Degree to which feelings impair functioning	The extent to which feelings either positive or negative impair normal functioning varies both within and between individuals.
• Degree to which feelings enhance functioning	The extent to which their positive or negative feelings enhance normal functioning varies both within and between individuals.
• Level of drive which feelings produce	The degree to which feelings generate motivation to act varies.
• Degree to which feelings produce physical reactions	The level of outward manifestations of emotional experience varies.
• Nature of physical reactions produced by feelings	The specific nature of outward manifestations of feelings also varies.
• Specific physical reactions produced by specific feelings	The degree to which specific feelings result in specific behaviours or other manifestations varies.
• Extent to which feelings manifest into psychosomatic disorders	For some people, feelings end up as psychosomatic problems. The extent to which emotions are the precursors of physical symptoms varies.

Questioning skills

Questions are a very powerful tool. They can empower your mind, direct your thinking and give you access to parts of your mind that are otherwise out of reach. They can do the same for your staff. All questions force the mind of the listener to concentrate on whatever area the questioner decides. The asking of questions is, by definition, directive. That accepted, what choices do you have when asking questions? Along which dimensions will your questions focus? The answer is anywhere between, and including, the following:

- the client or the problem
- fact, feeling or perception
- detail or generality
- time or timing
- purpose or process
- intimate or superficial detail
- the client or the involvement of others
- context or content.

Asking for examples

One of the most useful ways to reach an understanding of the client's problem is to ask the client to give you some examples. Asking for examples is best used when clients adopt a position without giving you enough to understand what they mean. They may even indicate they are doing so by using phrases like 'you know', 'know what I mean'.

Question types

We will examine the different types of questions in some detail but, before we do, bear in mind that questions you ask reveal an enormous amount about your attitudes and motives towards the client. Indeed some questions are so revealing of your intentions that they should only be used in stage 3 (reframing) and beyond; they are inappropriate for the early stages of rapport formation and seeking understanding. Such questions are marked*.

There are two main categories of questions – open and closed. Open questions are those to which an answer other than 'yes' or 'no' is required. Closed questions invite nothing other than a 'yes' or 'no'. The other categories can all be either open or closed. Questions have several specific uses. They can be used to show interest, to check understanding and so on. Examples of the range of questions are presented below in a tabular format:

- Open questions — What options do you have now?
- Very open questions — Tell me about each of your options?
- Closed questions — So, you prefer the first option?
- Socratic questions* — What is your next step now you have made this decision?
- Probing questions* — And how precisely will you do that?
- Leading questions* — How are you going to involve your family?
- Hypothetical questions* — What will you do if they don't approve?
- Justifying questions* — What makes you so sure that is the right thing to do?
- Feeling elicitation questions — How do you feel about that?
- Empathetic questions — You must feel good about that?
- Prefix/suffix questions — You are pleased you reached a decision, aren't you?
- Discrepancy questions* — Didn't you say you planned to stay until you finished the current project?
- Challenge questions* — How can you keep your promises and do what is right for you?
- Follow-on questions — Could you continue?
- Clarification questions — Could you explain that to me again/in another way?
- Elaboration questions — Can you elaborate on that?
- Evidence questions* — On what do you base that conclusion?
- Example questions — Could you give me an example?
- Demonstration questions — Would you like to demonstrate?

EXERCISE

Think of other types of questions.

Tone and structure   Questions can also be asked by tone and intonation as well as by structure. Note that some of the above questions are, in their written format, just statements with a question mark at the end. That means of communication is normal in everyday life, and, as such, should be used in counselling. Some counsellors spend much time and effort phrasing the perfect question every time, thereby interfering with their person-focus. Don't worry about the phrasing of the questions. Just reflect or ask what you feel is relevant in whatever way it comes out; simply continue in the way you converse normally.

Multipurpose questions   Did you notice that some of the questions were of two types? For instance the prefix/suffix question is also an empathetic question; it seeks to convey that you understand how the client is feeling. As just stated, ask your questions in whatever way seems natural to you.

Silence as a counselling tool

Silence   Counselling does not just involve talking to the client. You can use silence to the client's advantage. Silence is an extremely effective way of encouraging someone to express themselves. Most people tend to think 'it's my turn to contribute to the conversation' when a silence occurs, particularly if the stated purpose of a meeting was to solve a problem by means of discussion (counselling). Especially if you were the last to speak, the client will feel an intense desire to open up. Silence may also be interpreted as a non-verbal question: 'You have something you want to say?'

Silences are extremely productive events in counselling. Try to feel comfortable during them. Don't interrupt them. Be comfortable in the knowledge that your client is working. They may be: considering the conversation just had; thinking about the problem; experiencing some feelings; analysing some thoughts or feelings; shifting their thinking to a new position; redefining or reframing the problem; seeing the problem and its solution clearly; planning how they are going to implement the solution they have chosen and so on. Let the silence run as long as it needs to. However, if you suspect that it is turning into a game or a battle of wills, break it immediately otherwise it will destroy your hard won rapport.

Guidelines on when to ask what

How do you use the range of questions you have at your disposal? What can they achieve for the client? Questions in counselling are, at the most general level, closed when seeking facts, reflecting or confirming and (ideally) open or very open for all other purposes. (For a more in-depth consideration of questions and their uses, refer to *Coaching and Mentoring*, pp. 67–81.)

- *Open questions* help the client understand or think clearly.
- *Very open questions* help the client think in as much detail as possible on an issue.
- *Closed questions* confirm or test your understanding.
- *Socratic questions* help the client generate a particular answer without spoonfeeding them.
- *Probing questions* help the client to consider specific details which may be influencing them.
- *Leading questions* introduce something the client seems to have overlooked.
- *Hypothetical questions* help the client consider alternatives or evaluate solutions.
- *Justifying questions* help the client to explore/justify a statement you or they think is shaky.
- *Feeling elicitation questions* find out how the client feels.
- *Empathetic questions* demonstrate you do or are trying to understand how the client feels.
- *Prefix/suffix questions* reflect a statement or rescue yourself from having made a statement.
- *Discrepancy questions* invite the client to address discrepancies in their messages.
- *Challenge questions* confront or challenge the client about something (see page 150).

- *Follow-on questions* invite the client to continue.
- *Clarification questions* help the client clarify what they have said.
- *Elaboration questions* invite the client to expand on something they have said.
- *Evidence questions** invite the client to back up an assertion.
- *Example questions* invite the client to provide some examples of what they are discussing.
- *Demonstration questions* help the client demonstrate what they mean.

The fine line

There is a very fine line between asking questions which are clearly aiding your attempts at understanding and questions which are perceived as interrogation. Questions become interrogation when they take on an accusatory tone, are felt to be directed towards fact at the expense of feelings, are asked in rapid succession or are not mixed with acknowledgement and recognition of the client's answer in an empathetic way.

In summary, avoid the following when asking questions:

- rapid-fire questioning – it conveys interrogative intent
- picking up on every new issue the client raises – it continually distracts you from the main problem
- accusatory tones – it destroys rapport
- the temptation of using questions as a cover for what you want to say (at this stage)
- always asking closed questions – it conveys lack of interest.

Listening to and checking the answers

Note the ways in which questions are answered as well as the content of the answers. The points we said you should listen for earlier are the same points you should be listening for after you've asked your questions. But, as we keep saying, person-focus is far more important than any and every technique.

Naturally, as a counsellor, you should check that your understanding of what was said is accurate. However, don't be fooled into thinking that you will do so in a non-directive manner. That which you don't understand is likely to require checking. Why are you likely to understand some things rather than others (assuming equal clarity of communication on the part of the client)? Because, for example, you lack contextual understanding or some of the assumptions necessary to interpret what the client has said. So, what effect on the proceedings does that have? Well, it means that you will check areas that more reflect your ignorance than the client's needs. That clearly makes the process directive. It is directing the client to educate you in the ramifications of the problem you were unable to understand previously. This is not a bad thing, but it is not the non-directive counselling that the vested-interest professionals will tell you is possible. It is not possible. But don't let that put you off; you should still be checking statements and issues you don't understand.

Doing so is an excellent way of demonstrating that you are trying to understand. It is a great way of paying attention to the client.

Summarizing

Providing summaries for your clients is a very effective tool: it is a very useful technique for ensuring that you try to understand; it helps you maximize your person-focus when trying to understand; and helps you keep track of both the client's thinking and your own.

Summary types

There are many different types of summary – many ways in which you can consolidate and reflect what the client has said. But how do you decide what type of summary to use? Most importantly, your summary should reflect what the client has been discussing. The different summary types are more representative of what the client has been discussing than anything you want to achieve. You will automatically provide the right kind of summary if you just gather together what the client has been discussing. As you go through the following list, ask yourself: 'At which stage in the eight-stage model is this kind of summary likely to occur?'

Simple reflection summary   The content of the client's message is used as the basis of your summary.

Feelings and reasons summary   The feelings and/or reasons which the client has expressed form the basis of your summary.

Clarification summary   This is used when the client has expressed some fairly confused thoughts or feelings. You use your summary to convey the clarification of their message that you have been compiling in your head.

Context summary   The context of a problem is often critical to understanding both the client and the problem. You will, at some stage, be given the context of the problem. Providing a context summary shows the client you understand the wider picture.

Theme summary   The problem will often unfold like a well-told story. It will have a plot and various sub-plots each of which will have its own theme. Demonstrate to the client that you understand the theme in their messages. There may be one theme running throughout the problem or which characterizes certain elements of the problem. If you see them, reflect them.

Problem specification summary   Early on in counselling, the client will give you a first draft of what they perceive as the problem. That definition or problem specification usually changes as you progress through the early stages of counselling. Each time you detect a change in the client's specification of the problem you should reflect that change. This summary focus is very well used in the reframing stage of the counselling process.

End-of-session summary In the same way that you follow the work cycle in the achievement of normal business tasks, you should do so in counselling. Summarize, or ask the client to summarize, what you have achieved during each session. It is an excellent way to both keep track of what you've done and congratulate yourselves for your efforts.

Revision of previous session summary At the start of each new session, remind yourselves what you achieved with the last one, what goals you set in the interim period and what you plan to explore in this session.

Problem redefinition summary Although the formal period for redefining or reframing the problem takes place in stage 3, the client will probably gradually redefine the problem as you go through the counselling process. As and when that occurs, you should summarize the change. Although this summary has a slightly different purpose than the problem specification summary, it must be said that the line between the end of an evolving problem specification and the start of problem redefinition is hazy, broad and grey.

Information provision summary Occasionally you will have to provide the client with some information. When you have done so, summarize what was provided. Why? For two reasons. First, because we know it improves the likelihood of the information being remembered and, second, it gives the client an opportunity to express how they feel about the information and for you in turn to note whether or not the information provided has had the effect you had anticipated.

Client's decision summary Clients will make a series of decisions all the way through your counselling sessions. Summarize each decision as it is made, if only to show the client you are still trying to understand, support and follow their efforts to solve their problem.

Client's plan for action summary Reflect what your client plans to do in response to their problems. It gives them a chance to hear how the plan sounds coming from another person.

EXERCISE

Think of other possible types of summary.

Some of the most common barriers to understanding

The client can prevent you from listening well enough to gain an understanding of their problem in many different ways. Be aware of, and try to minimize the effect of, these barriers: deceit, pomposity, monotony, irrelevance, lethargy, stuffiness, hypersensitivity, patronism, formality, complexity, statistics, vagueness, insecurity, nervousness, distractability, inconsistency, mixed messages.

Presenting a professional facade

This is the kiss of death to an effective counselling session. Just be yourself – a competent manager who is also providing counselling as and when required. Your preoccupation with being something you are not will block your ability to listen. You don't have to go into counsellor mode and start affecting a 'sympathetic' voice. Clients instinctively know when you are being yourself, especially if they are working with you on a day-to-day basis.

Presenting a facade

Faking interest

Tempting as it may sometimes be, particularly when you are tired, avoid pretending to be interested. The effort going into the pretence will further diminish your ability to listen. If you can't pay attention for whatever reason, tell your client and reschedule the session.

Excessive desire to help

Being too keen to help will direct your attention on what you can do rather than on trying to understand. Seek understanding first; worry about how you can help later.

Attitude barriers

Any attitude other than respect and a willingness to help the client understand their own problem and to help themselves will effectively sabotage your counselling efforts. Any belief other than 'the client is the best person to help themselves with the assistance of a supportive other' will sabotage your efforts to understand.

Questioning inappropriately

While the question is the master tool in coaching, it is a hazard to be avoided in the early stages of counselling, when the client's emotional turmoil is at its highest levels. The asking of questions by counsellors is frequently seen by clients as the fact-finding stage before proper problem solving starts. To a large extent it is just that. And there is a specific time for that approach. It is not when you are trying to help the client to communicate how they feel. Remember, your objective is to demonstrate to the client that you understand them and their problem, *not* to drag that understanding out of them with a series of questions. Too much questioning takes control away from the client (unless the questions invite the client to decide what to do or explore next). As stated, there is a fine line between questioning appropriately to seek understanding and being more interested in the facts than the person.

EXERCISE

Consider how you feel when someone is asking you a chain of questions. Does it fill you full of a desire to cooperate? Does it make you want to offer information? Does it either alienate you or make you respond passively to what is asked so that, if the asker fails to ask the right questions, on their head be it?

Allowing the client to wander down blind alleys

What do you do when a client apparently becomes preoccupied with some side issue that has no real bearing or effect on the problem? Quite simply, ask them how 'this' issue will help solve the main problem. If it can, then carry on. If it can't, then ask the client to carry on with what they were discussing before they provided the interesting 'background piece'.

Many blind alleys will start off as interesting and relevant contextual background information. Having communicated their messages, clients may then continue down the same line of reasoning looking for an answer, but in so doing they move further from the crux of the problem.

EXERCISE

Think of other ways in which blind alleys will reveal themselves. How can you avoid reading something incorrectly as a blind alley?

Misinterpreting a significant shift

Often, when clients are at the point where they can see the problem clearly, they will become quiet, or at least quieter than normal, while they test the fledgling reframing in their minds. Don't misinterpret this apparent withdrawal as either a blind alley or a breakdown in rapport. The speed of your client's eye movement is a good guide here. If the eyes are glazed, you are watching a withdrawal. If the eyes are moving rapidly the client is processing their new insight. Observe your own behaviour. When do you go quiet in a serious discussion? What signals do you give off to reveal the different possible motives for your quietness? Observe others. What signals do they send?

Problem inexplicability

There will be occasions when the client's problem will seem totally inexplicable to you. If that is the case, don't bluff. Tell the client you don't understand. What are the likely causes of problem inexplicability? If you can't understand why something should be a problem for a client, or if the problem as presented doesn't make any sense to you, there is something missing. There is usually some piece of information, some shared assumption that you believe everyone holds, which the client does not. More on this in the next chapter.

Presented problems and actual problems

Clients will very often come to counselling with a highly specific problem. You will start the counselling process, and some other problem will materialize which puts the original problem in the shade. What's happening here? Is the client lying? Does the client not know the real problem? Do they only discover the real problem as counselling progresses? All of the above are possible, but the most common explanation is that the client wants to test you out. They want to use a presented problem to see how you are going to handle it. If you gain their trust you will be given the privilege of helping them with the actual problem. You may think the word 'privilege' is used inappropriately here. It is not. Giving someone permission to enter your inner life is a very risky business, and being granted that permission is something that very few people ever receive in their entire lifetime from anyone. Most people don't allow their spouse or partner to get that close. It is undoubtedly a privilege, and as with all privileges, it confers enormous responsibilities. Honour those responsibilities. Show the client that sense of responsibility with the presented problem and you'll be given permission to help them with the actual problem.

EXERCISE

When have you presented a problem which was not the real issue for you? Come on now, we've all done it! When have you talked of one of your problems as though it were 'a friend's'? What made you take the leap to subsequently present the real problem? And if you didn't, what held you back?

Trying to help or reassure before trying to understand

This is one of the few cardinal sins in counselling. Don't try to help or reassure before you understand the problem. Unless you understand your client they will have no faith in your ability to help. In any event, how could you possibly help before obtaining an understanding of what the problem is?

Acceptance and transition to the next stage

The client must be totally certain that you understand them and their problem. They must accept that understanding on your part is an indication that the two of you can work together to solve their problem.

Only those clients who desire more than understanding and a listening ear should progress to the next stage. Sometimes a clear signal of the time to move on is when the client is moving in circles.

Clients who are likely to withdraw at this stage fall into the following categories:

- those who feel supported in their own problem-solving efforts knowing that someone else understands
- those whose problem was that they needed to understand something which was confusing them – once they understand they know what to do about the problem
- those whose only need was to know that *you* understood their problem
- those who you feel will benefit from solving the problem themselves now they understand it
- those towards whom you feel negative once you understand the problem for whatever reason
- those who do not wish your input to the solution for whatever reason.

EXERCISE

There are plenty more reasons for terminating counselling at the end of this stage, what are they? What motives would you have for terminating counselling at this stage, and what motives would your client have?

Summary

Understanding is the purpose of person-focus. What most matters to clients is that you understand. In this stage we have explored a range of tools to help you reach that understanding. But remember that 'unqualified' counsellors are indistinguishable from the so-called qualified. That is, those who have no formal knowledge of the techniques just covered are just as good from the client's point of view. Simply directing your entire attention on trying to understand the client is as good as any and every counselling technique.

10

REDEFINING THE PROBLEM

Stage 3: Reframing

Objective

To help the client reinterpret or reframe the problem in terms that make it more resolvable or manageable.

How is the objective to be achieved? By helping clients to see the effects their choice of perception has on their problem. By helping the client to see alternative interpretations, meanings, perceptions which empower them to solve or manage the problem in skill terms by using various tools.

Which cues tell us that we are dealing with a problem requiring reframing?

A problem requires reframing:

- if the client has not solved their problem in the understanding stage
- if the client presents a problem that seems to defy resolution in its current format.

Clients enter this stage in counselling because their problem, as it is currently defined, does not permit an acceptable resolution. Some slight change in thinking is usually required. Sometimes only a slight change of perception is needed, or a new awareness of something they have missed. Perhaps a piece of information or knowledge is lacking. Maybe they lack the realization that their behaviours are self-sabotaging. See the list of dangerous thoughts in Appendix II, page 264, for further possibilities.

Reframing

Guidelines for confronting and reframing problems

Challenging and reframing: what are they and what is the relationship?
Challenging or confrontation is the principal tool for helping to reframe or
redefine the client's problems. It can bring about benefits other than reframing.
Indeed, it should be clearly stated that challenging is required separately from
reframing. Successfully challenging some minor inconsistencies, contradictions,
false premises, inaccurate attributions and so on may be sufficient for the client
to realize that the problem concerns their perception or thinking. Successful
challenging usually involves a small degree of reframing or redefinition.

Confrontation or challenging is most effective when it points out discrepancies and when it is invited from the facts, when the facts make it inevitable
and when it has been softened by a big dose of compassion. Humour can be of
great help in the process.

Reframing is a necessary stage before problem solving and problem-
management planning can begin. This does not necessarily mean that you must
have conducted the reframing with the client. Some clients may come to you,
after they have solved or redefined their problem, for help with choosing a solution that is acceptable to you, the manager, and the company or department.

Reframing involves a much more substantial change in perception than that
experienced with a normal challenge, although challenging tools are the mechanism which usually brings about a significant reframing. The client's whole

Challenging a reframing: the relationship

view of the situation is changed when they restate the problem in the new perspective. They may change their entire paradigm (see page 97 for more on paradigm change).

Managing confrontation and challenging

The client will usually have an understanding of the problem from a particular perspective. If that perspective were a close picture of reality (excluding those entirely factual problems, such as a death, redundancy and so on) they would have been able to solve or manage it. But, because their perception is flawed they can see no acceptable solutions. The purpose of this stage is to help clients reframe or redefine their problem in a way that makes a solution or resolution possible. To make that happen, you must challenge the existing definition of the problem.

Challenges and confrontations

A client's willingness to accept and respond to your challenges depends on the depth and quality of your rapport and understanding of their problem. Challenging should be conducted with compassion and sensitivity. It should be done slowly, softly and persistently. It should not be done to relieve your frustration: it is likely you will see the obvious solution to the client's problem early on in the proceedings – the timing of your confrontation should not reflect your increasing frustration that the client doesn't yet share your vision. Accept that your clients will need some slow, gentle encouragement.

At this point you can do something to further improve your rapport. Invite your clients to challenge you on your counselling approach or skills. Inviting them to confront you about anything they don't like about what you are doing with them will increase their acceptance of your challenges. Such challenges will enhance your rapport and the level of trust the client has in your motives. In general terms, a challenge from you should follow this sequence:

1   Confirm that you understand what has been said.
2   Obtain the client's agreement that you understand.
3   Then, and only then, challenge or confront what was said.

What should be challenged? Conflicting communication between: words and deeds; words and body language; deeds and body language. Inconsistencies: within information provided; between items of information provided; over time; over target of message. Beliefs, behaviours, attitudes which appear to be disempowering or self-sabotaging, including any of the following:

What to challenge

- evasion of issues
- beliefs (harmful and absence of helpful beliefs)
- values (harmful and absence of helpful values)
- self-esteem (harmful and absence of helpful patterns)
- actions, inactions (harmful and absence of helpful actions and inactions)
- thinking patterns (harmful and absence of helpful patterns)
- perceptions (harmful and absence of helpful perceptions)
- predictions (harmful and absence of helpful predictions)
- information (harmful and absence of helpful information)
- choices (harmful and absence of helpful choices)
- habitual games (harmful and absence of helpful games).

EXERCISE

The above list is by no means complete. Add to it from the list of irrational beliefs and dangerous thoughts in Appendix II, page 264.

At some point you will have to risk helping the client to clarify their flawed or disempowering perceptions. But when do you challenge? When the client has started to look for solutions or seems to be inviting input from you. Or when the client starts to recognize they are going round in circles because no acceptable solution exists in the current framing of the problem.

Challenging – a precursor to reframing

As you have probably gathered, there is a big overlap between reframing and confronting. Everything you can use to challenge a client can also be used to help them reframe a problem. Indeed, much challenging is the precursor to reframing. The following techniques can therefore be used to challenge smaller issues or reframe the bigger ones.

Challenging tools

What tools do you use to challenge and confront? There are several. Choose from them on the basis of those that suit you best – those which you would naturally and habitually use.

Humour   This is by far the most difficult challenging tool to use but, as you might expect, the most effective. If you can make a joke about your client's perception that will, on the one hand, amuse them and, on the other, show them the flaws in their thinking, you can instantly change the way they see the problem. Humour can be introduced to, and merged with, all the other methods.

A few years ago I was in a situation that illustrates the process of mixing and matching. I was with someone who was stressed out about what they perceived to be an inevitable and impending disaster: 'This situation is dynamite; it's going to blow up and there's nothing I can do about it.'

'Have you tried pissing on the fusewire?' It was all I could think of. You might consider this to be thoroughly tasteless and not that funny, but it was to the recipient. It also allowed them to change their imagery in such a way that they could take control of the situation and express a healthy irreverence for the problem. They went on to identify ways of preventing the situation getting out of hand, and then ultimately of removing the dynamite. You can imagine the chain of jokes about having a good bang coming out of that analogy, I'm sure.

Provocation   This is risky but effective. The risk is in alienating your client. The effectiveness comes from pointing out the consequences of their current thinking by presenting it at its most extreme to illustrate the point.

Teasing   Be very careful here. Mildly taking the mickey can help clients to see what the difficulty is with their perception or current framing of the problem.

Peer pressure   'How do you think your team would react to your thinking/saying that?' Or, 'What do you think my reaction is to you saying/thinking/doing that?'

Education   This involves demonstrating the effect of irrational and rational beliefs. Point out to clients the effect their thoughts and beliefs have on their lives. Show them the Pentagon Principle and the other diagrams demonstrating the effects of belief and inner dialogue on the problem.

Consequence analysis   'What do you think would be the consequences of that kind of thinking? What would be the consequences if you applied it to ... ' (another part of their lives or a similar situation). Ask them to predict what consequences would follow from the stance they have taken.

Probing   Probe when the client makes a statement which you would have expected to have been richer in detail, or in explanation, or one which leads you to believe there is a flawed assumption underlying it. Probe at the foundations of the problematic framing. Uncover the flawed assumptions. Ask questions which require the client to prove their assumptions. Caution should be exercised here; you may push the client to a point where they feel they have to defend themselves or their position, even though they recognize it as unreasonable. As soon as you have identified a shaky assumption, ask questions aimed at seeking a more empowering interpretation of the 'facts' uncovered.

Illustration of contradiction   'You say on the one hand ... but on the other ... '

Cognitive dissonance   When people are presented with two things they have said or done which are in direct conflict with each other, they have to resolve the resultant dissonance. One way to use this is to harness your memory of the client in the past to show them how they previously solved a similar or related problem: 'You solved this kind of problem before (last week/month/year), I have faith that you can solve this one too.'

Two behaviours result from this approach: either your client will immediately start looking for the ways they solved the previous problem for lessons (good), or they will tell you what is different about this problem and why the previous solution won't apply; a different one will be required (good).

Suggestion   Quite simply, suggest alternative explanations or framings of the problem or interpretations of facts presented.

Persuasion   Counselling is most obviously like persuasion in the challenging or reframing stage. Good persuasion always involves establishing a strong rapport and mutual understanding before attempting to change the recipient's view. Ask any of your leading sales staff if they would ever try changing a prospective customer's mind before establishing an excellent rapport. Also ask them whether they would try to win a favourable decision by going with, or against, the client's beliefs.

Sometimes by simply listening, the client will reach a point at which they challenge themselves. Other times, reframing will simply involve the provision of information or a very brief explanation of something about which the client was previously ignorant. See page 188 for more on persuasion.

Thought interrupting   Many of your staff will find themselves stuck in a destructive thought pattern. What do you do? Use one of the simplest and most effective techniques known of – thought interrupting. Break the pattern with something unexpected. If they are continually complaining about their job being boring suggest, 'It must be through by now.'

'What?' they'll say.

'It must have bored through whatever it is boring. What is that thing?'

Alternatively, if they are complaining about someone else's level of competence, you might ask them what level of competence a successful leader must have in dealing with incompetence of others. Regardless of their response to either example, you will have successfully interrupted the undesirable thought pattern.

Thought blocking/substitution/switching   Ask your clients to cease falling back into an existing and problematic framing of the problem by shouting 'stop' to themselves. This technique is most useful when a client is beginning to see the problem differently but keeps reverting to the old framing.

Silence and repetition   Sometimes the best way to challenge a position is to not respond to it at all. Say nothing until the client softens or changes their position. Alternatively, you can make your challenge and remain silent until the point has been taken. You might have to repeat your point a few times, with appropriate silence in between, to drive the message home that you think their position should be modified. But remember to show compassion. Do not make your point in an accusatory tone.

Thought interrupting

Imagery, metaphors and analogies   Altering the mental image or representation of the problem usually changes the client's ability to manage it. For instance, a tight deadline involving the completion of reams of paperwork might be pictured as a mountain weighing down on the client. Change that image to one of a pile of bricks, each one of which can be used to build a career.

Reframing may involve painting a different picture or repainting the same picture. The brushes for the job can be imagery switches, metaphorical continuation or helpful analogies. For example:

'My mind is like an emotional sieve – everything but the biggest nastiest lumps fall straight through.'

'What could you use to push the lumps through?' or

'Perhaps we could create the opposite effect by swapping your sieve for a settling tank? What could you use to cream off the nice bits and leave the lumps?'

EXERCISE

Analyse what facilitated the change when you last changed the way you looked at a problem.

EXERCISE

Make a list of any other tools you have used in the past to confront others.

Reframing – a summary of the key points

- Definition   Whatever the counsellor does to encourage the client to examine their beliefs, thoughts, feelings, or behaviours. Usually challenging or confronting.
- Objective   To have clients re-examine themselves and their perceptions to maximize the chances of problem solving/managing and of taking self-responsibility.
- When   After a good rapport has been established and you have obtained confirmation from the client that they believe you understand their problem.
- How (examples)   By challenging using various techniques:
  'You say on one hand that ... but on the other ... '
  'You've told me that ... but your ... tells me the opposite.'
  'You believe ... which seems to be causing ... '
- Emotional sensitivity   Describe what you see. Don't accuse.
- Types of reframing   Highlighting inconsistencies, conflicts between verbal and non-verbal messages, discrepancies/conflicts between words and deeds, inaccuracies, possible lies, distortions, projections, self-sabotaging behaviours, unused strengths, alternative interpretations, consequence highlighting and so on.

Tips on facilitating reframing/redefinition

- Start by reflecting what the client has said.
- Ensure that self-responsibility is sought in and by the client.
- Don't force the issue; the client should ideally confront themselves.
- Avoid threatening or defensive verbal and non-verbal communication.
- Don't patronize.
- Be willing to admit your own errors of judgement.

How do you achieve the objective in STM terms?

By seeking with the client to assess problems in terms of their skills repertoire. For many, that will be the case. But, for a few, all that will be needed is a general reframing of the problem in terms that make it manageable to the client. In order of priority, the following strategies are likely to effect beneficial change:

1 Maintain your person-focus.
2 Help the client reframe the problem.
3 Help the client reframe the problem in STM terms.

What cues tell us that we are dealing with a problem requiring reframing in STM terms?

- If the client presents a problem that seems to defy resolution with normal reframing.
- If the client presents a problem that defies early/rapid resolution in normal reframing terms when time pressure dictates a solution be provided quickly.

EXERCISE

Consider past occasions when you realized you needed to acquire skills to solve a problem. Analyse what you think facilitated that realization.

How to assess problems in terms of the client's skills repertoire

At the most simplistic level – usually the best place to start – use the successful living skills list (see page 75). Ask your clients to consider to what extent they engage in the skill described. That, in itself, can prove most effective. For instance, the client may realize (reframe their problem) that they don't have a confidant. Developing such a relationship then becomes the solution.

On the other hand, they may realize they lack a confidant and then become aware that their inability to relate well to others is the reason, in which case social skills training is one likely remedy. Another remedy is to explore the disempowering beliefs the client holds about others and consider more empowering alternatives.

Redefining problems in terms of the client's skills repertoire

To make progress with problems in the workplace, they must be redefined in commercially relevant ways. There is no virtue in defining the problem in terms of traumatic childhood experiences which have to be 'worked through', or any such like. There is no coherent system for 'working through' problems (whatever that is supposed to mean) despite what the psychodynamic counsellors will tell you. Even if there were, there is no time or place for a haphazard approach to anything in the workplace; the industrial miracle was, and is, based

Redefining problems in STM terms

on systematizing every conceivable human process. Counselling is no exception. But, of course, you will hear some bleeding hearts pleading a special case for counselling. (Now why would they want to do that, I wonder?)

How to redefine problems in terms of the client's skills repertoire:

1 Listen to the client.
2 Look for elements in the chain of events that could have been better handled had there been better skills available.
3 Ask the client to consider the chain of events while looking for things that could have been done differently.
4 Ask them how skill X could have helped (you may need to explain what skill X is).
5 Continue the exploration of the chain of events, asking for skill implications at each stage.
6 Present the full skill-oriented picture in the form of a summary.

Present the client with a rationale, or ideally help the client to offer their own rationale for the problem, defined in skill terms. For instance, 'If my social skills had been better, I would have been able to ask for help with this project, and not found myself in a snowed under position.'

The rationale should be based on the information the client provides and offered as a possible explanation – a hypothesis to be tested. Naturally the rationale should also be sensitive to the client's feelings (devoid of any blame, moralizing or any other 'you did wrong' meaning), presented in the client's language and in tune with their previous explanations as much as possible. Use the principal problem areas as a starting point and, after the client's acceptance, also include the smaller problem areas.

Stages of skill issue awareness in reframing

Clients go through several stages of skill issue awareness before or during reframing (and occasionally after an apparently failed attempt at reframing). Obviously the starting point on this list varies from client to client. It will help your persuasive efforts if you spend a few minutes asking questions aimed at determining in which of the following stages your client fits:

- ignorance of 'skill' as a factor in human problems
- awareness that skill may affect others' lives
- acceptance that skill may affect some parts of one's own life
- acknowledgement that skill issues may be involved as a contributory factor in one's problems
- acceptance that a skills deficit/problem was responsible for at least part of this problem
- awareness of what skills deficits/problems may have caused/exacerbated this problem
- acknowledgement that a skills deficit rectification is a possible solution to problems
- acceptance that skill development is the solution to this problem
- willingness to acquire or improve skills to solve the problem
- willingness to acquire/improve skills to anticipate, prevent, solve or manage problems in the future.

(There is a full listing of the stages of acceptance necessary for successful progress in counselling on page 266.)

Likely resistance to redefinition/reframing

Sometimes it is best to ignore small inconsistencies, contradictions and the like in favour of seeking to help the client reframe the principal misconception. That does not mean you should dive straight into the issue. Most people like to be gradually shown where they have gone wrong; they don't want it slapped in their face.

Another group seems to prefer to defend their current position; they need to feel that they are not the problem. Let them know that is the case; show them that those thoughts/thought patterns would cause anyone a problem.

Others will take the stance 'what I think, I am'. They view attempts at changing what they think as attacks on their very substance. How do you handle that? Point out that in the past acquisition of some basic skills they had to change the way they thought. Take reading skills, for example: as most people progress from being a non-reader to a competent reader they change the way they think about information; that which was previously inaccessible becomes available. Books change from being collections of paper to sources of knowledge. In the process of acquiring a new thinking skill (reading) the new reader gains access to something which enhances their lives.

Occasionally you will have a client who needs to have and win a good argument before they will accept the views of another. If you detect argumentative intent you have two choices. One is to let them dissipate their argumentative desires on some trivial issues, let them score a few points until they start cooperating, then move on to reframing the big problem, by which time they will have satisfied themselves that they can out-argue you if they so choose. Your second choice is to state clearly and simply that you are not prepared to argue, that your role is to help and, if that is what they want, you can deliver. If they want a debate, you suggest they go elsewhere and do it in someone else's time.

Likely resistance to redefinition in STM terms

Clients can be very reluctant to accept that their problem has been caused by their lack of skill, their use of the wrong skill, or their use of the right skill at the wrong time and so on. They can be very unwilling to accept that their skills repertoire (or lack of it) has been responsible for maintaining their problem once started. Reluctance levels are directly proportionate to the degree of external control that clients perceive the world has over their behaviour. People who take total responsibility for every aspect of their behaviour very rarely find their way to counselling. Yes, I know it is not politically correct to blame the victim for their circumstances, but counselling in the workplace is no time to enter into philosophical debates that go back three millennia. What you need is results. What you need is a staff member returning to full functioning as soon as possible. So the bottom line applies: people who take total control over their lives handle life's problems better than those who let events control them. The obvious, and only sensible, conclusion to reach, therefore, is that methods which help clients to take control over their lives are absolutely necessary in the workplace. The Skills Training Model I advocate gives your clients the vehicle with which to take control of their lives.

Paradoxically, some of the most emotionally disabled clients respond best to the Skills Training Model. Clients who blame themselves for everything that goes wrong in their lives are in the habit of looking to themselves for the cause of the problem. By giving them the Skills Training Model you give them a tool which makes a positive outcome of their habitual thinking processes possible.

Resistance to the STM

EXERCISE

List any other forms of resistance you think you are likely to encounter.

Barriers and difficulties in this stage

- The client is so tied to an existing belief that they refuse to change.
- The counsellor believes that his or her reframing is the only one possible.
- The counsellor suffers from the same skills deficits as the client and is therefore blind to their absence.
- The client refuses to believe that changes in their skills base will change their problem.
- The client fails to accept self-responsibility.
- The counsellor tries to pressure the client.
- The counsellor forgets that person-focus is more important than technique.
- The counsellor presents a solution which is unacceptable to the client before the client is ready to reframe, thereby giving the client an additional motive not to change.
- The counsellor inappropriately tries to reframe a problem-management issue into a skills deficit issue.
- The client is wary of taking on self-responsibility now for fear of being held responsible by you for other work-related problems in the future.

Acceptance and transition to the next stage

The client must accept the reframing of the problem.

Clients are ready to move into the next stage when they are indicating verbally that they are ready to start looking for a solution, or that they think finding a solution is now possible.

Clients who are likely to withdraw at this stage fall into the following categories:

- those who have established a new understanding of the problem which they now wish to manage on their own
- those who resent your attempts to help them see the problem differently
- those for whom reframing the problem was a solution in itself (they have changed their perception from 'oh, my goodness!' to 'so what?')
- those who find the awareness of their problem in skills terms sufficient to motivate them to acquire the skills on their own
- those who refuse to accept that their lack of skills has any bearing on their lives
- those who find your approach to problem solving (as their manager) something they wish to avoid.

Summary

Clients often come to counselling because the problem as it stands is in an insoluble form. Others come to counselling unable to face the obvious solution because it conflicts with something they hold dear. Whatever the cause of the impasse you will reach a point when it is wise to challenge, or encourage the client to challenge, some assumption or belief about the problem. With all the challenging and reframing techniques, compassion and sensitivity are required.

11

MANAGING SOLUTIONS

Stage 4: Solution searching

Objective

To identify a solution which is both acceptable to the client and is viable and likely to be beneficial in the long as well as the short term. Too many solutions are great in the short term but damaging in the long term. To give a light-hearted example, getting blind drunk removes the problem for a short while but causes long-term damage – not least of which is the destruction of innumerable brain cells which may have been useful in solving the problem!

General principles

- Maintain your relationship with the client.
- Encourage clients to empower themselves to seek ways of managing/solving the problem.
- Encourage them to empower themselves by believing solutions exist and that they can find them.
- Make the client, not the techniques, the centre of your efforts to help them find solutions.

Solution searching takes place in two stages:

1 finding possible solutions
2 deciding which solution to select.

While exploring possible solutions with the client, take notes (mental or actual) of the reasons various solutions are accepted and rejected. Very quickly you will see a pattern emerge. Those reasons can be formally used later as the basis for deciding on the best type of solution.

The solution may be very clear after redefining the problem in skill terms. It will be to acquire, improve, transfer or practise using appropriate skills. Alternatively the reframing may have led to a general awareness that a skills deficit was the problem, without specifying the exact nature of the deficit.

Should we always assume that the problem should be redefined in skill terms? No. The problem may be successfully handled if redefined in problem-management terms – that is, the issue should be redefined as one which is currently out of control where control is needed. Reframing should seek to regain control for the client.

EXERCISE

Formulate a list of the criteria you will use to decide if a problem requires a general solution or a skills-based solution.

Testing hypotheses – both counsellor and client

In this stage both client and counsellor will test a range of solutions. The client is trying to find a solution which is achievable, workable and acceptable. That means generating hypotheses and testing them against the client's criteria for achievability, workability and acceptability. What are those criteria? Well, they will emerge as you consider some possible solutions. As with scientific reasoning, the generation and testing of a hypothesis generates useful information, whether the outcome is positive or negative. Generating possible solutions and testing them is useful even if the solution(s) is/are rejected. Each time a solution is rejected, take a note (actual or mental) of the reason. Each of these reasons will become a criterion for determining the final solution.

What constitutes an acceptable solution?

Solutions should be in keeping with: the client's ability to control; the client's values and should also be sufficiently appealing to the client in order to instil them with enough commitment to push through the inevitable barriers. From your perspective, the above must satisfy the organization's needs for the restoration of full performance.

Choosing between solutions

If after having used the above-mentioned 'acceptable solution criteria', the client has several solutions to choose between, a further selection method is required. Since commitment and persistence are the best predictors of success in most fields, the levels of these attitudes towards each potential solution make a useful selection criterion. The ideal solution is the one to which the client has the greatest commitment, even if that solution is not the best in an absolute sense. An adequate solution with strong commitment is much more likely to be success-fully implemented than a brilliant solution with only adequate commitment.

Rejection of all solutions

If all the possible solutions suggested are rejected, it is probable that the client has not properly reframed their problem; they still have a problem which, in its current intellectual format, is insoluble. In this case, you should re-enter the reframing process, explaining your reasons (as above).

Solution searching in terms of the STM – a reminder

Skill deficit	Solution type
Identified skill strengths	Skill transfer/generalization to problem area
Identified skill absence	Skill training
Identified skill weaknesses	Skill improvement training
Identified inappropriate skill usage	Skill use cue training/application awareness training/objectives ...
Identified absence of skill usage	Skill use cue training/application awareness training/objectives ...

Factors to consider when seeking solutions

- Decide which options the newly framed understanding of the problem immediately suggests.
- Develop the less obvious solutions.
- Consider each of the options.
- Consider the positives and negatives of each.
- Identify which can be implemented as the client will allow.
- Identify which require the development of skills or other input.
- Identify which match the values/beliefs profile of the client.

Increasing client disposition towards choosing a solution

How do you encourage your clients to come to a decision, to choose a solution? It is not easy when they are still traumatized by the events which brought them to counselling. Here are some tips:

- Discuss issues around choice.
- Encourage the exploration of choices.
- Praise the client for their acknowledgement and consideration of different choices.
- Encourage them to explore alternative choices to the ones they immediately suggest.
- Confront the non-acknowledgement of choices.

- Encourage them to discuss their reasons for avoiding choosing a solution.
- Invite them to examine how they are defending themselves against choosing.
- Invite them to consider the consequences of not choosing a solution.
- Invite them to consider the consequences of not choosing a solution now.

EXERCISE

As an experienced businessperson, you regularly encourage people to come to decisions. What can you add to the above list?

Barriers and difficulties: breakthrough blues

Often, clients will experience a depletion in their spirits when they have reached a decision about how to tackle the problem. They suffer what I call the 'breakthrough blues'. They have just decided to give up a pattern of behaviour with which they have become familiar and, in some cases, comfortable. They have just agreed to make some significant changes in their lives which they know will involve much effort and discomfort. The emergence of breakthrough blues is a cue for you to return to the listening and understanding phase. Give your clients a chance to express their emotions surrounding their decision.

Breakthrough blues

Acceptance and transition to the next stage

The client must accept that their previous perception of their problem was hindering their search for understanding and that their new perception makes solution searching more likely to be successful.

Only those clients who, after having reframed their problem, wish you to help them solve the problem will progress to the next stage. Many will not need or want further input once they know what the solution is.

Clients likely to withdraw at this stage fall into the following categories:

- those who, having solved the problem, wish to implement the solution themselves
- those for whom the solution was a process or perception change and not a practical shift have no reason to proceed.

Since clients often reframe and identify a solution simultaneously, all the reasons why a client might want to withdraw after reframing also apply here.

Stage 5: Solution planning and commitment development

Objective

To help the client to decide how they are going to implement their solution and develop sufficient commitment to see it through.

General principles

- Maintain your relationship with the client.
- Encourage clients to empower themselves to manage/solve the problems.
- Encourage them to empower themselves with sufficient determination to see the process through.
- Encourage them to empower themselves to rectify the skills deficits.
- Ensure you have the competence necessary to train in any skills being developed.
- Ensure they have thought through the logistics of the implementation.
- Make the client, not the technique, the centre of your efforts to help them plan the solution.
- Structure the implementation in such a way that it provides early encouragement through preliminary successes.

Although we are using the STM, you should remember that the client is the focus of your efforts and not the STM. That may mean you must help the client to plan a solution which has nothing whatever to do with the enhancement of their skills base.

For managers who enjoy proactive roles, this will be the most fulfilling stage of counselling.

Solution planning

In the world of work, clients can't be left to develop a solution plan in their own self-paced way as they would in non-work counselling. You need results. That may mean using your personal authority to direct the client to plan their solution rather than waiting for them to decide when to do it. That does not mean you should plan the implementation for them. The most constructive, most potentially successful, method is to have the client plan the implementation themselves. In this way, they own the plan, it is their own creation and it is devised *for* them *by* them. When is your commitment level to a plan at its highest?

Solution planning in counselling follows the same general steps that you use to plan the implementation of virtually anything else in business. The structure of planning may vary but the content will normally include:

- objectives setting
- objective prioritizing
- sequencing sub-goals as required
- considering help to be harnessed
- considering hindrances to be managed or overcome
- specific actions planning
- planning implementation as a whole.

Factors to consider

What factors does the client usually consider when planning their implementation? What structure should they use to make sure they don't miss out any critical components? Should they use the who, where, what, when, how structure? Or should they use the helping and hindering factors structure by considering:

Presence of factors which help the solution	Absence of factors which help the solution
Presence of factors which hinder the solution	Absence of factors which hinder the solution.

There are many more structures which could be used. Consult the client. They may prefer to use the one most commonly used in your organization. However, the choice of planning structure should be theirs if they are to have maximum commitment to the plan. Whatever structure they use, here are some of the factors they and you will, and should, consider when planning the implementation of their solution:

Successfully overcoming the hindering factors

- maintenance of your counselling relationship
- what skills the client will acquire
- what skills the client can transfer or generalize from other areas of their life
- what skills will be taught afresh and which will require improvement
- how the client will raise and maintain their commitment to the solution
- what methods will be used to equip the client with the required skills
- how the newly acquired skills will be maintained
- who should provide input other than yourself and the client
- from what sources assistance can be sought
- how much time various options will take
- what the cost of the options will be
- in what order the various inputs should be provided
- what timescale the plan should cover
- relevance to workplace objectives
- maintenance of work/peer relationships
- the client's level of self-esteem
- the client's motivational level
- the client's level of resistance
- the client's level of intelligence
- family, social factors, gender, sexuality, age, religion and so on
- factors relating to the availability of support (including your input).

EXERCISE

List any other factors you can think of which could be added to the above list.

Some possible inputs by you at this stage include:

- coaching, behaviour rehearsal
- providing feedback on planned actions and possible consequences
- providing knowledge and information
- providing training in appropriate skills (that is, solution planning)
- goal-setting suggestions
- sub-goal-setting suggestions
- analysis of things done and not done which will help or hinder the goals
- anticipation of difficulties.

Eliciting and maintaining commitment

We have already made several references to how to obtain and maintain commitment. Now let us pull it all together:

1 Ensure that the means of making decisions are the client's.
2 Ensure that the decisions (about the solution plan) are made by the client.
3 Help the client to concentrate on the positive aspects of decisions made and the negative aspects of the previous situation.
4 Help the client to realize that success in their desires to solve the problems is best obtained by strong commitment to the plan they have devised.
5 Build rewards into the plan.

Have the implementation plan committed to writing. This serves three purposes:

1 It gives weight to the agreement.
2 It provides a record of the plan to which the client can refer.
3 It gives both of you a tool with which you can evaluate and modify the implementation plan.

Barriers and difficulties

Since you regularly help others to devise action and other plans, and subsequently help them to overcome the barriers to implementation which inevitably emerge, I will resist the temptation to teach you how to suck eggs.

Acceptance and transition to the next stage

The client must accept the plan and the method of implementation, and should be committed to achieving results.

Clients are ready to move into the next stage when they feel the plan is complete and are pushing you to agree to start the implementation.

Clients wishing to, or for whom you should, terminate counselling at this stage fall into the following categories:

- those who wish to implement the solutions themselves
- those who feel they have already taken enough of your time
- those who have lied about the acceptability of solutions and cannot bear to be exposed or carry out the plan you have both agreed
- those whom you feel can carry out the plan on their own for whatever reason
- those whom you feel after repeated solutions, plans, reframing, etc, will not pursue any course of action.

Stage 6: Implementation

Objectives

The primary objective is to help the client with their motivation, commitment and persistence while implementing their solution.

General principles

- Maintain your relationship with the client.
- Encourage clients to empower themselves to manage/solve the implementation.
- Encourage them to empower themselves with sufficient resilience to see the process through.
- Ensure you have your training material well prepared.
- Ensure you have thought through your rationales and presentations.
- Make the client, not the technique, the centre of your efforts to help them implement the solution.
- Make continual slight adjustments to the implementation plan. (If serious alteration is required the client will be tempted to move you on to the next stage.)
- Beware the client who uses the inevitable minor difficulties with any plan as an excuse for changing the plan or quitting altogether.

Much of this stage is like stage 2 – that is, listening and understanding and supporting. Clients are trying to solve/manage/cope with a problem which may have taken a long time to arise and may take a long time to manage. They will go through an emotional process very similar to the grieving process (see page 247) and the breakthrough blues (see page 166). Because your staff will have to consider and understand a whole range of complex interacting variables, the process of implementing a solution becomes a problem in its own right, requiring the listening and understanding of stage 2 and, occasionally, the reframing and solution searching of stages 3 and 4. Which of those skills do you think you will use most often at this stage?

Turning theoretical solutions into action for results

Theoretical solutions not implemented through lack of action are as bad as no solution at all. The client should be aware that all the work which has gone before is dependent on action at this stage in order to be of any value.

Making implementation more effective and more likely to succeed

- Demonstrate your understanding of the difficulties in the same way as you did in stage 2.
- Provide emotional rewards for steps taken; build rewards into the plan.
- Encourage clients to see the benefits gained from attempts which did not go to plan.
- Request the use of self-monitoring devices (logs, charts, diaries and so on).
- Help the client rehearse their proposed actions, new behaviours and so on.
- Help clients to identify and overcome the internal and external barriers which block their efforts.

Help the client to rehearse

Many of the skills you need here are the same ones you use to help your staff implement the myriad of changes common in organizational life today.

EXERCISE

Using your business experience as a guide, list the other ways in which you make the successful implementation of the solution more likely.

Preventive counselling during implementation

What do you do about preventive counselling with someone you are already counselling? Do you intervene, in non-counselling time, to help them avoid making a mistake which you have previously discussed in counselling? Or do you stand by and watch, taking mental notes on the sequence of events and the cause and effect links? The answer depends on your agreement with the staff member. With some you may have agreed only to intervene if requested; others may have asked you to point out mistakes as or before they occur; others may have requested you to intervene on no account and to save your input for the formal counselling sessions.

That sounds straightforward enough. But you can be sure there will be situations in which it is good for you, the department and the company to breach your agreed intervention policy. What do you do? I suggest telling the client at the time of agreement that those situations may arise and that you owe it to your mutual paymaster to intervene, whatever agreement you have.

That's one interpretation of the term 'preventive counselling'. There is another. Preventive counselling can also mean counselling people to anticipate certain situations – to help them prepare themselves for some possibility or eventuality.

Barriers and difficulties

There are many reasons for not being able to turn solution ideas into implemented realities: lack of clear objectives, of desire for a solution, of self-confidence, of a method to handle barriers and difficulties, of persistence, of self-management and of the requisite empowering beliefs. Other reasons for non-implementation include: unclear beliefs and values, conflicts of interest, fear of failing and fear of some of the consequences of succeeding, including fear of others' reactions. A few deserve special attention.

Fear of others' reactions   If the price of change is losing the affections of those who prefer your staff as they are, they may be tempted to sabotage the change plan. Most human beings prefer to belong in the mediocre majority. It is perceived as being too risky and too painful to rise above that level. The truth, of course, is the opposite. The rewards of achievement greatly outweigh the rewards of conformity and compliance.

Personal inertia   The plan may sound good to your staff member – they may even agree that its implementation is right for them – but the current situation is preferable to the pain of change even when the rewards available on the other side of change are taken into account.

Previous failure   When people have failed at each of their previous attempts to solve the problem, they have good reason to believe that this, too, will be a waste of effort. 'Better to learn to put up with it,' they think, 'than to bash my head against a brick wall forever.' Many beliefs can generate such an attitude including the beliefs that they don't have enough staying power, that the solution won't be accepted by others, that the solution will bring more pain than pleasure or that they are likely to make the wrong choice as they did in the past.

You could help the client tackle those disempowering beliefs in the same ways we discussed earlier – in other words, by moving to the reframing stage again. Moving between stages will happen naturally and frequently if you are making the client the focus of your efforts and not the stages or model.

EXERCISE

List any other beliefs that you consider to underlie other barriers listed.

You will find a more detailed analysis of the barriers preventing success in *Coaching and Mentoring*, pp. 183–209.

Acceptance and transition to the next stage

Clients must accept that there is enough of a workable plan to make it worth improving.

Clients who are starting to modify, improve or otherwise beneficially alter the plan will automatically make the transition to the next stage.

Clients likely to withdraw at this stage fall into the following categories:

- those for whom implementation went so well there is no need to progress to the next stage
- those whose self-monitoring and problem-solving skills are so good that to progress to the next stage would be wasteful
- those whose implementation went so badly and was so painful that they cannot bear to tell you they failed
- those who, despite several commitment building sessions, replanning attempts, subsequent resolution searching attempts, reframing and so on, will not carry out any agreed implementation.

Stage 7: Evaluation and adjustment

This will be a short section. We are going to assume that, as a competent manager, you are already skilled at evaluating and adjusting plans of all sorts. We will concentrate only on the issues of greatest importance to counselling.

Objectives

To evaluate how well the implementation went and to choose whether to modify it, and if so, how.

General principles

- Maintain the client as the central focus of your efforts.
- Avoid becoming defensive.
- Accept that your methods can be challenged without feeling under attack.
- Accept that the client may criticize you when their anger is actually with the methods or even themselves for failing to carry out what they have agreed.
- Encourage the client to be as constructive as possible with their adjustments to the plan.
- Seek to boost morale and re-ignite commitment.

You may also find that the client will evaluate not only the implementation but also everything else in the entire process. If they don't prompt such evaluation you should. An enormously useful learning experience awaits both counsellor and client in evaluating their journey together. Every stage of the expedition so far should be examined. Doing so will provide some useful pointers for the next stage.

Separating 'will' and 'won't' power

The decision you have to make most frequently in this stage concerns the cause of an implementation problem. How do you tell if a particular problem in implementation is related to 'will' power (or rather 'won't' power) or is the result of a genuine obstacle? Define it accurately and you identify the obstacle and plan to overcome it. Define it wrongly and you alienate your client. But it is not as simple as that. A progress barrier for me with my personality may be an aid to progress with yours. So what do you do? The most useful indicator in separating the two is the nature of the conversation you have about the subject. A client seeking to overcome the barrier ('will' power) will ask for help in finding a way through and in identifying the barrier, or will respond to your encouragement when you suggest they look for a way through. By contrast, a client exhibiting 'won't' power will ask for help in seeking another implementation and will be hostile/dismissive/evasive towards your response to make good the original plan. Observe yourself covertly refusing to do something which you are unable to refuse overtly. How do you behave?

'Won't' power

Handling 'won't' power

Once you have identified 'won't' power at play, what do you do? Ask the client what makes the plan, or part of it, unacceptable to them. You can then ask them to modify the plan to take account of the reasons offered. The principle at work here is to work with the client's motives. If you discover strong 'won't' power you can fight or flow with it. Flowing with it is usually most productive. However, if the client continues to exhibit strong 'won't' power in response to agreed implementation plans, you should return to the reframing stage; it is clear no solution or plan is acceptable in the current definition of the problem.

Barriers

Client-based barriers

- Clients may condemn a plan because it requires too much effort.
- Clients may seek to neuter a plan by apparently adjusting it.
- Clients may not want to evaluate a plan for fear of exposing their unwillingness to implement a plan to which they have agreed.

- Clients may wish to avoid evaluation for fear of exposing their inability to stick to a plan.
- Clients may unnecessarily seek evaluation of a plan just to keep contact with you, thereby interfering with a perfectly workable plan and possibly resulting in its sabotage.

Counsellor-based barriers

Most were implicitly listed in the general principles at the beginning of this stage.

EXERCISE

From the general principles, extract and list explicitly the counsellor-based barriers at this stage.

Acceptance and transition to the next stage

The client must accept that the problem has been solved or, at least, is now being managed.

Those clients who have solved or managed their problem and are starting to talk in terms indicating that they are ready to wrap up the process are ready to move on to the next stage.

Clients likely to withdraw at this stage fall into the following categories:

- those whose problem-solving and management skills are so good that to proceed would be wasteful
- those who, for whatever reason, are willing to forgo their opportunity to consolidate their new skills
- those who wrongly think they have mastered problem-management skills
- those who still refuse to accept self-responsibility for problem solving and who were pushed through the stages by you.

Stage 8: Ending and consolidation

Objectives

To give the client an opportunity to consolidate the skills they have learned in counselling and to provide an opportunity to end the counselling sessions in as constructive a way as possible.

General principles

- Provide opportunities to consolidate and build on the skills learned.
- Make a definitive end-point.

- Agree which factors will determine the end of counselling.
- End the process at any time if the client wants it.
- Maintain your rapport so that the door is left open for future counselling if it is needed.

Converting knowledge acquired in counselling to self-help skills

The final active stage in counselling consists of turning what the client has learned into long-term self-help skills.

Clients will also benefit from you teaching them some new self-help skills. Your role is (after all) that of a manager who wishes to counsel to improve your staff performance. You are not a full-time counsellor who is reluctant to teach your clients self-help skills for fear of putting yourself out of work. Your objective is for your staff to grow and develop in competence, and that means to be able to solve their own problems before they grow so unmanageable that they need counselling – in other words, before their problems begin to cost your organization time and money.

Self-help skills

Teach your staff to use the eight-stage problem-solving (skills training) model you have been using. That is:

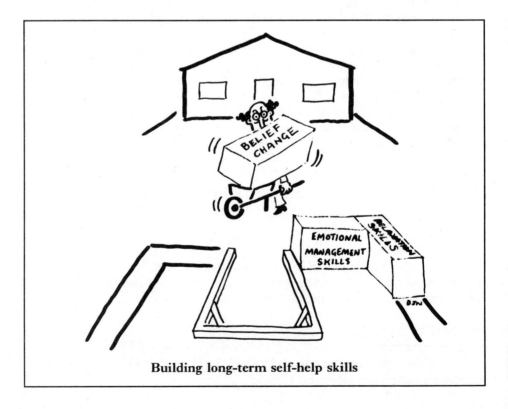

Building long-term self-help skills

1   Form an honest rapport with themselves.
2   Seek an understanding of themselves and the problem.
3   Reframe ... Complete this list from a self-help perspective.

Cultivating and keeping a positive attitude

On page 246 you will find a section which outlines the rules of happiness. Take those rules and convert them into a series of action or 'to do' points. Turn them into a list of 'actions/activities to obtain and maintain a positive attitude'. You could go a stage further and turn those points into a training course for your staff.

Self-change programme

Teach your clients how they can change their lives immediately. They can, if they develop and follow their own self-change programme. Devise one yourself. Here is an example:

1   What do you want to change?
2   What is the cost of not changing?
3   What pleasures will there be in changing?
4   What benefits will there be in changing?
5   How can you intensify your sense of pain at not changing?
6   How can you make yourself feel maximum discomfort at not changing now?
7   What enormous pleasures can you associate with changing now?
8   In what ways can you break the pattern of behaviour you want to change?
9   What will be your more constructive replacement?
10 Does the new behaviour suit your personal values?
11 Rehearse and practise the new behaviour until it is automatic.
12 Build your commitment and determination towards your new behaviour.
13 Make it so.

Helping the client to maintain their self-help skills

The following actions form a general guide:

- Encourage clients to engage in skill maintenance behaviour, practise the skills they have learned.
- Encourage clients to engage in behaviour pattern maintenance, regularly use the behaviours they have learned.
- Encourage clients to practise their thinking skills.
- Encourage clients to establish a skill/behaviour maintenance structure – a self-monitoring programme.
- Encourage clients to reward themselves for their efforts.

Self-monitoring devices

Self-monitoring devices

When anyone makes any significant change to their lives, they usually experience some difficulty in making the change stick. Answers to that problem vary in the specific, but are constant in the general – that is, some kind of self-monitoring or self-prompting and self-rewarding system is required to maintain and reinforce the change.

What should they monitor? Naturally, the answer to the question will be determined by the change being made. In principle it will always be some aspect of your client's beliefs, thoughts, attitudes, feelings, behaviours, skills and outcomes. Means of self-prompting and self-monitoring include: log books, checklists, reminder signs and posters, diary checks and so on.

When to end the counselling process

When the client's expectations have been satisfied

The end of counselling may come when the client has had their expectations satisfied. You may see the need to do more, but if counselling is what you are providing, you must respect the client's desire to end when they decide. Clients' expectations can vary greatly:

- Some want only understanding.
- Some want only to have their erroneous thinking exposed to them so they can solve the problem themselves.
- Some want understanding, to understand their problem and help with implementation of a solution.

In practical terms that will mean your client will terminate the counselling sessions when they have received what they wanted. You should, at all times, assume that the client will decide when sessions will end and, periodically, make that assumption explicit.

When you decide to end

If the client is not carrying out the assignments you have both agreed, you should terminate counselling yourself. Naturally, you should enter a contract for counselling (verbally or in writing) to that effect when you start counselling. Make the deal very explicit. The rationale could not be clearer: if a staff member is not prepared to invest their time and effort solving their problem for their benefit, why should you?

Harsh? Yes. Effective? Yes. Realistic in the workplace? Extremely! An effective indicator of who merits the investment of counselling? Very. A very large number of research studies have shown that clients who are neither prepared to invest time and effort in the counselling processes nor keep their counselling contracts are much more likely to drop out and fail to solve their problems.

Many ivory-tower counsellors are horrified at such advice. If you hear objections from that quarter you can remind them that they don't have to carry the cost of counselling unwilling staff members. They don't have to bear the lost opportunity cost deriving from wasting time with those who don't care enough about their own welfare to attempt to help themselves. They don't have to explain to your bosses and shareholders why you are tolerating the shoddy work being produced by a problematic staff member when there are hundreds of high-performing possible replacements applying to the company every month. They don't have to bear the costs of their open chequebook advice on your bank balance. Now, if they are prepared to come and counsel your problem staff free of charge, out of business hours, until the problems are resolved, that is a different matter. However, I don't suppose you'll have many offers of that kind today, or any other day.

EXERCISE

Pull together all the realistic expectations from counselling to which we have referred.

Ending the counselling sessions

If you have followed the tips mentioned in the counselling logistics session (page 123), this stage will be made easier. You will have agreed with clients how long counselling should last or what factors will indicate that counselling should finish. Nonetheless, clients will become attached to their counselling sessions, and ending something from which one benefits is not easy. You can ease the process by raising the issue of ending counselling again when it is clear that the end is in sight. As each session from that point on takes place you should be able to predict with increasing accuracy just when the last session ought to take place.

Possible problems

There are two potential areas of difficulty. Either the client becomes attached to you or the counselling sessions and engages in behaviour that prolongs their continuance, or you may become attached to the good feelings you experience from helping this person and engage in behaviour which prolongs the need for counselling. The best way to cope with this is to point out to yourself and the client that the longer counselling goes on, the more dependent on it you both become. You need it to feel good about helping; they need it to feel good about being helped. You are both in danger of becoming counselling junkies. Such addiction may sound unlikely but, believe me, the helping professions are filled with people whose need to help exceeds their clients' need to be helped.

If the counselling process has been long term, when it is nearly over, plan to end it with some kind of ceremonial display which you both will recognize

Counselling junkies

and remember as the climax of a successful joint project. We advised earlier that counselling should follow the work cycle. With this in mind, end counselling with a period of reflection, mutual congratulation and discussions about moving on to your next goal.

Acceptance of the final stage

Your client should accept that the problem is solved or under control, that they have learned and consolidated the relevant skills and that ending counselling is best for all in the long term.

Summary of the counselling model

With the application of only eight simple guidelines you can be a highly effective counsellor. Take those eight and tailor them into a commercially relevant counselling model, based on the cultural assumptions of our time, and you have the tools to be an even more effective counsellor in the workplace. Add to that your strong declared interest in having all your staff perform well, and the motives of your staff towards resuming normal performance ASAP to protect their jobs, and you have an enviable advantage over those counsellors who are paid regardless of outcome, and for whom outcome is only of indirect significance.

12

TOOLS FOR COMMUNICATION

Opening the door to counselling

It seems a little late in the book to be discussing something as simple as this, but how do you start the counselling process if the client has not come to you? How do you open the door, without sounding as though you are saying 'you need a shrink'? By using such generalized statements and questions as:

- 'What's the problem?'
- 'How can I help?'
- 'Do you want to talk about it?'
- 'You look as though you are experiencing some difficulty.'
- 'When do you want to talk about it?'
- 'This would cause anybody problems, wouldn't it?'
- 'There must be a way to deal with this, let's explore some options.'

EXERCISE

Devise some of your own door-opening statements or questions.

Even here there are difficulties. Do you say 'Can I help with a chat?' or 'I can help, let's have a chat'? The first is a closed question and invites a closed response – yes or no. Once the response has been made people might feel they need to stick to it, and may even defend what was an off-the-cuff response rather than admit that their instant reaction caused them to give the wrong response.

On the other hand 'I can help, let's have a chat' disempowers your staff member. If they agree, it may be simply because the boss has requested a chat, and not because they want to or feel they can benefit from it.

Opening the door to counselling

So, the principle is to offer the option to discuss the problems. There will be circumstances when, as line manager, you will have to impose a discussion. If so, make it clear that while you are performing your duties you will do so in as helpful a manner as possible, and as such offer the option of counselling.

Communication analysis

The role of thinking styles in listening

Transactional analysis (a counselling system based upon analysing the transactions between people and within the self) as a helping system makes the same mistakes that most other counselling systems make, but it does have something useful to offer. It provides a way in which we can think about our different thinking styles. As with most counselling systems, it hides very simple concepts behind a wall of apparently complex jargon and terminology. Those familiar with transactional analysis will note that I have dispensed with the rather unhelpful familial labels given to the different patterns of thinking and replaced them with less emotionally loaded and, hopefully, neutral terms.

There are three broad thinking styles:

1 Sometimes we are emotional and highly involved in, and responsive to, our feelings.
2 At other times we are rational, level-headed and decision-oriented.
3 At other times we are in an intellectual mode that can best be described as controlling and superior to all that is going on around us.

■: Believing/overseeing thinking patterns
◆: Rational/logical thinking patterns
●: Feeling/reacting mental patterns
→: Represents the thinking pattern from which the communication originates and the thinking pattern at which the communication is aimed.

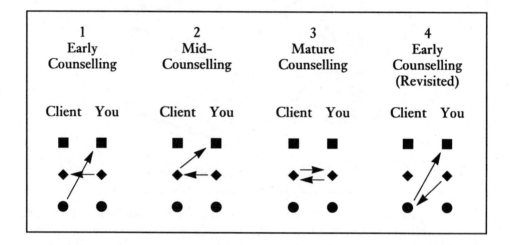

As counselling starts, the client typically views you, the counsellor, as a support-ive authority figure. They see themselves as being in much emotional pain. In short, they communicate with you using feeling-oriented thinking patterns, assuming that you are communicating with them using overseeing/directing thinking patterns. Naturally the client would never articulate what they think is going on in those words, but the behaviour they largely exhibit is based on some mental representation of those premises. You in turn, following a fundamental rule of counselling, wish to avoid patronizing your client and are treating them as a rational, logical human being (as illustrated in 1).

But you will fail to communicate if you address the client as if they were in one thinking mode when in fact they are in another. To be effective you should be sensitive to what thinking mode the client is in and communicate with them in those terms. If they are expressing emotions you should be relating to their emotions (as illustrated in 4). If they are being rational and logical, relate to them in those terms. If they are being judgemental/directive, then relate to them in those terms.

As the counselling relationship progresses, the client will gradually move from emotional thinking patterns to rational problem-solving thinking patterns. That will occur gradually as you move from stage 2 (understanding) to stage 3 (reframing). When the client has expressed their feelings – when they know you understand their pain and their problem – they will naturally begin to come to terms with, or resolve, the problem. They will naturally move from emotional thinking to rational thinking patterns. They will, however, on the whole, still see you as the supportive authority figure (as illustrated in 2).

That starts to change as you move to the solution searching and solution implementation phases of counselling. The client gradually begins to see you as a supportive equal who is trying to help them solve a problem. Ideally, throughout the counselling process, you should be the rational/logical support-ive other who is relating to the client in whatever thinking mode they choose to communicate (as illustrated in 3). But that does not mean you shouldn't be yourself. Be human. Remember that the person counselling and their rapport with the client is more important than any technique, including this one.

The communication cycle in counselling

Your thoughts, beliefs, attitudes and behaviours will affect your clients, and their beliefs, thoughts, attitudes and behaviours will affect you, in the following way:

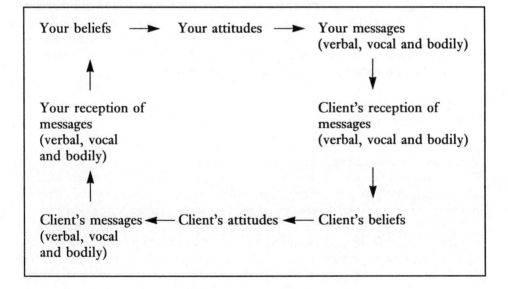

Levels of communication

You will know from witnessing and participating in polite exchanges that take place at parties and other large social gatherings, that superficiality is the norm. That level of interaction is totally useless in counselling. Further along the intimacy continuum there is another level of communication which is only slightly less useless – that is, the level you share with associates. A more useful communication is that you share with close friends. And nearly ideal is the level of rapport you share with your 'closest significant other' (excuse the clumsy politically correct language – it is a counselling book after all). That level of communication is only nearly ideal because you have to hold back some of what you genuinely think for fear of sabotaging the relationship. In counselling you have the same worry. You are the manager of the client, and don't want to sabotage the relationship. You are their boss; they don't want to sabotage the relationship. The ideal is out of reach.

Other ➤	Stranger ➤	Party ➤	Associate ➤	Friend ➤	Close ➤	Confidant ➤	Ideal
culture	talk	talk	talk	talk	friend	talk	talk
stranger					talk		
talk							

Communication intimacy continuum

Ideally you would like to get direct access to the client's uncensored inner dialogue, and be prepared to offer access to your inner dialogue on the same basis. That is out of reach. Or is it? Yes, it is out of reach for issues that will affect your relationship, but how many of those are there? Potentially, you should only censor that which you think will spoil your working relationship. If you can do that, you are in a better position to help the client with their problem. Ideal communication is inner dialogue to inner dialogue.

Persuasion in counselling

'Persuasion in counselling' understates the relationship between the two fields. The similarity between persuasion and counselling is striking. As we have already stated, counselling requires persuasion skills. Indeed, counselling may largely involve persuading others to change. If so, we should explore how to do so.

Every stage in counselling helps the process of persuading change. For instance, obtaining an understanding of the problem equips you with knowledge of how best to persuade the client to change. It enables you to master the client's language so you can present your persuasive message in their language. It enables you to present the facts in such a way as to ensure they are interesting and relevant to the client. In the reframing stage that knowledge enables you to steer the discussions in directions you know are likely to lead to reframings acceptable to the client. Searching for a solution is chiefly about persuading the client to look for a remedy. Solution planning very much concerns persuading the client to adopt a particular solution.

EXERCISE

*Complete the sequence stated above. Outline what each stage in coun-
selling seeks to persuade the client to do.*

Counselling as the acceptable face of persuasion

Research into persuasion has repeatedly shown that a forewarning of a persuasive message increases people's resistance to persuasion. We also know that
people are reluctant to admit to having been persuaded, preferring to maintain
that persuasion only works on others with more impressionable minds. What
do those two findings tell us? Emphatically, if counselling is presented as
persuasion, people will be more reluctant to use it, and if they do receive
counselling/persuasion, they will be more resistant to its objectives. Persuading
people to change their beliefs, attitudes, behaviours, mind set, skills base and
so on must be disguised as something else. That something is counselling.
Counselling is the acceptable face of persuading people to change. What other
reasons are there for disguising the persuasive nature of counselling?

How close is counselling to persuasion?

Are the client's beliefs and attitudes changed in counselling as they are in
persuasion? Yes. Successful persuasion is strongly correlated with belief
change. Successful counselling is strongly correlated with belief change. Do the
client's beliefs change towards those of the counsellor's, as is the case with the
audience moving towards the views of the source in persuasion? Definitely.
Numerous research studies have shown that the client's views change towards
those of the counsellor with whom they have contact, and away from those
with whom they have no contact. The views of an audience change towards
those of the source of the persuasive message, and away from those to whose
message they are not exposed.

Does counselling operate within the same parameters as persuasion? You
bet. The factors relating to the source, the audience, the message are the same
in counselling as in persuasion. Let us look at how they are related and what
that tells us about how to be an effective persuasion-realistic counsellor.

Source/counsellor factors

The same factors which determine the acceptability of a counsellor coinci-
dentally (?) determine the acceptability of a persuader – that is, expertness,
trustworthiness and attractiveness. The word 'coincidence' suggests chance
but, as must be clear by now, it is not chance that is behind the similarity
between counselling and persuasion, it is design. Counselling (beyond the point
of listening) must motivate clients to change their beliefs, attitudes and behaviour if it is to be successful. Persuasion must cause or facilitate similar changes
for the same reasons.

Message/ counselling factors

In both counselling and persuasion, the message must have a clear and obvious structure. When persuasion has no structure it is ineffective. When counselling has no structure, disillusionment sets in. The message and counselling are both presented in a way that has relevance to the audience/client. Information between counsellor and client is almost 100 per cent relevant to the client. The message is in a language style appropriate to the listener, either by establishing shared terms at the outset or by altering a set message to suit the particular audience. Both persuaders and counsellors demonstrate interaction and involvement with the client by reacting to the listener's responses.

Client/ audience factors

People uncertain of any issue are more easily persuaded than those not. By definition, anyone coming to counselling is uncertain of how to handle the particular situation which brought them there. Marketing experts worldwide will tell you that the more involvement you can create in your prospective customers, the more they are likely to buy your product or service (ever wondered why car sales people always insist you sit in the driver's seat?). Counselling techniques necessarily create involvement. And those which are highly involving are especially effective, such as counter-attitudinal advocacy, role play and role rehearsal (details of which are in Appendix IV, page 269).

We also know that the effect of persuasive messages can be diminished if the audience is given the chance to make any negative inner dialogue statements during the presentation. Marketing gurus and sales experts are well aware of this and use a range of strategies to defend against negative inner dialogue. Similarly, counsellors use techniques designed to make the client feel guilty if they think or express negative thoughts about the wonderful changes which will take place in their lives if they only comply with the recommendations.

Commitment to results is a significant predictor of efficacy in both persuasion and counselling. People who are committed to achieving results in a particular field are more easily persuaded by messages that are aimed at helping their achievement. In counselling, those clients who are highly committed to solving their problems are more easily persuaded to adopt empowering beliefs and other behaviour changes to solve their problem.

Can there be any reader who still doubts that counselling is a persuasive tool? Is there any wonder that the world's business leaders are probably the best counsellors too?

Do the same phenomena occur in persuasion as occur in counselling? Certainly. People are known to be more persuadable when in a reclining position. And in what position is the world's most famous counselling method, psychoanalysis, conducted? Now why does that come as no surprise to you?

Persuasion in counselling

EXERCISE

Take any counselling style with which you are familiar and explore how it provides each of the above components. To any academic reading this book, I challenge you to find any counselling method which cannot be described in the above terms – which cannot be clearly shown to be 'persuasion by numbers'. Happy hunting.

What factors should you consider when planning a persuasion attempt? Such factors as the client's language usage, their thinking style, their needs and motives and so on.

EXERCISE

Everything you need to establish a set of rules for effective persuasion in counselling is embedded in the preceding text; draw it out and form a set of principles.

Counselling is neither a methodological saviour nor a Machiavellian Satan. It lies somewhere in between. People are persuaded by counselling to conform to social and company norms. People's beliefs are changed in counselling to those more likely to make them succeed in the host company. There is mild Machiavellian intent in counselling. Subtle persuasion techniques are used, but it is in both parties' best interests that positive change takes place. All effective counsellors can therefore benefit from a good knowledge of how to be optimally persuasive.

Many counsellors claim not to use persuasion in counselling. They argue that, in counselling, the client maintains control while, in persuasion, the persuader takes control. Their claim not to be using persuasion perfectly illustrates the point. The counselling process is inherently persuasive; no conscious effort of persuasive intent is required. You would expect to hear such claims of 'no persuasive intent' for other reasons too: telling clients that persuasion is taking place will make counselling less acceptable to them, and therefore much less likely to be effective.

You would also expect some kind of manifestation of the need to give the client a sense of being in control. With all effective persuasion the 'persuadee' has, or is deliberately given, the illusion of being in control. What do we see in reality? Claims that counselling is 'non-directive', claims that the client is 'in control'. As we have already demonstrated, there is no such thing as 'non-directive' counselling. All human interaction is unavoidably directive. For 'directive' read 'influential' or 'persuasive'.

Summary

Since counselling is a communication-based set of skills, it helps (but is not essential) to have some models to assist your understanding of what is happening. People think in many different styles for many different purposes in many different contexts. We have explored three popular thinking styles and pointed out that it is useful to be sensitive to your client's thinking style.

Counselling is very similar to persuasion – so similar, that it is difficult to avoid concluding that they are one and the same thing. If counselling is the acceptable face of persuading people to change, you, as a change master, ought to be knowledgeable about persuasion.

Part IV

Issues and problems

Now you have spent time and effort developing your skills on a general basis we ought to explore their specific application. In Part IV we first explore some of the problems you will encounter and explain how to overcome or, at least, manage them before moving on to discuss specific issues and counselling for common problems.

Whether you are counselling for specific problems or overcoming difficulties during counselling, you will be doing so in an organizational and ethical context. We also examine some of the organizational and ethical issues which will face you and suggest how best to manage them.

13

PROBLEMS WITH COUNSELLORS

In this chapter we will examine some of the problems you will encounter because of your (and my) human frailties. We will help you to identify the problems and suggest ways in which you can overcome them.

Variations in counselling

Variations in counselling are necessary and desirable. Don't confuse normal variation with some of the numerous problems. As you have seen, counselling can start or end at any of several stages. The period of time for which clients will need counselling can vary too. It can be short, medium or long-term – although, realistically, if a member of your staff needs long-term counselling that ought to be done in their time, not yours, and at their expense, not yours. Some employee health schemes may cover long-term counselling intervention, although it has to be said that few do.

The actual input you offer varies depending on what the client needs. A client who just wants to get something off their chest will be less directed by you than one who clearly needs new skills to solve a problem. A client who has a fair understanding of the problem, and has come to terms with the need to solve it, will require less emotional nurturing and more logical solution planning assistance. Already we have three dimensions along which counselling input can vary:

Time input:	Short	Medium	Long-term
Emotional/ Logical input	Emotional needs	Combination	Logical needs
Your input:	You listen	Balanced	You train

195

There are many more dimensions along which counselling varies. As long as you maintain a strong person-focus, these dimensions are of mere academic significance.

Counsellor characteristics and behaviours which cause problems

What words would you use to describe a counsellor? Which characteristics would you say they should possess in light of our discussions so far? Amongst the many are: analytical ability, patience, judgement, warmth, alertness, resilience, communicator, trustworthiness, self-restraint, focus, experience, confidence, bravery, calmness, assertiveness, prudence, integrity, realism, sensitivity, discretion, tolerance of people and ambiguity, self-knowledge, interest in people, liking for people, acceptance of non-perfection, ability to cope with lack of clarity and confusion, ability to cope with one's own hypocrisies and contradictions. All of these qualities are applicable at one time or another, but the most important factor is – and you must be sick of hearing it by now – person-focus.

The opposite of all the above qualities can produce problems in counselling. Some of the more common traits that counsellors bring to counselling and which cause problems are: anxiety, emotional baggage, a personal agenda, a tendency to focus on weakness while ignoring strengths and so on.

Some other obvious and commonly made errors to avoid are as follows:

- inflexibility – sticking to a stage or set of skills
- having unrealistic rules about helping others – such as taking responsibility for others
- inappropriate self-disclosure
- faking attention
- refusing to acknowledge client's feelings as they are
- attempting to cheer up the other person – it is perceived as undermining their emotions
- immediately trying to seek a solution or, worse still, trying to provide one
- trying to do something for the client, as if practical help was always the solution for emotional problems.

Trying to be something you are not

People new to the recognition of being counsellors tend to believe they are required to behave differently. One way you can avoid the temptation to put on an act is to show the client the sequence of stages you wish to go through to help them. You can then be 'you' following a process, rather than being 'an alternative you' shaped by the process.

Faking attention

Perfection? Forget it!

There is no such thing as the perfect counsellor. Don't even try to be the perfect counsellor; it will 'mess up your head'. Accept that you will make mistakes. Accept you will say the wrong things. Accept that you will totally fail to understand some of your clients. Accept that you will fail to understand some aspect of virtually all your clients. Accept that, to some clients, you will be utterly impotent. If you can handle those probabilities without worrying unduly, you'll make a much better counsellor than one who seeks perfection and continually falls short of their own expectations.

Not knowing when to advise and when to counsel

As a guide it is best to let clients offer their own advice; it helps them to empower themselves and, in any event, they will be more committed to their ideas and solutions than to any you can offer. The only time that advice is acceptable is after the client *knows* you understand the problem.

However, clients may hint, or explicitly state, at the start that they want you to advise them on a particular issue. In this case, you face the dilemma of deciding whether to end the counselling session and offer advice as their manager or to continue the counselling session and resist giving advice. This is a difficult choice. To help you decide, we should consider the basic responsibilities of management – to help your staff do their job as effectively as possible – and the basic responsibilities of a counsellor – to help the client help themselves. Quite clearly, there is a conflict in role responsibilities here.

How to decide on whether or not to give advice

1   Try to gauge how seriously the client is seeking advice. The more intense their desire, the less they want counselling in place of advice. The less intense their desire for advice, the more they need counselling. Granted, this is not a very scientific, or even systematic, way of making the decision but it's as good as, if not better than, any other methods I've seen to resolve this dilemma.

2   Resolving the dilemma is not a once-and-for-all decision, you'll be pleased to hear. If on receiving the advice the client retorts with something like, 'Yes, but ... ', it usually means 'I want advice, but not that advice. I know that's what I should do, but I can't face it.' This is a cue to return to counselling and help the client to gradually realize why they are resisting the obvious solution.

3   If you can see the client will harm themselves without the information or guidance you can supply, you should offer the advice. But present it as a case history of someone similar to them or as a question or series of questions. For instance:

'Someone I know refused to delegate the important responsibilities to their staff. They always had good reasons for not doing so, like the staff are not sufficiently skilled/knowledgeable/motivated etc. They had a nervous breakdown twice before learning the lesson. The lesson was, the only way they were going to equip staff with the necessary skills was to train and coach them.'

Adopting counselling methods for which you have no credibility

Counsellors, in a workplace context, work most effectively if they operate (beyond the rapport formation and understanding stages) as life skills trainers. For all trainers, credibility is critical to success. Which of us respected the college lecturers who never practised, in real life, the principles they preached? No answer required. By contrast, you as a manager have worked successfully in the real world. In the eyes of your subordinates you have credibility. Couple that with the other responsibilities you have for ensuring your staff are sufficiently skilled to do their jobs. Your staff expect you to attend to their skill development and therefore to be more skilled in life skills than they. Thus, for your staff, you are the ideal counsellor – as long as you practise the Skills Training Model. If you adopt other counselling roles which clash with your staff's perception of you, your credibility and effectiveness will take a nosedive.

Credibility in counselling

How would you react if your superiors starting using Freudian techniques to counsel you? Would you be less than impressed?

Excessive rationality

If you are in the habit of handling life on a rational basis, you may find it difficult to understand how anyone could allow their emotions to interfere in their problem solving. But most people are not rational and do need to have the validity of their emotions understood, recognized, and even appreciated before they can begin to cope. If you are an arch-rationalist, remind yourself regularly that most other people are not. Watching a good tearjerking movie can work wonders for maintaining your understanding of the emotional side of life. It works for me – try it. What other ways can you use to remind yourself of the emotional side of life?

Current emotional problems

If you have serious emotional problems, you should not be counselling. Counselling requires you to be on an emotional even keel. If you are not, your understanding of the client will be filtered through your current emotional problem as well as through the rest of your emotional baggage. Don't counsel. Paradoxically, many (probably most) counsellors become involved in counselling because they have had problems themselves and the counselling helped them. That's the up side. The down side is that most counsellors, therefore, have a proven history of emotional instability. Oh dear. What does that say about you and me? Well ... let's quickly move along, shall we?

Self-esteem

Counsellors with either very low or excessively high self-esteem don't perform very well, although they do well with clients who have similar levels of self-esteem to themselves. We know that people with low self-esteem tend to find people with high self-esteem arrogant. Those with high self-esteem see others with high self-esteem as being appropriately confident to achieve results. However (time for a harsh reality), few people with high self-esteem ever find their way to a counselling session. Most clients will be low on self-esteem by the time they reach your office. Couple that with the human tendency to meet people halfway and it doesn't take much to realize why counselling is such a high turnover profession; it lowers counsellors' self-esteem.

If your self-esteem has become temporarily low, it does not preclude you from counselling, but you should think carefully about the effect it will have on your staff. It could cause them to doubt whether it is worth solving their problem. You, after all, are assumed to be a well-adjusted, successful person. If you are suffering low self-esteem, why should your staff bother to solve their problems if that is where it gets them? That attitude, in turn, may bring you down, and there begins a negative self-perpetuating cycle.

Reacting emotionally

Some clients will behave in such a way that you will feel anxious (if you allow yourself to). Sometimes you may immediately be able to pinpoint what they are doing that triggers your reaction, but it could take you some time to work out what is going on. Suspend counselling until you can resolve the issue or until you can find out what you are allowing to make you anxious or emotional and do something about it. If you can't, you should pass the client on to someone who will not react as you do.

Reacting negatively to trigger words, phrases, behaviours and attitudes

Something that drives me wild is pretentious and histrionic behaviour. I cannot, and will not, counsel people who behave in those ways. If such a disposition is not immediately evident from a person's dress code, voice or body language (it usually is), it becomes clear from the use of certain phrases or words. As soon as I detect these, it's time to withdraw and refer the client to someone else. Now I have exposed one of my counselling weaknesses, can you honestly put your hand on your heart and say there is no type of person you are unable to counsel because of your emotional reaction? Be honest enough with yourself and your clients to say so.

'Aha,' I hear you shout, 'but some of the types I cannot stand are members of my staff, so what should I do?' Yes, it is a bit of a dilemma. It's easy to say 'no' when you don't have to work with a person on an ongoing basis. It's easy to say 'no' when you aren't going to be faced with some staff members asking why others are being counselled by you, yet you refuse to counsel them. Oh, dear. Well, there are several options. You can find a way of learning to like the characteristics you previously hated (not an easy or rapidly completed task). Or you can tell a white lie and state that some problems are outside your remit/skill level/experience/proven competence (likely to be demonstrated as false when you counsel someone with an identical problem in the future). Or you can be honest, and say that the client's need for counselling is too important to allow your emotional reactions to block the likelihood of a positive outcome, or (my favourite) that someone else is better equipped emotionally to handle their problem (also very true).

EXERCISE

Define what kind of people or behaviours elicit a strong emotional reaction from you, either positive or negative. Decide how you will tell them that you cannot counsel them. If there are no types you will not counsel, I suggest you counsel no one; you are not being honest with yourself.

Prejudice, stereotypes, ignorance, attitude barriers, fears

Behind the above reactions there is certainly an element of prejudice. Let's not kid ourselves, we all have prejudices. Some are empowering, some are disempowering. Whether they are empowering or disempowering, they will have an effect on your counselling relationship if someone possesses the characteristics against which you are prejudiced. You will not be able to listen to and understand such a client in the same way you would be able to with a client who has characteristics you admire or, at very least, are neutral towards. So what should you do? Overcome the prejudice? This is a possible solution; counselling always has been just as much an agent for change for the counsellor as for the client. Be honest and declare that you are not emotionally equipped to help the client? Yes, this is the best option. You won't do either of you any favours by forcing yourself to listen through a powerful prejudice, stereotype, attitude barrier or fear.

Using counselling clichés

It is all too easy to begin to use the same phrases or sentences over and over again without even realizing it. However, clients will be quick to notice it and may interpret your repetitions as meaning you have lost interest or that you've gone into autopilot mode. This can be potentially damaging to your counselling relationship. Here are some clichés that I've habitually used in the past:

- 'If I understand you correctly ... ?'
- 'So what you are really saying is ... ?'
- 'What I hear you saying is ... ?'
- 'So, to summarize ... '
- 'I hear what you are saying.'
- 'I'm picking up ... '

EXERCISE

Make a list of the clichés you habitually use.

From automatic phrases to autopilot

Using the same old phrases is just the start of your clichéd behaviour. Once you've got some serious counselling hours under your belt, you may even find yourself listening to the start of sentences and then only periodically paying attention just to confirm that, yes, this case is just like the 40 others of this type you have seen this year. You then listen to the end of their statement (you know when it is coming because of the tonal change signals) just to check they haven't thrown in anything unusual. No, they haven't, how disappointing; cue the same summary you've used so many times before. And wait for it – yes, their reply was just as predicted, to the syllable. Perhaps (?) you should write the counselling scripts in advance and ask clients to read them before counselling starts and only discuss anything that varies from the norm. Gosh, that would really cut down your workload. And prevent you from suffering a boredom-induced early grave!

Emotional exhaustion/burn-out

If you find yourself starting to think and behave like the above, you are suffering classic symptoms of burn-out. Take a break from counselling. If you've had enough of counselling you won't be able to listen effectively, no matter how hard you try. Take a break from work if necessary. You won't do yourself or your clients any favours by continuing with that kind of disposition. Believe me, I know – I've been there.

Burn-out prevention

Limit the amount of counselling you do to keep it interesting. Yes, that is selfish. No, you are not going to help as many people as you could. Surely that is better than ending up not being able to help anyone in counselling ever again? Of course it is.

EXERCISE

Compile a list of those signs which will indicate that you are starting to burn out.

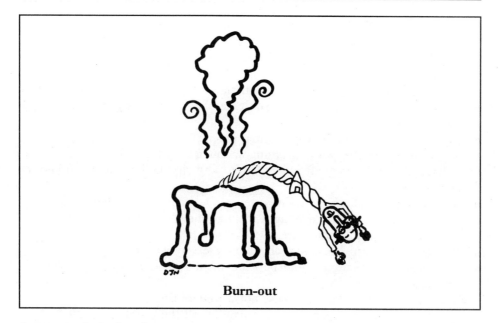

Burn-out

Automatic behaviour patterns

Some of your behaviours will make it very difficult to listen to the client properly. You must have encountered people who finish your sentences for you. Or people who start to ask you their next question or make their next statement before you have finished what you are saying. If you confront such a person with their behaviour, you may be surprised to learn they are astonished that they behave in such a way. We all have some undesirable automatic behaviour patterns, whether mental or physical. Identify and rectify them. Ask your clients if there is anything about your behaviour which made it difficult for them to communicate with you.

Common reasons for being reluctant or hesitant about counselling

There is no shortage of sensible reasons for being reluctant to engage in counselling. In fact, after reading this list you may ask yourself why you should bother:

- I won't know what to say.
- I won't know what advice to give.
- I can't solve their problems for them.
- What if they break down emotionally in front of me?
- What if I say the wrong thing and make it worse for them?
- What if I say the wrong thing and sabotage our working relationship?
- I don't want my impartiality to be clouded by getting involved in a confidential relationship.

- I don't want to be blocked from particular actions because it would appear like a breach of confidence.
- I don't want to become angry and frustrated because I can't do anything for them.
- What if I end up agreeing with them and compromise my position?
- Once I can see the solution, I won't be able to stop myself from telling them to 'get on with it'.
- My job is to manage healthy, normal people.
- I solve my problems without crying about it, why can't they?
- I don't let my feelings affect my work; why should I encourage others to do just that?
- If they've got problems, they'd better not let them affect their work.
- This welfare business encourages malingering: look at the level of unemployment in socialist countries.
- If I fail to perform I lose my job; that's the way we work here.
- Time spent counselling could be time spent recruiting a non-problematic replacement.
- This is a money-making business not a welfare agency.
- We have a welfare department that handles all the problem people.
- Counselling is a low-status activity; I can't be seen doing that and still be in the fast stream.
- Counselling and other forms of psychological help are for wishy-washy, left-wing, social worker types, not high-powered business executives.
- Counselling equals inadequacy: it is provided for inadequates, by inadequates.
- Promotion is based on results in our company; I can't afford to have some weakwilled individual have me look as though I failed to get results counselling them.
- It is politically wise to distance oneself from those who look like failing; it is not wise to be the person who failed to prevent them from failing.

What other reasons are there which might make people reluctant to counsel?

But ... you should bother, because it works. Yes, there are risks, but when has anything worthwhile ever been achieved without taking some risks? Perhaps the most compelling reason you should engage in counselling is to obtain the deep and profound loyalty that all business leaders need from their staff to achieve excellent results. You receive that loyalty by first giving it. Good leadership principles suggest that officers should always make sure the troops are fed and happy before eating or entertaining themselves (but there are cut-off points which we will discuss later).

Realistic personal guidelines for counselling

- Perform as competently as you can without feeling the need to be perfect.
- Approval of clients is not necessary to help them help themselves.

- Acknowledgement that counselling is uncertain and unpredictable, and tolerance of those factors will make it easier to handle.
- Person-focus in counselling is more important than any technique.

Summary

Oh, the pain of being human! There are, alas, so many ways in which you can, knowingly and otherwise, sabotage your own counselling efforts. In many cases, knowledge is the best defence against the problems listed. You now have that knowledge. For other cases, various strategies can be used to minimize, or even prevent, the problem. You now have those strategies.

14

PROBLEMS WITH STAFF

Client characteristics and behaviours which cause problems

There are many ways in which your staff members can make counselling problematic. Here are a few with some suggested remedies.

Rambling

Some clients will ramble aimlessly about their problem. That is a measure of their clarity of thought about the problem. Help them by placing a structure on the discussions, or asking them what structure they would like to use to conduct the discussions.

Embarrassment and guilt

Some clients will be reluctant to talk because they feel ashamed or guilty about the problem. If you establish this to be the case, allow them to express their guilt; don't undermine their emotions by telling them there is nothing to feel guilty about.

Leaving and re-entering counselling at different stages

Generally, clients will terminate counselling when it is right for them to do so. That, you should make clear to them, is their absolute right. You should also make it clear that the door is open for them to return at a later stage. Some will, and there are many reasons for doing so. Some clients will leave after having gained an understanding of the problem. They will take some time to process that new understanding and then return at a later stage. In the interim they may have redefined the problem and now wish to seek a solution. They may have done both and now seek some help with planning and implementation, or they may have totally solved the problem and return to get help with acquiring the skills they need to ensure it never happens again.

Avoidance of change

Some people will go to great lengths to avoid changing the way they think. They will vigorously seek to prove there is no need to change. Most will spend more time and effort 'proving' they don't need to change than they would have needed to effect the beneficial change. Point it out to them.

Undisclosed maintenance factors

Often, there may be motives for maintaining the problem which the client prefers not to, or is unable to, disclose. The motives are rarely simple, but the rewards the person receives from the environment for having the problem make it easier to continue with it. If you find yourself unable to understand why the client is sabotaging your efforts to help, it is worth re-exploring the rewards obtained from the problem.

Destructive inner dialogue

One of the most difficult factors to influence in counselling is the client's inner dialogue. The statements they make to themselves inside their heads are invisible to the onlooker. The client can completely destroy all your good work with one simple and destructive statement to themselves. Educate them. Tell them all about the power of inner dialogue. Show them the chain of events which are started by the inner dialogue. Show them how to control and choose what to say to themselves.

Reluctance to accept the STM

Some members of your staff will recoil from the notion that they alone are responsible for what they think, feel and do. Those same people will find it virtually impossible to imagine that there are skills which successful people use to cope with life's problems. Even the notion that such skills exist will be resisted. Why? Because admitting they exist is also an admission that they do not possess them. It is an admission that they were not even clever enough to realize such skills existed. It is an admission that they failed to think about why some people thrive on problems and others are crippled by the same problem. It is an admission that they've been responsible for their own misery over the years. The more competent and achievement-oriented a person is, the more likely they are to accept these premises. So, for your high achievers the persuasion job will be easy. For your low achievers the task will be much more

Destructive inner dialogue

demanding. Remember, it's a persuasion job, not a counselling job. Plan such a persuasion in the same way you would plan any other business persuasion.

Lack of belief in self-responsibility

The most difficult client of all is the one who continually refuses to accept the notion of self-responsibility at all. At the risk of sounding heartless, this staff member is not equipped to respond to counselling in the workplace. They require more input than you have time or resources to offer. Psychiatric wards all over the world are full of people who deny that they are responsible for their beliefs, thoughts, attitudes and behaviours. You have to set a cut-off point for work-based counselling: this is one of those points.

Summary

The list of problems clients can bring to counselling to sabotage – deliberately and otherwise – your counselling efforts could fill several volumes. We have listed the more common and suggested remedies. You, as an experienced manager, don't need several volumes to tell you about the ways people can thwart your efforts. You have been identifying and managing such problems for some time. Draw on that experience when you encounter problems with the people you are counselling. In this respect, management as an art and a discipline is far ahead of counselling.

15

PROBLEMS WITH THE PROCESS

There are many process problems in, and barriers to, counselling. We have commented briefly on several throughout the book. Here is a more detailed analysis with suggestions to contain or resolve the problems.

Making good progress

You will often have a clear view of how a client ought to progress with their problem solving and be tempted to tell them. You will be tempted to 'hurry them along' because they are taking an inordinate amount of time over a simple decision. You will see ways in which you can take short cuts through the counselling process and be tempted to follow them. Don't, don't and *don't!* Now that is as clear as can be. But why not? For three reasons. First, clients need time to come to terms with the changes they are making; they have to prepare themselves. Trying to speed up the process takes more time in the long run – after trying and failing, you have to go back and take the time you would have had to take in the first place (that's if the client hasn't lost faith in you in the meantime). Second, if you do manage to persuade them to bypass the process or speed up, you will almost certainly miss part of the adjustment process mentioned above. The client will gradually become uncomfortable with their current position, sensing that, somehow, it just doesn't seem right. You will then have to tackle the 'something which just doesn't feel right'. Third, clients will believe, and have more faith in, their own solutions, discoveries and theories than in yours. They will have commitment to their own solutions, if they have discovered, nurtured and planned them. How will you prevent yourself from hurrying the client for your benefit rather than theirs? How will you reconcile this advice with your business pressures?

When to understand and when to act

This is yet another corollary to our original principle. But, first, let's set the scene. You have come for counselling. Very quickly it becomes clear that the person offering the counselling has the solution to your problem in terms of some practical help they can offer you. But they have to follow the rules of counselling. They insist on continuing to try to understand your problem. How are you going to react? Calmly? Or with extreme frustration? With frustration, of course. That is the reason you should offer help, direct action, to the client if it is clear that that is both what they want and the best way to solve the problem. As a counsellor–manager, you will encounter this scenario more frequently than a non-managing counsellor. Quite frequently it will become clear that what has started out as a counselling session should have been a normal manager's 'problem-solving-followed-by-action' session. Is that an accurate assessment? If you have been counselling over the last year, what percentage of problems that started out as counselling problems ended up as management problem-solving issues?

Coping with strong emotions

Counselling gives people permission to express their deepest, darkest and most intense emotions. You may have dealt with such intensity of emotion only very rarely. If so, you should prepare yourself to cope with it if you wish to genuinely help your staff. The two most common emotions seen in counselling are anger and sorrow (as manifested by crying).

Anger

The verbal ferocity you will witness occasionally is difficult not to take personally. How do you handle it? By inviting the client to express why they feel that way and then, point-by-point, conveying your understanding. You do not have to agree; just make sure you understand. Does this sound familiar? It is exactly what you do in the understanding and listening stage.

Anger at you

The worst thing you can do in response to anger against you is to employ the kinds of responses used by much-hated politicians. The kind that blames the victim of corruption for causing that corruption. The kind that blames blatant lying on the person who was deceived because they failed to ask if they were being deceived. The kind that asks the complainant to resign because their leader took action without consulting the complainant and thereby subsequently sabotaged their efforts. If your staff are angry with you, let them express it; they only become angry because they care. Let them put their case. If they are right, admit it. Yes, that is right, admit it. People will always forgive mistakes. In fact they find it difficult not to admire and respect someone who is big enough to admit their mistakes and immediately sets in place the mechanisms to ensure they don't happen again. But they will never trust you again if you have made mistakes and use all sorts of political and deceitful strategies to cover them up. Politicians take heed. Even if the reason your staff are angry with you is not a mistake, listen to them and let them see the reasons you did what you did. Your objective is not to avoid blame, but to engender loyalty and commitment in staff. Blame is as easily avoided as loyalty is sabotaged; the two are inextricably linked.

Sorrow

A member of staff breaks down in your office. They are crying hysterically. What do you have to do? Nothing. That's right, nothing. You do not *have* to do anything. In fact, it is the feeling that you have to do something yet know you can do nothing that makes dealing with the crying of others so uncomfortable. You could touch or hold the person if that is appropriate. You can encourage them to let it flow. But do not patronize by uttering such platitudes as 'There, there, it'll be alright.' Do not ask them not to cry; crying is as natural as laughing – it is a heartfelt expression of emotion. As with the expression of all other emotions, you should acknowledge its occurrence. Let the staff member know that you know how upset they are. You might even go as far as expressing your appreciation that the staff member feels able to cry in front of you (or at least acknowledge this inside your head). It probably means they really trust and respect you. They believe you will understand and can potentially help. You are probably the first person to whom they have expressed their true depth of emotion.

Avoiding dependency problems

Some clients will be tempted to become dependent on you. Well, maybe that is not quite true. Surely no one would deliberately allow themselves to become dependent? Let's examine the sequence of events which can lead to dependency to find out whether temptation is the right description:

1   You show interest in them as a person.
2   You develop a good rapport.
3   You demonstrate understanding and respect.
4   You tolerate their character flaws.
5   You try to help them improve their lives.
6   You are willing to discuss things their way.
7   You do not coerce or rush them.
8   You are available to help as is needed.
9   You help them to feel good about their abilities to cope.
10 You 'make' them feel valued, worthwhile and appreciated.

Does that sequence remind you of anything else? Such as, perhaps, the ingredients of a successful courtship or bonding? Yes? Yes! Now, if someone provided you with that kind of input as and when you wanted it, you might be tempted to seek more and more and more. You might form a counselling habit, you might find yourself obtaining all your feelings of self-worth from the relationship. You might well become dependent. Unethical counsellors depend on this process for their livelihood.

For you, however, that is a nightmare scenario. You will quickly have a staff member who is unable to make decisions for themselves. How do you avoid it? Or, more precisely, how do you avoid forming dependency-based relationships in such a way that you do not sabotage your counselling efforts? It is not easy. One way is to explain to the client what could happen. Ask them to beware of emerging dependency. Tell them also that you will draw their attention to it if you detect dependency-type behaviours emerging.

EXERCISE

What are dependency behaviours? They are embedded in the preceding text; extract them and form a list.

Projection

Projection

This was mentioned earlier (page 90), but not explored. Projection is a cinematographic technique by which the images of a real and permanent part of one substance, usually film, are transmitted by means of an optical lens and strong light on to a surface which previously appeared to have no image. In fact that's a fairly good definition of the human kind of projection too. One person transmits something in themselves on to another by means of their emotional light, focused by the intensity of their like or dislike of the whole or a part of the other person. Of course, seeing something in others does not make 'it' real; neither does it remove 'it' from ourselves. Clients will project on to you and others. You and I do it too. How do you resolve it? By asking the client, or yourself, if what you admire or detest in others is what they are currently claiming to see in the person on to whom they are projecting.

Transference

Transference

What is transference? It is the projection of feelings, which can be described as those other than strictly professional, by one or both parties on to the other. The feelings can be positive, negative or, more usually, ambivalent. They can be direct, or as a response to the projections of the other party. Projection from the counsellor to the client (and vice versa) is called transference. The reactive projection back from the client to the counsellor (or vice versa) is called counter-transference. There are also negative transferences and contradictory counter-transferences. For instance, one party may project positive attributes on to the other, but receive negative projections in return (contradictory counter-transference). Have I lost you yet?

Good! Had I not lost you, I would have been worried about the level of your RQ – your Realism Quotient. Why good? Because, despite what some will tell you, we simply do not have the methods to analyse communication of such complexity. In fact, we can't even analyse a simple one-way communication with any degree of accuracy. So, to suggest that we can analyse contradictory (or synchronous) counter-transference is, quite simply, optimistic delusion.

So, what do we do about this barrier to successful counselling – a barrier beyond our understanding? First, being unable to understand something does not mean being unable to sense it. If you do sense some unconscious communication going on, observe it for a while, then draw the other party's attention to it. Ask them what you could be sensing. They may be able to tell you, albeit in a roundabout way. Whatever their response to the question, your response should be that neither party can afford to allow these emotions to interfere with the efforts of counselling.

As you might imagine (from the description of the similarity between counselling and courtship), you will experience a great deal of positive transference. While that is clearly good for the development of rapport, there is a point when it becomes destructive to counselling. Explain the risks and agree where to draw the line.

Establishing the cause of problems

Some counsellors fall into what I call the 'aetiological certainty delusion'. They make what seems to be a small leap from noting that certain clients seem to be predisposed to certain kinds of problems to thinking they can identify the cause of any client's problem. They believe without reservation that a particular chain of events and factors led to the client's problem. If you challenge them on their conclusion, they will forcefully defend their 'professional judgement' against what they perceive as ill-informed criticism; they know their clients, and *you* don't. Previously you might have assumed that their years of experience made psychologists, psychiatrists and counsellors able to determine the cause of any problem. It is not so. They (and we) are unable to determine the cause of problems. You should know the reasons, otherwise you will delude yourself in the same way the majority of the mental health profession deludes itself (with the same consequences – low levels of efficacy). Let's apply some of this 'professional judgement' to examine how likely it is that you will identify the correct causal pattern of a person's problem. Prepare yourself for some surprises.

Why no one can establish causal patterns

If we are to identify the factors and sequence of events that have caused a problem, then clearly we need to be able to analyse how various factors interact to cause a problem. What kinds of factors interact and how many of them are there? To start, we need to make some assumptions. First, let's assume that there are only 16 personality characteristics which can have an effect on a person's life (multiply that number by at least 10 to get closer to the truth). Why 16? A famous psychological indicator uses that number.

Those of you who are numerically inclined might want to start working out the number of possible interactions between these variables. Here is the statistical formula for calculating permutations:

$$P = \frac{N!}{(N - R)!}$$

P is the number of permutations in which R variables can interact with N variables when account is taken of the ordering of the variables. ! is the factorial of any number (factorial $4 = 1 \times 2 \times 3 \times 4 = 24$).

How many interactions are there with 16 variables? Well, there is little point in providing the answer because the figure is so large as to be meaningless. But, to put it in some kind of perspective, it means that if you were to count from 0 upwards at the rate of one per second for the next 10 000 years, you still would not reach the number of possible ways the limited number of variables we have explored can interact. But we haven't finished yet.

Now let's assume that each of the 16 variables can have one of three effects: positive, negative, or neutral (a ridiculously simplistic assumption). Let's introduce some skills which have a bearing on life performance, such as social skills, rational thinking skills and so on. Assume we have only 10 of these key skill areas (a ridiculously low number). And, as before, let's assume that the skill can have a positive, negative or neutral effect depending on the circumstances in which they are used (every skill is a strength in some contexts and a weakness in others). For good measure, let's add in a number to represent the number of experiences that could happen to influence our lives. Events like death of a parent at 1 year old, 2 years old, 3 years old ... Events like being bullied at school at 5 years old, at 6 years old ... Events like friends moving away with their parents when you are 7 years old, 8 years old, 9 years old ... Events like your parents being made redundant when you were, say, 12 years old, 13 years old, 14 years old ... Events like discovering your sexuality before or after your peers, by 1 month, 1 year, 3 years ... And so on. But, for simplicity, let's allocate a small number such as 10 (we've listed more than that).

Try calculating again. The number of possible interactions is simply beyond comprehension (you could count them if you had a few millennia to spare). Surely nobody in their right mind could claim to be able to say they *know* what causes a person's problem with that number of permutations in the background.

Definition difficulties

As if that was not enough, there are further difficulties which make claims of 'knowing' what caused a particular problem more ludicrous. We can't even

Definition problems

agree on what certain problems are. There are very few acceptable definitions of individual emotional problems. At a higher level we can't even define 'personality' properly. And if you can't define something, how on earth can you hope to measure it accurately? You can't. Can you imagine functioning as an engineer without being able to measure the material with which you were working? No? Well, that's what trying to assess causal factors of a problem is like. Except we can't even define what it is we would measure if we could measure it.

The correlation problem

There is also the omnipresent correlation problem. Most of us instinctively assume that when things occur together they are causally related. In trying to understand the cause of a problem you will witness many things occurring together. For instance, you observe that your client breathes more rapidly and sweats more than people without the problem. So, you conclude, rapid breathing and sweating are obviously the cause of the problem and if only you could cool them down and slow their breathing, the problem would be solved. 'Ridiculous' you might say, the client is merely manifesting symptoms of stress. Maybe so, but people do reason as stated. The history of medicine is stuffed full of such amazing reasoning. Of course, we don't do that today, do we? Think again! ECT – electroconvulsive 'therapy' – is used to 'treat' mental health clients. The 'rationale'? If you put a voltage through the 'clients' ' brains, their symptoms seem to be reduced in severity. You may also have noticed that if you put a slightly larger voltage through someone strapped to a specially designed chair, *all* their symptoms disappear permanently. ECT 'works' for a tiny percentage of people because it destroys large parts of the brain; it effectively fries your neural pathways. With large parts of your brain fried your behaviour is obviously going to be different after cooking than before. The correlative reasoning flaw is 'it changes behaviour, so it works'. 'Works' is a charitable term; ECT randomly destroys neural pathways. For some people it will destroy the problem-causing pathways, along with innumerable others. For most it just destroys, period.

Correlative link direction problem

It can be even worse. Not only may there be intervening variables causing the apparent causal link between two factors, there may also be confusion over the direction in which a causal chain is working. Medical scientists believed for a long time that there was a link between the amount of blood in a patient and their illness. So physicians 'bled' their patients. If the patient died it was 'because' of their overwhelming illness. If they survived it was 'because' of the efficacy of blood-letting. There was a link between blood quantities and prognosis but not in the direction it was assumed to be; bleeding killed, when it was thought to cure. The physicians of the time noticed a link, but perceived its subtleties incorrectly. These were not stupid people, they simply did not have all the facts to determine the nature of the link they were observing. So in your context, even if you could accurately rule out coincidence when witnessing a correlation, and rule out intervening variables creating the link you thought was direct, you still have to be able to correctly determine the direction of the causal link.

More flawed correlative reasoning

ECT is not the only mental health treatment based on flawed correlative reasoning. The hearing of voices is often associated with schizophrenia (the basket term used by psychiatrists, psychologists and the like when they know someone is behaving in an odd manner, but for which they are unable to provide an explanation), so much so that this phenomenon is described as a symptom of the illness. We now know that most voice-hearers lead normal lives and do not suffer any other 'symptoms'. Only recently have people been willing to admit to hearing voices. In the past, they were so afraid of being carted off to the nearest asylum, they kept it to themselves and carried on with their otherwise normal lives. Have you never heard a voice? Have you never been sure you heard someone calling your name who could not have done so at that time and in that place? Most people have, and most people live normal lives.

Variation taken as deviation

Even in those whose voice-hearing ... Stop! Let's change the term 'voice-hearing', which implies a delusional state, to one which reflects what we now know is going on – 'excessively powerful inner dialogue' (EPID). Even in those whose inner dialogue is extremely powerful and who also display bizarre behaviours, those behaviours are usually a response to the dialogue and not a symptom of illness. The behaviours are wrongly interpreted as schizophrenia. We pointed out earlier that labelling can stop you trying to understand. Well, until very recently, labelling 'voices' as schizophrenic symptoms blocked our attempts at understanding. Even now the majority of the mental health profession does not accept the views just expressed.

The key point is that correlation is *not* causation, but even highly intelligent people can be duped into thinking it is. Even if correlation does signify causation, the direction of the causal link is rarely clear. Does EPID cause bizarre behaviour or does bizarre behaviour cause EPID? Or is some hidden third variable responsible for both? We don't know. Yet we offer 'treatment' based on a reasoning so flawed that it would fail a school-level scientific reasoning test. Most school-level scientists know that correlation does not prove causation. But somewhere between casting off teenage fashion and becoming established in professional life, that small fact seems to be forgotten. Don't think that these are isolated incidents. Or that EPID is the only normal variation of behaviour which is interpreted as a symptom of madness. It is not. Don't imagine that we don't have modern-day equivalents of bleeding – we do. Lots of them.

We could stop here: the case against being able to establish the causal pattern for any emotional problem is certainly established beyond all reasonable doubt. But we won't. We'll use this topic as a means to convey some other problems you will encounter in counselling your staff, and how you can overcome them.

Cognitive capacity problem

Your short-term memory, the part available to process information, can only handle seven plus or minus two chunks of data. That is, the range of variation between 'normal' human beings' short-term memory capability is five to nine pieces of information. How do you use such limited capacity to process a problem which has, say, 14 causal factors which have a total of 34 active interactions? You can't. Pure and simple. Even advanced multi-variant analysis statistical techniques conducted on a computer would have problems with those few variables. And those few do not even begin to scratch the surface of the average client's problem. Client problems with only 1–5 active interactions just don't exist. Even a single causal factor (unheard of) interacts with a multitude of variables in a client's life.

What effect does that information have on day-to-day counselling? Try to handle small amounts of information at a time. When you think you are reach-

Cognitive capacity problem

ing overload (that is, more than $7 +/- 2$ chunks, stop the client and try to summarize. Doing so gives you a chance to (unwittingly) transfer the information into long-term memory. It also gives the client the chance to remember what you know and understand about them and their problem. How will you know when it is time to summarize?

Preferred theory informing explanation

Your interest and training influence your ability to perceive causal factors. If you have trained in one style of counselling, you will be on the look-out for the causal factors which that school espouses and will be ignorant of the plethora of other possible causes. Even if they jumped up and slapped you in the face, you still wouldn't see them (see also the section on conceptual repertoire deficits, page 222). Prove it to yourself. Ask any group of people to explain any complex event. Mentally note each person's explanation. Follow up by asking each individual what theories they have about those kinds of events. You will be sure to see how their explanation was informed by their theory. If they change their theory they will change their explanation of the cause.

Quite clearly, explanations offered tell us more about the theories of those offering them than the cause of the problem they are trying to explain. In fact their theories may be so strongly held that it blocks them from seeing hard evidence in the same way the flat-earthers were blind to Galileo's evidence.

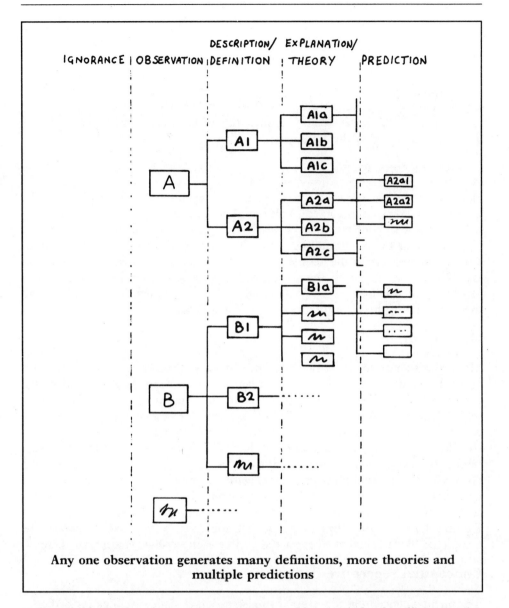

Any one observation generates many definitions, more theories and multiple predictions

You don't need to know what caused a problem to help the client to solve it. This is one of the wonders of the common principles and Skills Training Model approach.

Client secrecy

Client secrecy can also block your attempts to uncover a cause. Have you ever told anyone everything about yourself? Have you ever revealed all those things in your past of which you are deeply ashamed? Of course not. But you can be sure that they have had an effect on your life. Some may even be among the many factors which caused problems for you. But you cannot tell what effect they had or how they interact with other variables.

Don't expect your client to reveal their deep, dark, nasty secrets. You don't need to know them. Knowing them would not help. In fact it may hinder your ability to be compassionate towards them. And it will certainly confuse you even further, or, worse, lead you into the aetiological certainty delusion – 'I found the one what did it, Guv.'

Client acquiescence

Have you ever told someone what you knew they wanted to hear just to make life easy for everyone involved? You bet. And your clients will do it too. They will comply with your favourite theories and agree with your inspired hypotheses, thereby further confounding your slim chances of getting to the bottom of a problem. Be alert to the acquiescent client. They agree with everything you say. They agree to do all the intercounselling session exercise that you plan together, but don't deliver. When faced with such a client you should invite them to explore the consequences of their acquiescence.

Memory problems

Memory also interferes. We've all experienced something as being a memory of a real event which was in fact a dream and vice versa. We've all forgotten something which was of great importance to our lives. We've all falsely remembered something which we've been told happened to us as children. These are only a few of the problems with memory. The full range of memory phenomena alone could sabotage all your aetiological investigation attempts. In counselling be aware that human memory is a flawed and unreliable creature. However, it can function well with some prompting. Start and end your counselling sessions with some memory prompting. Summarize the previous session. Remind your client of how the counselling relationship was going. Remind them of the objectives you set together in the last session to be completed by the current one. At the end of each session, summarize again.

Conceptual repertoire deficits

The client's conceptual repertoire can also sabotage your investigations. If they don't understand some of the concepts behind some of the causal factors, you can't expect them to report accurately what happened to them. How could they? At the time of whatever events you are exploring, they didn't have the conceptual repertoire to process what was happening. They therefore didn't have the ability to store an accurate picture of the events. How can you then expect them, after goodness knows how long, to be able to reinterpret the events with any degree of accuracy? You can't and neither should you (unless you are seeking a reinterpretation for the purposes of providing a reference experience for a changed belief – in which case accuracy is of no consequence).

Summary

Now you have seen the host of problems associated with trying to determine the cause of a problem, you can better appreciate why the common principles approach is preferable to those approaches which advocate 'finding causes'. Any one of the problems listed can sabotage any attempt at determining a causal pattern. Collectively they make effective causal investigation a pointless fantasy. For the same reasons, the Skills Training Model is preferable to those which explore cause. There can be no accurate determination of the cause of any problem. That accepted, the best solution is to equip clients with skills for effective performance in life.

16

ISSUES IN COUNSELLING

What companies mean by counselling

Some companies are genuinely concerned for the welfare of their employees. They genuinely want to help their staff shake off their problems. They set up truly confidential counselling services, staffed by business-experienced people who have also acquired counselling skills. The staff trust the organization to manage the counselling system in the way they promise to manage it. The managers trust the staff not to abuse the system. Mechanisms are in place to detect and remedy a breach on either side of the counselling contract. Evaluation systems are set up to measure the short- and long-term benefits of providing counselling as a whole and in the way it is currently being provided. However, that is by no means common practice. Some counselling systems are set up for less than admirable motives, are staffed by people with less commercial experience than the average social worker, and are widely abused by both management and staff.

Corporate abuses of counselling

Counselling has been documented as being abused for the following purposes in some very large companies. When you read this list, consider what effect this kind of behaviour will have on staff morale, output and loyalty. Then ask yourself if you would trust the companies engaging in this kind of activity, as an employee, customer or supplier.
  Counselling has been inappropriately used:

- to gather information about staff for the company
- to gain confidential information about some staff from others

- to establish the personal motives of staff
- to cover directing employees to change their behaviour
- as a cover for disciplinary action
- to enable the company to present a caring image (while not really offering counselling at all).

In what other ways could counselling be abused?

Short-term advantage at the cost of long-term effectiveness

There will be many temptations for you to abuse/misuse the trust your staff place in you as a counsellor/manager. Many short-term advantage apples will be dangled in front of your nose. Direct your mind past them to the long-term orchard. Taking a nibble of the only short-term apple will destroy your crop of the long-term variety. If you exploit the trust placed in you for short-term gain, your trustworthiness for the long term will be destroyed. After such a breach, with what can you be trusted? With recruitment decisions? Promotion decisions? Appraisal decisions? After such a breach, who can trust you? Your staff? Your peers? Your superiors? If you break a confidence to help one of your superiors, how can they ever trust you not to break *their* confidence? They can't and, more importantly, they know they can't. How will that affect your promotion prospects?

Priority of interests conflicts

Every good manager knows that their company's interests come first, right? No, let's be honest. Every street-wise person knows that each individual's interests are their own top priority, but that they will pretend to place the interests of their company first. It's a small game of deception that everyone knows and everyone plays, so let's admit it for the purposes of understanding your motives in terms of counselling. What implications does that have for the counselling manager's hierarchy of interests? They will be as follows:

1 your interests
2 your department's interests
3 your paymaster's interests
4 your profession's interests
5 the client's interests.

So, in which circumstances are managers, providing counselling, likely to place the client's interests higher up the list? When the five interests coincide. When is that? When solving the client's problem helps you, the department and the company. Specifically, when solving the client's problem will improve the performance of your department. If it will not, you have a conflict of interest. If helping your staff member places a burden on your department and is therefore likely to detrimentally affect your performance (and therefore your promotion prospects) are you still going to provide counselling? If it would be cheaper to replace an awkward employee than counsel what would you do? If a staff member who was not performing as well as the rest needed counselling for another issue, would you provide it or use the problem as an opportunity to remove them and increase the performance of your department as a whole? If an employee who was a threat to your next promotion needed counselling, would you provide it or look after your future?

That is just a small sample of the kinds of dilemmas you will face. Some will be much more complex. And those are just the dilemmas that affect you. How much more difficult it becomes when we also add the needs of the organization into the equation.

Realistic resolution of conflicts of interest

Even the best-intentioned companies experience conflicts between their needs and the needs of their staff. The goal of the organization is to solve an employee problem as quickly, cheaply and permanently as possible. The goal of the employee may not be as clear-cut. Certainly to them cost is of little concern. Speed of resolution is likely to be threatening; it takes time to accept that a change in one's life is required to solve a problem. The permanence of a resolution is logically of value, but not if you are in great pain and want immediate short-term relief. The company must, and should, make a cost-effective decision about its staff. If it is going to cost more to solve an employee's problem than he or she is likely to be worth to the company, the company ought to be making decisions to protect its own interests. Included in this calculation should be an element which reflects the period of time an employee is likely to stay with the company. The company ought to provide help if the staff retention figures indicate that the employee will probably stay with the company for the period of time necessary to recover the investment in solving their problem.

Costs of counselling

If the company does not make such a decision, and publicize the fact that such a decision will be made, it can expect to see the situation which has occurred in the UK. The number of people claiming 'sickness benefit' (an allowance paid by the state to those incapable of work due to illness) doubled in a ten-year period despite the dramatic improvements in the health of the nation over the same time. Why? Because the payment was automatic and required no independent verification for an employer to recoup the costs from the state. Since a legislative change, large companies now have to carry that cost. As a result, they have introduced a wide range of checks where previously none existed. You should apply similar principles to the provision of counselling. It should not be an open-ended arrangement. Your company is not a charity.

It is simply not fair to ask customers to carry the cost of a company which chooses to behave in such a manner. In any event, such a company won't survive for long; competitors will rapidly emerge to provide the customers with products and services which don't carry a social welfare premium.

Costs of not counselling

The above rationale is at one end of a continuum, the opposite end of which is the rationale that good-quality employees will not be prepared to work for a company because it demonstrates no welfare concerns whatsoever. The cost, in that case, is incurred in having to pay nearly equal wages to low-quality staff for much lower levels of performance and output.

The cost-effectiveness of counselling

Your company may also be faced with an almost overwhelming case when its financial advisers point out that the return from counselling is uncertain and extremely difficult to quantify. By contrast, they will say, the costs are all too obvious and extremely easy to measure. They will be able to present a very strong argument for not providing counselling of any kind. At least they will if you don't set up your counselling system with some very quantifiable results-oriented measures built in. Set up measures to assess the cost-effectiveness of counselling.

We will explore those measures in 'Some guidelines for running effective counselling, page 228. First, however, we ought to point out the general principle which applies to virtually all systems: what a company perceives counselling to be will determine how it is applied and consequently what outcome will be obtained. In short, operating perceptions will determine outcome performance. So, if a company perceives counselling to be the way to look attractive to prospective employees or shareholders, that is all it will achieve; existing employees will see through the cynical sham with all the consequences that that will have for morale, loyalty, and staff retention.

Employee assistance programmes (EAPs)

Such programmes are set up as the answer to many of the dilemmas that organizations and counselling managers face. Worldwide there are tens of thousands of effective EAPs in operation. There appears to be a correlation between the level of enterprise culture in a society and the number of EAP schemes operating within it. That is, the less socialist in orientation a country is, the more companies will see it as wise to look after their employees. And the more socialist a country is, the more companies will leave their employees' welfare to the state – which, of course, usually means their needs are not attended to at all. The most capitalist country in the world, the USA, has the largest number of EAPs.

Why did I mention that correlation? Because it illustrates that enlightened self-interest is the best reason to introduce an EAP. The pursuit of wealth is the best way to help those in need. The need to make profit through superior performance is the strongest reason to have a system to maintain the performance levels of staff. Capitalism has been universally effective in harnessing the motives of most human beings. It transforms the ugly motive of greed into beautiful results. To make money, each of us has to serve each other willingly.

EAPs vary enormously in their nature. Indeed, each is likely to be unique. Some have external counsellors on call to cover all potential problems; others are set up after providing line managers with sufficient training to make them effective counsellors for most problems, with a range of specialist counsellors being brought in as and when required, to cover problems matching their speciality. Still others are set up with a team of specialist counsellors in-house. Others are set up via healthcare companies which provide counselling via the health package offered to all employees of the customer organization.

Some guidelines for running effective counselling

If you wish to set up an external service – that is, counselling provided by an individual or a team other than the employee's line manager, ensure that the following are in place:

1   Have a formal written policy which is actually available for staff to access without having to ask for it. As you've probably noticed, many companies have policies for just about everything, but accessing the policy guidelines requires supreme persistence. And when you do locate them, you often have to justify to some mindless bureaucrat why you should be allowed to access it.
2   Allow staff to refer themselves to the programme without their supervisor's permission.
3   Enable supervisors to refer their staff to the programme.
4   Make it possible for counsellors to refer clients to external specialists.
5   Make the programme available to the immediate families of employees.
6   Ensure that the providers are experienced businesspeople, with counselling skills, who can demonstrate positive outcomes. If they cannot supply outcome evidence or measure outcome, do not award them the contract.

   There is little point in sending your staff to a service which is run and delivered by psychologists, psychiatrists or counsellors who are unfamiliar with pressures and realities of commercial life, who have never run a business or at least held a senior commercial position long enough to understand the subtleties of the business environment. Formal qualifications are no guide to competence; no qualification-awarding organization of which I am aware uses *any* counselling outcome measures to judge the competence of its trainee counsellors. 1 001 reasons are offered for this omission, none of which would cut any ice in the real commercial world.

7 Ensure that the counselling service is evaluated using the measures *you* decide. Many counselling organizations offer customer companies feedback on their performance as counsellors. The reports are compiled by the counselling organization about their own services. Unbelievably some companies actually accept these reports and base their judgement of the counselling organization on them! It is bad enough that foxes are guarding the hen house, but when one discovers that the hens have invited the foxes to do so, one is left speechless.

8 Ensure that the counselling organization seeks and responds to feedback from the customer company. If they do not have such a system, do not use them.

EXERCISE

Add your own criteria to this list.

Evaluating counselling

No company should introduce a system without also introducing the means to evaluate it. As you will have doubtless noticed, that cardinal rule is broken more often than not in business. With a system like counselling there is more need than usual to make sure the system is being evaluated. Those who take a hardline view of staff (perform or leave) will have to be convinced that counselling saves more money for the company than it costs.

However, some companies are reluctant to evaluate their counselling programmes whether they be internal or external. As we have seen above, it is not unusual for companies to place the evaluation of the programme in the hands of those who have a strong interest in extolling its virtues. Why? Why would a company not want information or not want accurate information? For a few very simple reasons:

- 'The counselling programme is a public relations exercise. As long as we can show we care, there will be no interest in, or expenditure on, evaluation.' (A hypothetical head of any very real company.)
- 'Of course it is extremely difficult to measure the effectiveness of something as subtle and multiskilled as counselling. There is no effective evaluation system we know of.' (A very real head of a counselling service in the UK.)
- 'Evaluating the EAP draws attention to the numbers and scope of problems we have in the company. That is not congruent with our shareholders' objectives.' (A very real CEO of a very large company.)

EXERCISE

From the list of reasons people are reluctant to counsel (page 203), predict other motives for being reluctant to measure the effectiveness of counselling.

What kinds of measures can you use to evaluate the effectiveness of a counselling programme? Whatever measures are used must provide comparative rather than absolute information. You need to know to what extent counselling is working compared to both other methods and non-interventions (that is, no counselling).

Productivity

Measure productivity or performance as follows:

- before and after the introduction of counselling or an EAP
- in divisions or departments with counselling provision compared to those without
- in comparison to other similar companies before and after counselling
- in comparison to companies with no counselling and others with counselling
- in individuals before and after they have received counselling
- in individuals with problems who received counselling in comparison to those who did not.

Retention of staff

Use the same six measures as above.

Absenteeism

Use the same six measures as above.

Accidents and injuries

The occurrence of accidents is strongly related to emotional state and mental health. Use the six measures above to assess.

Medical visits

The number of times people make visits to their medical practitioner is related to their health and morale. Evaluate the effectiveness of your counselling programme using the six measures above.

Sick leave

The number of days taken sick per year is a very strong measure of morale, emotional state and general health (both physical and mental). Evaluate the effectiveness of your counselling system using the above six measures.

Disciplinary and dismissal actions

Counselling can be very effective at giving people an opportunity to air their frustrations before they manifest themselves as behaviours requiring disciplinary action. Evaluate the effectiveness of your counselling programme using the six measures.

Recruitment

In the longer term, an effective staff management and counselling programme will manifest itself in more people wanting to work with your company. What quality and number of applicants do you receive? Compare your system using the measures above which seem appropriate.

EXERCISE

Make a list of other measures you could use.

Evaluating counsellors

Naturally once you have relearned the basics of counselling, you will want to improve your performance as a counsellor. Do so by taking a step which your staff will love and admire. Ask them to assess you as a counsellor. That's right, ask your staff to judge you. Yes, I know it is usually the other way round, but that's why this technique will be so effective. If it has never been done before in your company, your staff will be surprised that you value their opinion so highly. The really effective performers in virtually every field – the best leaders, the best politicians, the best managers, CEOs – are known to ask for this kind of feedback regularly.

Some of your peers will be frightened of asking their staff to evaluate them for fear of what might be said. But you, being a dedicated professional (you wouldn't be reading this book, let alone this section, otherwise), will welcome all information you can use to improve your performance. So how should you get that information? Give your staff a 'Counsellor Rating Questionnaire', which might take on the following format and which should be completed anonymously.

Statement	Disagree Strongly	Disagree	Neutral	Agree	Agree Strongly
The counsellor made it easy for me to talk about my problem.	☐	☐	☐	☐	☐
I felt as relaxed as is possible talking about a difficult problem.	☐	☐	☐	☐	☐
I trust the counsellor to maintain absolute confidentiality.	☐	☐	☐	☐	☐

(Cont.)

Statement	Disagree Strongly	Disagree	Neutral	Agree	Agree Strongly
I trust the counsellor will not breach my confidence if there is a conflict of interest between roles.	☐	☐	☐	☐	☐
The counsellor made every effort to understand me and my problem.	☐	☐	☐	☐	☐
I was absolutely positive the counsellor really understood.	☐	☐	☐	☐	☐
The counsellor did not pass negative judgement on me.	☐	☐	☐	☐	☐
The counsellor helped to calmly explore the various aspects of the problem.	☐	☐	☐	☐	☐
The counsellor helped me to understand the situation more clearly.	☐	☐	☐	☐	☐
The counsellor helped me to see the problem as being manageable/soluble.	☐	☐	☐	☐	☐
The counsellor helped me to find a solution/resolution to the problem.	☐	☐	☐	☐	☐
I felt the counsellor helped me to make a decision which I had been putting off.	☐	☐	☐	☐	☐
I felt supported when planning how to implement my solution.	☐	☐	☐	☐	☐
The counsellor supported me with the implementation of my solution.	☐	☐	☐	☐	☐
The counsellor helped me learn/develop some useful skills.	☐	☐	☐	☐	☐

(Cont.)

Statement	Disagree Strongly	Disagree	Neutral	Agree	Agree Strongly
I felt we evaluated and learned from the counselling experience.	☐	☐	☐	☐	☐
The counsellor helped me to consolidate what I had learned in counselling.	☐	☐	☐	☐	☐
I felt the counsellor handled the ending of counselling with sensitivity.	☐	☐	☐	☐	☐
It was easy to make a request for a counselling session(s).	☐	☐	☐	☐	☐
The time the meetings were held was convenient.	☐	☐	☐	☐	☐
The location for the meetings was convenient.	☐	☐	☐	☐	☐
The facilities at the venue were appropriate.	☐	☐	☐	☐	☐
The number of meetings was appropriate to my needs.	☐	☐	☐	☐	☐
The level of privacy of the meetings was appropriate.	☐	☐	☐	☐	☐
I would use the counsellor again.	☐	☐	☐	☐	☐
I would recommend the counsellor to colleagues.	☐	☐	☐	☐	☐

EXERCISE

Develop your own counsellor evaluation form.

Moral and ethical issues

Contracts and referrals

First things first. If you find you are out of your depth – if you find the client
has a problem that requires specialist knowledge in addition to basic counselling

skills – you should refer them to someone who has this extra knowledge or, at the very least, to someone who is able to locate such a specialist.

Contracts for counselling are highly effective. I recommend you never counsel on anything other than a one-off basis without a contract. Of what should the contract consist? Simply stated, it is an agreement between you and the client about what you expect each other to do and not to do. It should state the terms and conditions under which you are prepared to counsel. It should state the reasons you reserve the right to terminate counselling, such as non-cooperation by the client or failure to carry out agreed action plans. It should also state that the client has every right to cease being counselled when and for whatever reason they wish. Devise such a contract.

Discretion and confidentiality

The rule for confidentiality in counselling is simple and unequivocal. Break a confidence once and you are finished as a credible counsellor. Word will get out. No one will trust you, and neither should they. You pass your information to no one. Not to personnel, not to the welfare officer, not to your boss. To no one.

A wise counsellor will have someone with whom cases can be discussed, but always anonymously. Discuss your staff with someone who has no involvement with, and no interest in, your staff or company, but do not discuss them by name.

The ethics of persuading clients to change

Is it ethical to attempt to persuade a client to change their beliefs? Perhaps not. But if you reframe the question to: 'Is it ethical to stand by and watch a client harm themselves because of the manifestations of a belief you could easily help them change?' it becomes clear that persuading clients to change is acceptable, ethical and desirable.

Is it ethical to use sophisticated persuasion techniques on people without their knowledge? Well, it goes on in every industry worldwide, 24 hours a day. Advertisers use the most sophisticated methods known and continue to improve on them. They don't stop at the end of the advert to tell you what method is being used. Since advertising is legal throughout the civilized world, one can assume that governments don't consider using persuasive methods without telling you is unethical. At least with counselling, there is no doubt it is the client's interest you have in mind. With some advertisers that would be a generous statement in the extreme. However, some would say companies only counsel because it affects the bottom line. That's probably true. But it also helps the employee to keep their job and maybe even improve their performance.

Should you lie to your clients?

Sounds straightforward enough – 'no' is the sure-fire answer. Wrong. There are certain circumstances in which it is not only wise, but beneficial, to lie to clients. Physicians have to do so regularly. If you have ever had a relative

Should you lie to your clients?

dying of some terminal disease, you will know that physicians will withhold information from the patient, but will tell you, the relative. If you've also witnessed your relative asking directly what the problem is and its likely outcome, you will have seen some smart manoeuvring on the part of the physician: 'We're still conducting tests', 'It's so difficult to say at this stage', 'We should be able to give you a definite answer on the prognosis in two weeks' (or two months or some time after they're fairly sure the patient will be dead).

Don't think badly of physicians for lying – they have to. You will have to too. You will have to sacrifice the smaller truth for the greater good. But be sure you are doing it in the client's best interests and not just to protect yourself from a painful situation. Undoubtedly you will be tempted to lie for your benefit and not for the client's. Personally, I wonder how many people are denied their right to know their fate for their own good and how many for that of their physician. This is an ethical minefield. What general principle is being used to decide when to lie? If knowledge of the truth is extremely likely to lead to enormously more harm to the client than ignorance, then lying by omission seems the preferred option. (Lying by commission is quite another matter!) Be very suspicious of your motives if you find your judgement leading you to the most comfortable option for yourself. My personal view on this issue is informed by how I anticipate reacting if I were on the receiving end: I'd always want to know the truth.

EXERCISE

Make a list of the potential situations in which you feel that you will have to lie to your clients. Justify your decision by explaining why it is for the client's good.

Clients can be angelic and satanic

Ways in which clients will abuse you

Virtually every counselling book you can obtain will tell you all about the abuses of the client you should seek to avoid. All very apt. But not very balanced. No counselling book I know of gives you, the counsellor, information about the ways in which the client can abuse you, or how to identify and remedy such abuse. The imbalance highlights the superior and patronizing relationship most conventional counsellors expect to have with their clients. It is time to remedy that imbalance. As a manager, you will already have experienced the ways in which people you are helping can abuse you. Let us put a structure on that knowledge to help you protect yourself.

Seeking rapport development

Clients can enter counselling simply to form a good rapport with you – a rapport they wish to use for personal gain, such as favourable appraisals, 'the ear of the boss', increased chances of promotion, a means of doing down others and so on. They can tell you something in confidence during counselling, which will be designed to have an influence on you but which, if said in other circumstances, would be taken as troublemaking.

Sympathy

Those who fear dismissal and other negative consequences may use counselling to gain sympathy.

Jealousy

Those jealous of others' performance may use counselling to tell damaging stories – which you will be powerless to refute or confirm because they have been provided during confidential counselling sessions.

Hate

Someone who hates another can use counselling to blame the other for their problems. How will you decide whether the target of hatred is the victim or perpetrator, or a bit of both? The confidentiality of the counselling role puts constraints on you. So what do you do if the client will not agree to some kind of peace negotiations with the third party? Are your views on the third party going to be unaffected? I think not.

Revenge

Counselling can also be used for revenge. During confidential counselling sessions, I've had people revealing the alleged wrongdoing of others and others making false claims about wrongdoings.

False credit

You may have seen the more deceitful of your colleagues discreetly creating disasters which only they can remedy (publicly). Your staff will behave in the same way: some will experience enormous problems simply to gain credit in your eyes for having managed something above and beyond the call of duty.

Loyalty

Some staff may even come for counselling out of loyalty to you. On announcing your availability for counselling, some may present you with problems simply because they wish to support you in your new role.

Sex

Yes, some people will seek counselling from you, as a vehicle to spend time with you, for the intention of engaging you sexually. Counsellors are regularly subjected to temptation from people who have sought counselling on the basis of an agenda that has little to do with any problem.

Laziness

Oh, what a wonderful way to skip work for an hour here and an hour there. Yes, that's right, some clients will seek counselling to avoid work. It adds nicely to their armoury of funerals (some people have more grandparents than fingers), dental appointments, medical check-ups, domestic repair visits and so on. Have you ever wondered why your dedicated staff never have these kinds of things to attend to whereas the slackers have a never-ending chain of them?

Pride

What? Pride? How can pride bring someone to counselling? Easily. They have been working on a project; it is not going well. They think they are going to fail. Rather than ask for help while help could still be useful, some will develop a problem which needs counselling as a means of protecting their pride: 'Of course, if I hadn't had that awful problem, I'd have succeeded with the project. Bad timing and bad luck, wasn't it?'

Confidentiality

While you are universally expected to keep the confidence of your client, you will quickly discover that some clients have a slightly different view. Some will use the positive things you have discussed to present themselves in a better light to their peers. Others will store the information exchanged in counselling for a time of strategic importance to them. Still others will talk about what was said and done in counselling.

For all the above, there are innumerable motives. Some are personal; others are political. Clients have a whole host of reasons to lie, deceive, misrepresent and abuse you. The best defence is to make it very clear that you will terminate counselling permanently if you detect any nonsense. More controversially, make it very clear to the client that if they breach your confidences in counselling, you will feel less honour-bound to keep theirs. For those who believe counselling is a balanced relationship that will present no problem. For those who claim counselling with them is balanced, but in fact patronize their clients, such a proposition will be unacceptable. In their view, they stand above their clients and would never do any such thing even if their client breaks the deal. I'm not suggesting that you should actually break a confidence, simply that you should tell clients that confidence is a two-way deal which only holds if both parties keep it.

EXERCISE

List other ways in which staff can abuse your counselling.

Summary

Counselling and counselling systems can be wonderfully used or wilfully abused. Even when operating optimally, counselling and counselling systems present many conflicts of interest between all the involved parties. Most experienced managers are more than capable of resolving those conflicts of interest – they do it regularly every day. However, an issue which is rarely tackled is one of the cardinal sins of management: introducing a system or method and failing to set up a means to evaluate its effectiveness. There are 1 001 reasons offered for this failing, none of which should cut any ice with someone genuinely interested in results.

We have taken a trip down the dark side of counselling life. There are many people who will abuse you in counselling for many different reasons. Fortunately most of them are not all in your workplace at the same time. If they do abuse you, stamp on them fast and hard. This is not the kind of counselling fairy story you could read about in most counselling books. This is the real world. If you think I'm being too harsh, you might like to know that the average time before burn-out for mental health professionals is between five and seven years. The turnover of staff is enormous – much higher than in other professions. You now know why. On the plus-side most of your staff will benefit from your counselling and will be entirely honourable and grateful for your help.

17

COUNSELLING FOR COMMON PROBLEMS

The most common problems as they actually occur in the workplace – rather than as they are perceived to occur – come in the following order:

1 Relationship problems
2 Family and marital problems
3 Pregnancy
4 Career development/block/change worries
5 Stress and anxiety
6 Lack of support
7 Lack of confidence/self-esteem/happiness
8 Bereavement
9 Depression.

The following, although they have a socially high profile, present much less often. That is not to say that they have less impact on the sufferers – their impact is often devastating. Perhaps that explains why, although these problems occur less frequently, they receive disproportionate publicity:

- Redundancy, retirement, redeployment, organizational change
- Financial problems
- Illness and disability
- Sexual harassment
- Other forms of harassment and discrimination – race, disability, sexual preference
- Violence at work
- Domestic violence
- Disciplinary issues
- Drug, alcohol and other dependency problems.

You will have good indications of a problem occurring when you see detrimental changes in:

- input performance – effort in
- output performance – results out
- relationships
- punctuality
- attendance
- attitude.

EXERCISE

List other cues that might indicate the occurrence of a problem.

Relationship problems

The most common problem in the workplace is with other people. Most people would take that as read, but few would be able to pinpoint the causes of problems. What are the possible causes?

- failure to listen to or to communicate with the other party
- misunderstanding or miscommunication with the other party
- possession of conflicting objectives (overt or covert)
- differing perspectives/understanding of the issues under debate
- different values, beliefs, standards of integrity, expectations of performance ...
- mutually incompatible core needs (those needs which are so important that they cannot be compromised)
- habitual disposition by virtue of personality, or job requirements.

The obvious remedy to each of the above is to encourage the parties to:

- listen to or communicate with each other
- identify and clarify the misunderstanding or miscommunication with the other party
- reveal all motives/objectives and seek a resolution or, ideally, a means of cooperating
- learn about and acknowledge the other's right to hold a differing perspective or understanding of the issues under debate
- acknowledge the variety of different values, beliefs, standards of integrity, expectations of performance – and agree to accommodate each other's preferences as much as possible
- manage mutually incompatible core needs (those needs which are so important they cannot be compromised) with mutual tolerance and an agreement to keep a distance from each other

- examine which parts of the personality and job requirement habit patterns are essential and which are open to modification (in both parties).

The most useful skill with which you can equip those having relationship problems is conflict anticipation, prevention and resolution skills. For more information on managing conflicts and relationship problems see *Coaching and Mentoring*, pp. 227–34.

Family and marital problems

There is a large overlap between relationship problems and family and marital problems. Families are far from the ideal environments they are often made out to be. In fact, they can be more accurately characterized as a perpetual problem creation and solution unit. The creation and solution link works well so long as communication is good. However, small problems escalate into crises when communication stops, is impaired or otherwise blocked (for the reasons mentioned above). But, as we have said, there is rarely any merit in analysing successful outcomes. So, what are the ingredients of successful marriages and relationships? What do people who have successful marriages/intimate relationships do that others don't? They:

- express affection verbally, materially, physically and sexually
- express appreciation and admiration
- express their real self
- offer each other emotional support
- accept demands and tolerate character flaws
- share time alone together and common interests
- are interested in the other's individual interests
- work at keeping the relationship interesting.

With some (obvious) changes, this list can be amended to describe the nature of a successful relationship between any family members, or indeed between any two people. In the past, how have you successfully resolved your relationship and family problems?

Pregnancy

Pregnancy in itself is not a problem (if it is wanted), but it can create problems beyond the usual sickness and fatigue. Having to take maternity leave is a disturbing event. It is like being temporarily and involuntarily redeployed, with all the insecurity and concerns that triggers: 'Will my job be secure, in my absence? Will things have been changed or reorganized by the time I get back? Will my absence be abused by others in all sorts of possible ways?'

That's just the tip of the iceberg. There are also worries about health, the baby's health, strains on the marriage (if there is one) and so on. If the pregnancy is unwanted or unexpected and the staff member is anti-abortion, the issue becomes even more stressful. A female counsellor who has had a pregnancy/baby while at work is the ideal person to counsel such a problem. Yes, that is sexist, but first-hand experience is more important to the client than political correctness. If the staff member is pro-abortion and planning one, there are specialist counsellors who can help. Your role should be one of secondary, non-specialist counsellor. Someone to support a colleague who has taken a very painful decision with extremely serious consequences.

Career problems

Career block

Career block is the term which applies to those who are ready to take on more responsibilities but who are prevented from growing because there is no vacant position for them to move into. The less likelihood there is of a position becoming available in the foreseeable future, the more severe will be the reaction. Typical feelings and reactions include: frustration, anger, understimulation, stagnation, apathy, a drop in performance standards, a desire to leave and a desire to create stimulation (by such devices as self-sabotage, troublemaking, political game-playing and so on).

The reaction to a career block may not always be negative. Some view a career block as a cue to take a rest from strenuous effort. They make a conscious decision to take it easy for a while until the possibility of a vacancy makes itself visible.

Career ceiling

Becoming aware that you have reached the height of your powers and are facing the possibility of doing the same job at the same level until retirement is not a comfortable experience. Counselling a person in this situation can take on several forms depending on what the client wishes. As a rule, you should follow the normal counselling sequence. Some common feelings in this situation include: depression, hopelessness, apathy, drop in self-esteem, drop in standards reflective of someone no longer striving for advancement, 'mid-life crisis', desire to leave, desire to change career, denial (attributing ceiling to poor management by one's bosses, to company structure or to industry type), desire to re-enter education to raise one's potential and envy of those who have potential still to exploit.

As before, not all people who reach their career ceiling react negatively. Many people are pleased; they know they don't have to push themselves as

Career ceiling

hard as they used to. Some people only start to really enjoy life when they reach this point. But, from a commercial point of view, that can be the worst possible reaction.

Stress and anxiety

The most difficult part of counselling for stress is persuading the client to recognize and admit it. There are all sorts of macho and political reasons for not wishing to admit to being a sufferer of stress. Your challenging and confrontation skills will be well tested with the average stress client. Once you can encourage them to admit the problem, the remedy is fairly straightforward.

Stress is experienced by those who perceive a mismatch between the challenge they face and their ability to cope. It is more usually associated with challenges beyond our control. Those within our control are perceived as exhilarating. Stress can have its roots in both overload and underload.

Stress is best identified by a range of pointers, the more of which are present and the further down the list the pointers occur the more 'stressed-out' the victim is:

- frustration
- refusal to turn down work, spending less time with friends and family
- taking work home
- blaming others for failures
- expressing strong feelings of fatigue
- irritability
- poor time management
- reduced work output
- increased work hours input
- taking on commitments which clearly cannot be honoured
- expressions of discontentment, anger, resentment, apathy and guilt
- emerging signs of emotional distance
- extreme and visible fatigue
- taking extreme positions over minor issues
- alcohol or other substance abuse
- regular and/or prolonged absence from work
- regular physical illnesses
- refusal to communicate with others
- voluntary or involuntary isolation from former colleagues
- emerging strange behaviours.

Stress can be managed or prevented using several tools ranging from rational approaches – such as encouraging the client to ignore the stressors they cannot control and tackle those they can or to choose to take total control of what they can control (namely, thoughts, beliefs, attitudes, feelings and behaviours) – through to practical approaches – such as recommending they take time out; discussing a change of role; providing more control over their work and so on. For more detail refer to *Coaching and Mentoring*, pp. 169–80.

Lack of support

Data from exit interviews reveal that a feeling that support is not being offered is the most common reason cited for leaving a job. First-rate managers would never allow a member of their team to feel unsupported, and, if such a complaint was raised, he or she would immediately take steps to rectify the problem. In short, this one is down to you. Do what is required to support your staff member, or be prepared for an uncomfortable discussion with your superiors after the exit interview report.

Lack of confidence/self-esteem/happiness

Confidence, self-esteem and happiness are very closely linked. Do you remember the three irrational beliefs held by well-adjusted people? Fortunately there are many more ways in which you can make yourself happy.

Guidelines for confidence, self-esteem and happiness

- Choose to be happy; make happiness a goal; see happiness as an active rather than a passive event.
- Do those things which make you happy.
- Take responsibility for your own confidence, self-esteem and happiness levels.
- Think positively and avoid thinking negatively.
- Do what is known to lead to success (see page 75).
- Help others and help others to be happy and confident.
- Arrange your values in such a way that it is easy to be happy/confident.
- Arrange your values in such a way that it is difficult to be unhappy or lacking in confidence.
- Have as few 'musts' as possible.
- Adopt those beliefs which lead to happiness, confidence, high self-esteem.
- Discard those beliefs which make you unhappy, unconfident, lacking in self-esteem.
- Think and believe you are happy and you will be happy.
- Your mind will prove what you wish it to – wish it to prove you are happy and confident.
- Count your blessings.
- Make affirmations of happiness, confidence, self-esteem.
- Make positive statements about yourself to yourself.
- Eliminate anything from your life which makes you unhappy and unconfident.
- Forgive others for their wrongdoings (but remember to protect yourself in the future).
- View problems positively – problems usually occur if you are striving to achieve something.
- Use imagery regularly to picture yourself being confident and happy.
- Share your positive thoughts and feelings with others.
- Express gratitude to others for their contribution to the world.
- Keep depressive and negative people out of your life.
- Draw inspiration from the millions of people who maintain their happiness, confidence and self-esteem while experiencing the most appalling conditions, illnesses or disabilities.
- Resolve to be happy/confident *now* – not tomorrow, next week, after your next promotion or payrise, after you are married/divorced, after you have kids, after the kids are at school, after the kids have left home ... after, after, after. Be happy now, not in the after-zone.
- Remember that *you* are the only person who can make you happy and confident, and *now* is the only time you can be happy and confident.

Add to this list the other things you can do to make yourself happy. Teach your clients these principles. Help your staff to practise the skills of happiness management.

Bereavement

Bereavement is something which will affect every member of staff. They may grieve over something as profound as the loss of a partner or other close relatives, or experience sadness for something as common as lost youth, missed opportunities and missed promotions. Grief is a deep and profound emotional pain in response to the loss of something or someone highly valued. The grief process follows a fairly predictable pattern:

- denial
- depression
- acceptance
- recovery
- post–recovery.

The first stage, denial, is usually characterized by a combination of shock and various manifestations of attempts to deny or psychologically minimize the loss. In the depression phase, there is a degree of letting go and a deep and profound sense of sadness at having to do so. In the acceptance phase, the worst of the pain is over and a period of discovery of the new self (without the person or object of loss) begins. In the recovery phase full and normal functioning gradually returns. In post-recovery, the client is able to look at the loss without feeling overemotional about it. The loss, and the learning experiences deriving from it, have become part of them; they have integrated the loss.

Other phenomena also occur in the grief cycle, but affect fewer people. Some people will go into shock in response to a loss. After the initial shock some go on to display a panic reaction. After the denial phase, some experience either anger or guilt, and sometimes both. Some people come out of the depression stage by entering into some kind of bargain with whatever spiritual values/entity they believe in. Such bargaining can also be witnessed occurring during a panic reaction.

Your role as counsellor to a person suffering grief is to listen, listen, listen. Be aware of what phases they are likely to experience. You need, for your own good, to understand what is happening to the person in front of you. Explaining the grief cycle will be of no use. Comments like 'you'll get over it' are equally unhelpful. Listen and make it clear that you are there to listen and support; that you are prepared to be with them when they cry, when they express anger at the unfairness of the loss, when they plead with the world not to let this happen. Most people feel extremely uncomfortable with someone in grief. So much so that they offer help, then promptly disappear. Most people express their condolences and make it clear that they don't want to talk about the loss in anything other than in the most superficial terms. If you, as a counsellor, make it clear that you are prepared to genuinely listen you will be, with that act alone, doing more good than all the condolences the world can offer.

Some people in grief may wish you to help with the practicalities of the loss. Others will see those tasks as part of the mourning process, and insist that they do them. Help your client go through the grief cycle in whatever way they wish. How does this advice compare to your own experience of grief?

Depression

Depression is manifested by the following:

- withdrawal
- social isolation
- a negative view of the world and/or people
- apathy
- lethargy
- lack of hope for, or faith in, anything
- lack of facial or vocal expression
- reduced level of physical activity – all physical actions appearing to take great effort
- lethargic dismissal of all suggestions for improving the situation as useless.

Resist the temptation to explore cause, unless you quickly discover there is a recent loss of some kind in the client's life. Why? Because it is virtually impossible to determine. But more importantly, in this case, attempting to explore further exposes the client to the myriad factors which they feel are making them depressed. The most useful skills depressed people can learn are how to reward themselves and how to gain approval and reward from the environment. Some of the other skills depressed people usually lack can be found on page 79 in Chapter 6.

Redundancy, retirement, redeployment and organizational change

Redundancy

Many people have their whole sense of identity linked with their work role. Common feelings in those being made redundant include: betrayal, anger, resentment, fear, insecurity, low self-esteem, a sense of victimization and loss of identity. These feelings are made more intense when the client knows (as is frequently the case in business) that it is they, and not the job, which is being made redundant (this might be against UK law, but we are dealing with the realities here).

What are the objectives of redundancy counselling?

1   To help the person cope with the news:

  - to help them express their feelings
  - to help them separate thought from feeling and regain clarity of thought.

2   To help them cope with the usual change of identity experienced in redundancy:

  - to help them cope with the anxieties of letting an old identity go
  - to help them manage the insecurities and feelings of inadequacy experienced in taking on a new identity.

3   To help them find an alternative source of income:

  - to help them decide what kind of alternatives they wish to explore
  - to help them with resources for job-seeking
  - to help them with job-seeking skills (self-marketing, interview skills and so on).

In Western culture many people derive their sense of worth and identity from their work. Their work is the vehicle through which they feel involved in and important to society. Refer to the list of factors which denote healthy adjustment (page 75) and you will see that many of them are work-related. Take someone's work away and you make a great hole in their life. Commercial reality dictates the necessity of redundancy as a survival tool for the greater good. If you have to do it, you have to do it. Naturally, as the consummate professional you are, you will do it as effectively and as compassionately as possible. You will not forget that your decision is going to massively disrupt someone's life. Neither will you allow that awareness to tempt you to shirk your responsibilities. You don't want your remaining staff to lose faith in you by hearing that you weren't big enough to look after a previously loyal member of staff. You might be tempted to remove the departing staff member from the premises immediately in the hope that news will not spread. Don't kid yourself; people who work together also socialize together, at least occasionally. All it takes is a telephone call and your story about 'a compassionate and thorough redundancy counselling session' is blown along with your trustworthiness.

But, again, such news is not gloom and doom for everyone. Some people will be delighted at being made redundant. It gives them a reason to leave a job they hate and they are paid for doing so – can't be bad! Delighted they may be, but your other staff will be watching (directly or down the telephone line) and they need to know that you support people in what they perceive to be a difficult situation. If you have ever been made redundant spend a few minutes remembering your fears, concerns and feelings at the time. If you have had no experience of redundancy, ask a friend who has about how it feels: you will understand your clients better with the information.

Survivor syndrome

After a redundancy programme, many remaining staff members will feel vulnerable and insecure and even angry. They know their workload is going to be changed or increased in the reorganization which follows. They will be wondering if it will be them next. They will be feeling betrayed – you did, after all, make loyal people redundant. They are loyal – or at least they were until the redundancy programme – but it is clearly everyone for themselves now. Offer your survivors counselling and other support. Feelings will run much deeper than those just mentioned. They will need support, and there are many good specialist agencies providing precisely that plus other 'outplacement services'. If you have not been made redundant, the chances are you have been a survivor. List your concerns, fears and worries from memory.

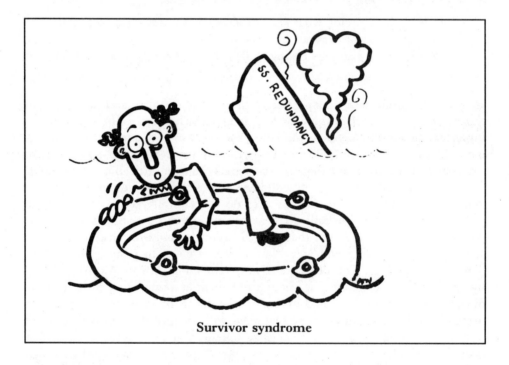

Survivor syndrome

Retirement

Retirement is a mixed bag. We know that people who sit around doing nothing usually die soon after retirement. Why? Because, to paraphrase a rather old book, 'Without purpose the people will perish' or, in other words, 'Without individual purpose, individuals perish.' Those who engage in purposeful activity are much more likely to thrive and survive in old age. Some look forward to, and cherish, retirement. Others view it as fixed-date redundancy with the level of impact redundancy usually has.

Common concerns that people have about retiring are as follows:

- Health   deterioration worries
- Income   substantial decrease
- Social life   removal of work-based social life
- Purpose   removal of prime purpose
- Status   loss of position and identity in society
- Prejudice   worries about society's prejudice against older people.

You may want to remind any of your staff who are approaching retirement that there are innumerable positive aspects to retired life.

EXERCISE

Compile a list of benefits offered by retirement.

Redeployment

Being moved around within a company may seem easy enough, but it is almost as stress-inducing as being made redundant. It involves the loss of work colleagues, facing the feelings of insecurity and inadequacy that taking on a new role and new peers creates. It creates feelings of loss of control, feelings of helplessness, fear of the new role, fear of being set up for redundancy, fear of being put into an impossible job with a view to instigating dismissal proceedings for incompetence. If you think any of these feelings reflect a paranoid disposition, you have not lived in the real world for very long. Many of the fears and concerns in redeployment apply to survivors of a redundancy.

Organizational change

Similar feelings and fears emerge in those people on the receiving end of organizational change as exist in those people being redeployed. They include feelings of suspicion and helplessness, loss of colleagues ... as above.

Financial problems

It is not your business to involve yourself with your staff's financial affairs since, as their manager, it puts you in a conflict-of-interest position. However, you can listen to their concerns and understand the problem, help them reframe their understanding of the problem and seek solutions. Seek outside expertise in debt and financial counselling.

Illness and disability

There may be little you can do for such problems other than support the person and keep in regular telephone contact. You can listen, you can give the staff member an opportunity to air their frustrations, sense of loss, anxieties and so on. Counsel at home or in hospital if necessary. You can make arrangements to allow the person to carry on working in some capacity if they want to, during their recovery. If the problem is permanent, you can alter the working environment to allow them to continue. In the age of sophisticated communication technology, you could even make it possible for the person to work from home.

Sexual harassment

This area is a minefield. The situation has not been helped by some successful, overzealous prosecutions against people whose behaviour would be considered natural and expected in any other environment. However, don't let that cloud your judgement of complaints, many of which are entirely genuine. You may be approached by the complainant for the purposes of registering and actioning a formal complaint. Or you may be approached with a view to counselling prior to taking any action, or with a view to resolving the situation without taking action. You have roles here of both counsellor and investigator. Not a comfortable or viable position. Separate the roles. Have someone else in the organization take one of the roles.

Other forms of harassment and discrimination – race, disability, sexual preference

Racial harassment is slowly declining, at least in multicultural cities all over the world. However, in rural areas worldwide, racism is still at the levels reported in medieval times. Your role here, too, could be a dual one. You are both the person who would initiate action and the person who will counsel both the alleged victim and alleged offender, and, again, you should separate the roles. The word 'alleged' is very significant. You will very rarely be able to prove whether the complainant is genuine or malicious.

Disability harassment and discrimination is much more universal. Amongst the well-educated it is much more mild but is still nonetheless present. Most companies employ no disabled people whatsoever. It may never be expressed, but it is a widely practised and accepted discrimination.

Discrimination and harassment on the grounds of sexual preference is still common in virtually every society worldwide.

The more civilized societies have some kind of anti-discrimination legislation to cover the above problems. Nevertheless, the determined perpetrator can always find ways of harassing or discriminating against those whose level of ability or sexuality is different from theirs.

EXERCISE

What forms of discrimination have you experienced? If none, speak to some people who have in order to gain a better understanding. If you are not prepared to do so, do not counsel victims of discrimination.

Violence at work

Violence, or the threat of it, is more common than you might imagine. The more male-dominated and working-class the culture, the more likely you are to have to counsel this kind of problem. Paradoxically, the more likely it is to occur, the less likely the victims are to report it or seek help for it; the potential reprisals are feared to the extent that it is usually easier to leave the company. You may then find yourself being sued for failing to provide a safe workplace or for condoning the practice (it won't be the first case of its kind and it certainly won't be the last).

Domestic violence

This is yet another minefield. Most usually, the victim feels trapped and unable to leave the perpetrator. Refer the client to one of several specialist agencies who can offer support.

Disciplinary issues

A member of staff who is being disciplined for some wrongdoing can be counselled by following the STM. That is, by equipping them with the skills to ensure there is no repetition.

Drug, alcohol and other dependency problems

You might imagine we are talking about illegal narcotics here. Not necessarily so. Caffeine and tobacco addiction can cause serious problems at work. Caffeine, despite what most people believe, impairs judgement quite markedly. What? Yes, it is true. It gives the illusion of mental alertness, but actually produces so much stimulation that clarity of thought is dramatically impaired.

Other drugs produce similar consequences for their own biochemical reasons. Even chocolate addiction can, like most addictions, produce dramatic mood swings, irregular behaviour, variation in attitude, extremes of performance and physical changes. These changes are common to most addictions.

Performance appraisal

It may seem improbable that you could use your counselling skills during performance appraisal sessions, but this is an experience that even the most robust of people find anxiety-inducing. They are presenting themselves for evaluation by someone they admire and respect or someone they hate and have to tolerate. Either way they are involuntarily presenting themselves for evaluation by someone whose opinion matters to their future. Not to be a little apprehensive would be asinine. The use of your counselling skills, as and when they are required, will make your performance appraisal sessions much more effective. Some possible and common thoughts and feelings in your staff that may require the help of your counselling skills are: insecurity, fear of criticism, fear of emotional hostility, fear of career blight, fear of unjust evaluation, fear of expressing genuine feelings, envy of others' performance, resentment that disliked others are being held up as an example of high-level performance, resentment that the real high performers are not being recognized, fear that political factors come before performance fairness, failure to acknowledge the realities of poor performance, failure to take responsibility for poor performance, failure to agree a course of action to rectify a poor standard of performance and so on.

EXERCISE

Define what you would like your boss to do to make your appraisals less stressful.

Life stage problems

Many of the problems you counsel will have their origins in life stage changes. Each stage needs its own skills profile to manage it successfully. Some changes are highly significant, while others are insignificant but have strong emotional impact. For example, the appearance of one's first grey hairs may be a physically trivial, but emotionally significant, experience ... Oh, stuff the emotion – where are the tweezers?

An overview of the principal life stages will help you understand your clients:

Family stages

Life phase	Changes	Identity
Late childhood	'I'm right, they're wrong.' Seeking independence	'I'm me'
Young adult	'Eek, that's responsibility.' Becoming adult	'Hey, that other me is nice.'
Adult	'Best get on with it.' Foundation building	Me + me = We From we, to we plus new mes

Mid-adult	'Hold on, what's this? I'm 40!'	Wee mes become big mes
	Real world 101	Goodbye to parents
Late adult	'Who's that wrinkly in the mirror?'	Bye, bye big mes, hello again we
Very late	Sell-by date approaches	Tee, hee the big mes have little mes
Overdue	'Come in no. 1, your time is up!'	Bye me, bye me.

Career stages

Career phase	Changes/decisions	Expression
Exploration	'I know what I'll do.' 'No, I don't, yes I do.'	'What's out there?'
First attempts	'Hey, let us try this!'	'Teach me.'
Stability and commitment	'Now let's get serious.'	'Here we go. Today the world, tomorrow ... '
Realistic ambitions	'Oops. Great. Oops.'	'OK, so I'm human!'
Mid-career	Time to pass it on	'Hey, I'll teach you.'
Peak of responsibility	'Let's keep it going.'	'Let's protect this baby.'
Late career	'OK, your turn now.'	'Take good care of my baby.'
Retirement	'Wow, all this free time ... '	'Let's use it wisely – voluntary service.'

EXERCISE

Write down what thoughts and feelings people will experience in the transition between each of the above stages.

Summary

As you have probably gathered, we had only a 'bare essentials' look at the most common problems. You can't hope to be an expert on all the problems listed. But you can expect to do enough to help the person with the workplace implications of their problem. And you can certainly do more now than you could before.

18

FINAL CONCLUSIONS

Anyone can provide counselling. In fact virtually everyone does in some form or another. Most well-adjusted people have a lifetime's experience of receiving and providing counselling. Long years of training are not required to be a successful counsellor/manager. Indeed, as we have seen, that may be counterproductive. Before you read this book you were probably unaware of just how extensive your existing counselling skills and experiences were. Certainly you lacked the theoretical knowledge and the jargon of the 'professionals', but you had the skills nonetheless. Now you are familiar with much of the jargon and also have the confidence earned from the acquisition of knowledge. Hopefully, you will also have the confidence gained from knowing you have a range of powerful tools at your disposal. At your disposal you have the eight common principles if you want to keep your counselling simple, and the eight-stage model and the Skills Training Model if you want to carry out more sophisticated and commercially-focused counselling.

There are many different approaches to counselling. As you now know, the differences between counselling approaches are irrelevant. What matters – and what determines effectiveness – is what they have in common. The common principles delivered with any technique you choose will achieve beneficial results. For your purposes as a manager, you should follow the common principles in a way that has added benefits – in a commercially relevant way that equips clients with skills they previously did not have or use properly.

Since the causes of problems are impossible to determine, and since you don't have time to look for them anyway, we should counsel in a way that equips clients with solutions as quickly, cheaply and effectively as possible. That way is by using the Skills Training Model.

This book is entitled *Counselling for Managers*. It is also designed to give you everything you need to help you become a 'manager who is for counselling'.

For counselling, because of all the performance management benefits it can bring. For counselling, because it can be fruitful and fun.

Enjoy your counselling as much as you can; enjoy its benefits even more.

Appendices

APPENDIX I

SOME PROBLEM CAUSES

As we stated earlier, it is impossible to determine with any accuracy the causal pattern of any emotional problem. That, as we have seen, does not prevent the majority of mental health professionals offering 'cures' which are based on the premise of a particular cause. The arrogance of their position is amazing; first they assume they can identify a cause and, second, they deem by default that that is the cause of most disorders. I say 'by default' because none of the many therapies or counselling methods I have studied have been humble enough to specify which cases they are unable to help. It is a testimony to the human search for certainty in an uncertain world that anyone, let alone so-called 'professionals', could be duped into believing such a claim. But, in fairness to those people, the pressures to follow such a line are enormous: not only do they need to satisfy their own need for certainty, they also must satisfy their bosses' need to feel that their underlings know what they are doing and, probably most powerfully, their clients' demand for an explanation for their condition.

You, too, will be subjected to those pressures. So, although you can never know if you are right, you will need to provide some explanations for a client's problem. We have already given you the skills explanation. Here is a further menu from which you can choose. Choose wisely; choose your proposed cause on the basis of its plausibility for that client in that context, on its relevance to them, their background, position, knowledge, beliefs, expectations and so on. And choose your proposed causes on the basis also of how credibly you are able to offer such explanations:

- Inappropriate skills being used for a situation
- Poorly learned skills being used in the right situation
- Lack of skills (including those above)
- Holding harmful beliefs (including those below)
- Applying beliefs inappropriately to a situation
- Incomplete beliefs causing confusion/ambivalence in a range of situations

- Work/life overload
- Work/life underload
- Chemically-induced stress (caffeine and so on)
- Dietary imbalance
- Problem developed to achieve the long-term ends for which it was intended
- Problem developed to gain some specific short-term aim
- Failure to live in the present – paying too much attention to future needs
- Stress, which causes different long-term symptoms in different people
- Failure to express emotions causing build-up of stress levels
- Anti-emotionality
- Failing to communicate with people who are seen as causing a problem
- Holding on to particular feelings (for whatever objective)
- Posture-related problems causing stomach pains which are then misattributed to stress
- Posture-related problems causing a wide range of problems which are misattributed to other causes
- Misattribution of cause and effect – for example, blaming the boss for stress levels instead of poor relaxation skills
- Sexual problems affecting social interaction and vice versa
- Inflexibility of belief and value structure – holding onto beliefs that were appropriate in one time and place and are inappropriate in a different time and place
- Overpowering need for truth and purity of motive
- Inaccurate attributions about the rhythm of life (feeling relaxed is misinterpreted as being depressed)
- Refusing to allow the rhythm of life to flow freely
- Maladaptive life style – smoking, drinking, burning the candle at both ends, not taking exercise and so on
- Lack of life knowledge
- Inappropriately learned automatic responses to cues/stimuli
- Inappropriate vicariously learned thoughts, beliefs, feelings and so on (for example, being frightened of spiders in a country which has no poisonous spiders because one or both of their parents were so afflicted)
- Learned helplessness – tie a string to the foot of a baby elephant and the same string will restrain a full-grown adult
- Moral problems – overzealous moral/religious education (which is implicated in a large percentage of mental health problems)
- Learned attribution patterns (along internal–external, global–specific, stable–unstable dimensions)
- Too many life changes in a short period of time
- Traumatic events
- Excessive self-criticism – insufficient self-stroking
- Self-valuation rules set at too high a standard to be fulfilled
- Self-valuation rules set at too high a standard to enable sufficient self-stroking (we all need about 10–12 positive emotional experiences per day to be happy – all can be provided internally or externally)

- Lack of rewarding feedback from the environment – either by inability to obtain, or by inability to seek, strokes or by unavailability of strokes from a hostile or indifferent environment
- Refusal to accept that strokes are genuinely given, or that the source of the strokes gives them any value
- Sarcastic or hostile environment
- Inability to let go of control occasionally
- Lack of fit between the skills required in the environment and the skills possessed by the person
- Too wide self-esteem gap – that is, the gap between the ideal self and actual self is uncomfortably large
- Social rejection – for any number of reasons (facial appearance, personal hygiene, accent and so on)
- Seeking entry into inappropriate social groupings (too high or too low)
- Social rejection from lack of willingness to engage in normal social deceit and white lie telling
- Perceptions of control over environment either too great or too little
- Perceptions that control over the environment extends beyond actual skill levels
- The pursuit of inappropriate or unrealistic goals (for example, a disabled 60-year-old seeking to be an astronaut)
- Insisting that decisions are for life (staying in a marriage which is harmful to all parties)
- The frequent making of negative, self-fulfilling prophecies
- Continual avoidance of reality – too much escapism
- Too other-directed to know themselves
- Too other-interested to attend to their own needs – typified by parents whose children have just left home and now experiencing long periods of depression and aimlessness
- Too other-reward-dependent to know themselves
- Living up to (or down to) one's expectations of oneself
- Fear of something – preoccupation with that something making it more likely
- Fear of the actions which are known by the client to be the solution they need
- Learned avoidance of situations which is now impossible to maintain
- Learned commission of a behaviour which is now impossible to commit.

APPENDIX II

COMMON IRRATIONAL BELIEFS AND OTHER DANGEROUS THOUGHTS

Irrational beliefs

There are a number of beliefs which are commonly held and are very damaging to the mental health of all concerned. They are:

- that one is responsible for other people's emotions
- that one should be able to control everything in life
- that beliefs, thoughts, emotions and behaviours are beyond one's control
- that one should be able to do and cope with anything
- that one should be able to explain everything
- that others can hurt one emotionally
- that others control your self-esteem
- that one should be loved by everyone
- that one's happiness is externally caused
- that perfect solutions are available and required for every problem
- that threats and possible disasters should be constantly dwelt on
- that one's history controls one's present and future
- that others' history controls their present and future
- that one should be dependent on others.

In short, any belief that disempowers the self is irrational.

Dangerous thoughts

Some thoughts/behaviours which are involved either in causing or maintaining problems are:

- seeking perfection rather than acceptable results
- catastrophizing – extremizing
- reading too much into normal bodily changes/reactions
- excessive consciousness of what others think
- self-deprecation (above and beyond humour)
- focusing on defeats rather than victories
- focusing on negatives rather than positives
- focusing on the future or past to the exclusion of here and now
- demanding that one must ...
- demanding that one should ...
- imposing undue emotional significance upon a problem thereby making it more difficult to solve
- believing that 'all' or 'always' is the case when only 'some' or 'sometimes' is true
- believing something on the basis of very limited or selected evidence
- overstating a position, problem, or difficulty
- justifying a flawed argument/stance with a complex analysis/rationale
- avoiding confronting a problem or some undesirable part of oneself because it is too complex or painful
- supporting conclusions with irrelevant evidence
- avoiding solving a problem because the alternative is wrongly perceived as being less palatable than the problem
- choosing a problem because it is perceived as the mid-point between two other problems
- choosing a belief/behaviour based on flawed premises
- resolving problems by opting for one of the extremes rather than one of the many possibilities in between
- failing to resolve a problem by using the factual conflict between solutions to deem them the same
- failing to seek a solution because the problem can't be defined
- accepting a problem because other high-status individuals have it
- failing to act on a problem because it is thought to be understood on the basis of having been labelled – for example, dyslexia
- failing to tackle a problem because 'even the experts don't understand it'
- continuing a problem because some expert says it's alright to behave like that
- justifying a problem because it is associated with favourable other factors
- seeking reassurance from others that a problem does not exist by presenting the issue in favourable terms
- avoiding a problem by twisting received wisdom – 'we all have problems'
- balancing the pros and cons of a problem to justify taking no action.

APPENDIX III

STAGES OF ACCEPTANCE IN PROBLEM RESOLUTION

- Accept that others have solved/coped with this problem in the past.
- Accept personal responsibility for solving/coping with the problem.
- Accept that you obtain positive and negative rewards from the problem.
- Accept that you obtain pains and pleasures from the problem.
- Accept that there is one point in which all desires and efforts to solve/cope with the problem reach a 'commitment point'.
- Accept personal responsibility for getting to this decision point.
- Accept that some of your behaviour contributes to/exacerbates the problem.
- Accept that the way you feel about the problem may exacerbate it.
- Accept that the way you think about the problem may exacerbate it.
- Accept that you can control the way you behave.
- Accept that you can control what you feel.
- Accept that you can control what you think.
- Accept that you can control the way you believe.
- Accept that you can control the way you behave in relation to the problem.
- Accept that you can control what you feel in relation to the problem.
- Accept that you can control what you think in relation to the problem.
- Accept that you can control the way you believe in relation to the problem.
- Accept that what you believe determines what you think.
- Accept that what you think determines what you feel.
- Accept that what you feel determines how you act/react.
- Accept that how you act/react determines the results you obtain/how others act/react towards you.
- Accept that, by analysing your motives towards solving your problem, you can find ways of enhancing your desire to find/devise a solution.
- Accept that, by analysing the barriers against you solving the problem, you can find ways of overcoming them.

- Accept that certain beliefs you hold may be disempowering and may maintain, worsen or even cause the problem.
- Accept that your beliefs may at least partially be presenting barriers to you finding an acceptable solution.
- Accept that you can hold empowering beliefs if you want to.
- Accept that human beings can always find a rationale for holding any belief they wish.
- Accept that you can adopt empowering beliefs if you create sufficiently strong reasons for doing so.
- Accept that there are strong experiences in your past which you can use as the basis for your new belief.
- Accept that using certain words can maintain, worsen or even cause your problem.
- Accept that certain words can dramatically change your perception of any problem.
- Accept that, by using empowering words to think about your problem, you can change your perception of the problem.
- Accept that certain events can change your perception of your problem in an instant.
- Accept that you can create events in your mind at any time you choose.
- Accept that you can create events in your mind deliberately to change your perceptions.
- Accept that you can change your mental state in an instant by choosing what to think.
- Accept that you can develop a system whereby you can change the way you feel in an instant.
- Accept that you can make the use of this system habitual and automatic.
- Accept that certain things/thoughts/activities make you happy.
- Accept that engaging in these activities will lift your spirits.
- Accept that you can use those activities/thoughts/things to take control of your happiness.
- Accept that by creating a list of activities that make you happy, that you can do any time, you can be happy any time you choose.
- Accept that your problem may resurface unless you take ongoing maintenance/prevention measures.
- Accept that you have responsibility to maintain your freedom from the problem.
- Accept that you either control the problem or the problem will control you.
- Accept that, if the pain of having the problem becomes greater than its benefits, you will change.
- Accept that, if you take measures to make the pain intolerable, you will change.
- Accept that, if the pleasure of changing becomes stronger than staying as you are, you will change.
- Accept that, if you make the pleasure of having changed stronger than the pleasure of staying as you are, you will change.

- Accept that the costs of not changing now are enormous.
- Accept that the benefits of changing now are enormous.
- Accept that you are ready to change now.
- Accept that you are permanently changed for the better.

APPENDIX IV

ADDITIONAL COUNSELLING TOOLS

Counter-attitudinal advocacy When people are asked to argue for a case which they would have preferred to have argued against, their views change. They adopt a less extreme position towards their previous stance and move towards the position for which they were requested to argue. Experienced counsellors use this phenomenon to great effect: 'I know you could never believe that you are responsible for the way you feel, but what would you expect me to say are the benefits of taking responsibility for believing that?' or 'OK, so it looks as though John's attitude toward you caused the row. What do you think John would say caused the row?'

Role play This technique has as many applications as you can imagine. For instance, it can be used to give your client a great opportunity to express how they really feel while using the role as a disguise. Alternatively it can be used to enable your client to see the world through the eyes of whoever they play.

Role rehearsal An excellent means of getting your clients to practise a new role they wish to adopt in a particular situation.

Provision of achievable tasks Gives a sense of achievement and of control – boosts self-esteem.

Defining life goals Gives purpose.

Reciprocal inhibition No one can experience two competing emotions at the same time. Inviting the client to engage in relaxation, for instance, makes it very difficult for them to experience anxiety.

Shaping A gradual changing of one behaviour to another by a series of small steps, each of which is rewarded.

Flooding/extinction/repertoire exhaustion Engaging in an undesired behaviour until the willingness and ability to continue it are exhausted.

Behaviour rehearsal The practice of any behaviour which is desired.

Vicarious learning instruction Learning by watching or listening to others.

Attention switching Moving attention from an undesired to a desired focus.

Thought stopping Blocking an undesired thought with a particular word – 'STOP'.

Thought substitution Substituting one desired thought pattern for one undesired.

Self-reinforcement/self-stroking Self-praise to boost self-confidence and self-esteem.

Inhibition factors unmasking Identifying and addressing the factors which are causing the client to be inhibited about any particular course of action.

Bodily feedback If you stand erect and confidently, you soon feel erect and confident. Ask your clients to adopt the physical pose that reflects the feelings they want to have.

Indirect suggestion A very subtle but highly effective technique: 'Our mutual boss would be very disappointed if we failed to resolve this problem.'

Hysterical counterwill Inviting the client to do something when you know they will do the exact opposite. Your intention is to have them do the very thing they end up doing. Most useful with deliberately obstructive clients (yes, they exist).

Relaxation and suggestion Helping the client to accept suggestions they know are good for them by inviting them to relax and self-suggest.

Permission giving Sometimes clients come to counselling just to get permission to do something most people would see as their right to do anyway.

Bibliotherapy People who read motivational material are better adjusted, happier and more successful than those who do not. Recommend to your client a few motivational texts, and perhaps even keep some specifically for lending.

BIBLIOGRAPHY

Alexander, F. (1950), *Psychosomatic Medicine*, New York: Norton.

Alexander, F., French, T.M. and Pollock, G.H. (1968), *Psychosomatic Specificity*, Chicago: Univ. Chicago Press.

Arowson, E., Turner, V. and Carlsmith, M. (1963), 'Communicator credibility and communicator discrepancy as determiners of opinion change', *Journal of Abnormal and Social Psychology*, 1967, 31–6.

Atkinson, R.L., Atkinson, R.C. and Hilgard, E.R. (1983), *Introduction to Psychology*, London: Harcourt, Brace, Jovanovich.

Barak, A., Patkins, J. and Dell, D.M. (1982), 'Effects of certain counsellor behaviours on perceived expertness and attractiveness', *Journal of Counselling Psychology*, 29, 261–7.

Beecher, H.K. (1962), 'Pain, placebos and physicians', *The Practitioner: Symposium on Anaesthesia and Analgesia*, 189, 141–55.

Berne, E. (1964), *Games People Play*, London: Penguin.

Bettinghaus, E.P. (1980), *Persuasive Communication*, 3rd edn, London: Holt, Rinehart and Winston.

Beutler, L.E. (1979), 'Values, belief, religion and the persuasive influence of psychotherapy', *Psychotherapy: Theory, Research and Practice*, 16, (4), 432–40.

Beutler, L.E., Pollock, S. and Jobe, A.M. (1978), 'Acceptance values and therapeutic change', *Journal of Consulting Psychology*.

Blincoe, C. (1993), 'Effectiveness of counselling services', *Employee Counselling Today*, 5, (5), 19–23.

Chapman, E.N. (1987), *How to Develop Positive Attitude*, London: Kogan Page.

Clare, A. (1980), *Psychiatry in Dissent*, 2nd edn, London: Tavistock.

Cochrane, R. (1983), *The Social Creation of Mental Illness*, London: Longman.

Cousins, N. (1989), *Head First: The Biology of Hope*, New York: E.P. Dutton.

Craighead, L.W. and Craighead, W.E. (1982), 'Implications of persuasive communication research for the modification of self-statements', *Cognitive Therapy and Research*, **4**, (2), 117–34.

de Board, R. (1983), *Counselling Skills*, Aldershot: Gower.

Deaux, K. and Wrightsman, L.S. (1984), *Social Psychology in the 80s*, California: Brooks Cole.

Delgara, F.J. (1972), 'Effects of involvement, competence and discrepancy on opinion change', *Journal of Social Psychology*, **87**, 301–9.

Elder, S.J. and Frentz, K.G. (1978), 'Operant control of surface body temperature', *Bulletin of Psychonomic Society*, **2**, (1), 53–4.

Festinger, L. (1957), *A Theory of Cognitive Dissonance*, Illinois: Row.

Frank, J.D. (1973), *Persuasion and Healing*, Baltimore: Johns Hopkins Univ. Press.

Garfield, S.L. (1982), 'Eclecticism and integration in psychotherapy', *Behaviour Therapy*, **13**, 610–23.

Garfield, S.L. and Kurtz, R. (1977), 'A study of eclectic views', *Journal of Consulting and Clinical Psychology*, **451**, 78–83.

Goffman, E. (1976), *Stigma*, London: Penguin.

Haslam, M.T. (1982), *Psychiatry Made Simple*, London: Heinemann.

Helmstetter, S. (1992), *Life Choices*, London: Thorsons.

Henrick, R. (ed.) (1980), *The Psychotherapy Handbook. The A–Z handbook to more than 250 psychotherapies as used today*, New York: New American Library.

Highley, J.C. and Copper, C.L. (1993), 'Evaluating employee assistance counselling programmes: practical problems', *Employee Counselling Today*, **5**, (5), 13–18.

Hill, J.A. (1969), 'Therapist goals, patient aims and patient satisfaction in therapy', *Journal of Clinical Psychology*, **25**, 455–9.

Honey, P. (1980), *Solving People Problems*, Maidenhead, UK: McGraw-Hill.

Huse, E.F. and Bowditch, J.L. (1977), *Behaviour in Organisations*, London: Addison Wesley.

Kerr, B.A., Clairborn, C.D. and Dixon, D.N. (1982), 'Training counsellors in persuasion', *Counsellor Education and Supervision*, **22**, (2), 138–48.

Kessler, D.J. (1966), 'Some myths of psychotherapy research and the search for a paradigm', *Psychological Bulletin*, **65**, (2), 110–36.

Kiesler, C.A. (1971), *The Psychological Commitment*, New York: Academic Press.

Kuhn, T.S. (1970), *The Structure of Scientific Revolutions*, Chicago: Univ. of Chicago Press.

Langs, R.J. (1983), *Unconscious Communication in Everyday Life*, London: Aranson.

Leahay, T.H. (1980), *A History of Psychology*, New Jersey: Prentice Hall.

Lowinger, R.K. and Dobie, S. (1969), 'What makes placebos work? A study of placebo response', *Archives of General Psychiatry*, **20**, 84–8.

MacLennan, N.T.R. (1994), *Opportunity Spotting: Creativity for Corporate Growth*, Aldershot: Gower.

MacLennan, N.T.R. (1995), *Coaching and Mentoring*, Aldershot: Gower.

McLaughlin, B. (1971), *Learning and Social Behaviour*, London: The Free Press.

McWilliams, J.R. and McWilliams, P. (1991), *You Can't Afford the Luxury of a Negative Thought*, London: Thorsons.

Meyer, A.E. (1982), 'What does clinical research in psychosomatics imply?', *Psychotherapy and Psychosomatics*, 38, 201–5.

Morse, S.J. and Watson, R.I. (1977), *Psychotherapy: A Comparative Casebook*, New York: Holt, Rinehart and Winston.

Nelson-Jones, R. (1993), *Practical Counselling and Helping Skills*, 3rd edn, London: Cassell.

Palladino, C.D. (1989), *Developing Self-esteem*, London: Kogan Page.

Peal, N.V. (1985), *Positive Thoughts for the Day*, London: Cedar.

Pease, A. (1981), *Body Language*, London: Sheldon Press.

Petty, R.E. *et al.* (1983), 'The effects of recipient posture or persuasion of cognitive response analysis', *Personality and Social Psychology Bulletin*, 9, (2), 209–22.

Reddy, M. (1987), *The Manager's Guide to Counselling at Work*, Leicester: British Psychological Society.

Robbins, A. (1992), *Awaken the Giant Within*, London: Simon and Schuster.

Rogers, C.R. (1951), *Client Centred Therapy*, London: Constable.

Rosenthal, D. (1955), 'Changes in some moral values following psychotherapy', *Journal of Consulting Psychology*, 19, 405–12.

Rusk, T. and Rusk, N. (1988), *Mind Traps*, London: Thorsons.

Selye, H. (1976), *The Stress of Life*, New York: McGraw-Hill.

Sifneoes, R. (1973), 'The prevalence of alexithymic characteristics in psycho-somatic patients', *Psychotherapy and Psychosomatics*, 22, 255–62.

Slaboda, J.A. *et al.* (1993), 'An evaluated staff counselling programme in a public sector organisation', *Employee Counselling Today*, 5, (5), 4–12.

Smith, M.L., Glass, C.V. and Miller, T.I. (1980), *The Benefits of Psychotherapy*, Baltimore: Johns Hopkins Univ. Press.

Smith, P.B. (1980), *Group Processes and Personal Change*, London: Harper and Row.

Sperling, A.P. (1967), *Psychology Made Simple*, London: W.H. Allen.

Stewart, W. (1992), *An A–Z Counselling Theory and Practice*, London: Chapman and Hall.

Szasz, T.S. (1981), *The Myth of Mental Illness*, London: Granada.

Thompson, G.J. (1993), *Verbal Judo: The Gentle Art of Persuasion*, New York: Morrow.

Torrey, E.F. (1972), 'What western psychotherapists can learn from witch doctors', *American Journal of Orthopsychiatry*, 42, (71), 1–9.

Totman, R.G. (1979), *Social Causes of Illness*, London: Souvenir Press.

Trandis, H.L. (1971), *Attitude and Attitude Change*, New York: Wiley.

Walmsley, H. (1994), *Counselling Techniques for Managers*, London: Kogan Page.

Weiss, T. and Engel, B.T. (1971), 'Operant conditioning in heart rate in patients with premature ventricular contractions', *Psychosomatic Medicine*, 33, (4), 310–22.

Wienstock, C. (1983), 'Psychosomatic elements in 18 consecutive cancer regressions positively not due to somatic therapy', *Journal of American Society of Psychosomatic Dentistry and Medicine*, **30**, (4), 151–5.

Welkowitz, J., Cohen, J. and Ortmeyer, D. (1967), 'Value systems similarity: investigation of patient-therapist dyads', *Journal of Consulting Psychiatry*, **31**, 48–55.

Wolpe, J. (1982), *The Practice of Behaviour Therapy*, 3rd edn, Oxford: Pergamon.

Zimbardo, P.G. (1969), *The Cognitive Control of Motivation*, Univ. Illinois: Scott Foresman.

INDEX